Weems, John Edward.
 Peary, the explorer and the man : based on his
personal papers / John Edward Weems ; foreword by
Sir Edmund Hillary. -- Los Angeles : J.P. Tarcher ; New
York : Distributed by St. Martin's Press, c1988.
 xvii, 362 p. : ill.

Originally published: Boston : Houghton Mifflin, 1967.
Includes index.
Bibliography: p. [351]-352.
03315606   LC:87026732   ISBN:0874774691 (p
bk.)

(SEE NEXT CARD)

PEARY

The Explorer and the Man

Also by John Edward Weems:

A Weekend in September
The Fate of the Maine
Race for the Pole

PEARY

The Explorer and the Man

Based on his personal papers

JOHN EDWARD WEEMS
FOREWORD BY SIR EDMUND HILLARY

JEREMY P. TARCHER, INC.
Los Angeles
Distributed by St. Martin's Press
New York

Portions of the description of Peary's journey across the Arctic Ocean ice from February 28th to April 1st, 1909, appeared in an earlier book by the author, *Race for the Pole* (Holt, 1960). Some material from Peary's personal papers, not previously available, has been added to it here.

Library of Congress Cataloging in Publication Data

Weems, John Edward.
　　Peary, the explorer and the man/by John Edward Weems.
　　p. cm.
　　Bibliography.
　　Includes index.
　　ISBN 0-87477-469-1
　　　1. Peary, Robert E. (Robert Edwin), 1856–1920.　2. Explorers—United States—Biography.　3. North Pole.　I. Title.
　　G635. P4W4 1988
　　919.8'04-dc 19　　　　　　　　　　　　　　　　87-26732
　　　　　　　　　　　　　　　　　　　　　　　　　　　　CIP

Copyright © 1967 by John Edward Weems
Originally published: Boston: Houghton Mifflin, 1967.

Requests for such permissions should be addressed to:

Jeremy P. Tarcher, Inc.
9110 Sunset Blvd.
Los Angeles, CA 90069

Manufactured in the United States of America
10　9　8　7　6　5　4　3　2　1
First Edition

For three young explorers—

Our grandsons, Jason, Daniel, and Joseph Ballew

Contents

Illustrations

Acknowledgments

SINCE 1910 no one outside the Peary family has had unlimited access to Admiral Robert Peary's voluminous papers. This includes the authors of two major biographies: *Peary*, by William Herbert Hobbs (1936), and *Peary: The Man Who Refused to Fail*, by Fitzhugh Green (1926). Peary never wrote an autobiography.

He kept the diary and the observations of his trip to the North Pole and back in a safe-deposit box, a security measure that was continued after his death. His other papers were boxed in sixty-two large cartons and stored on Eagle Island, Peary's home in Casco Bay, Maine, until 1940, when they were brought to the mainland for further storage. After Peary's death in 1920 Isaiah Bowman, director of the American Geographical Society and later president of Johns Hopkins University, suggested that neither the diary nor the observations be made available to the public, to prevent Frederick Cook's supporters from possibly manufacturing refutations or otherwise twisting the contents to suit their own use. Neither were the papers in the sixty-two cartons made public.

For allowing me unlimited access to the papers and for talking with me at intervals over a period of three months I want to thank Marie Peary Stafford of Brunswick, Maine, Robert Peary's daughter, and her brother, Robert Peary, Jr., of Augusta, Maine. Mrs. Stafford's assistance was particularly helpful, because of her tireless preliminary work in connection with the papers. She had filled eighty-seven scrapbooks with Peary material; and she has devoted a good deal of her time to getting the papers in order, for eventual presentation to the National Archives. I am also grateful to Mrs. Stafford for her generous permission to use many of the photographs which appear in this book.

This biography is based largely on Peary's collection of personal material, which includes not only his own writings but other accounts pertaining to him and to his work — both published and unpublished, favorable and critical. Peary's record of his life as maintained in his papers was remarkably complete and objective. Because of the large number of quotations drawn from this material I have, for the sake of readability, edited for style — to assure consistency of spelling, capitalization, punctuation, and so on — but words have not, of course, been tampered with. I have not dwelt on technicalities such as the Cook controversy or Peary's navigational observations made during his trip to the North Pole. The Cook controversy was my subject for an earlier book, *Race for the Pole* (1960), and Peary's personal papers have provided even greater proof that his recognition as the "discoverer" of the North Pole is proper — as that book states. Peary's original navigational observations are intact in the papers, but I have not quoted them herein; they were verified in computations by experts from the National Geographic Society, Royal Geographical Society, and Coast and Geodetic Survey after Peary's return from the North Pole, and I found no reason to question the accuracy.

My appreciation also goes to the American Philosophical Society of Philadelphia for financial assistance during the research; to the late Vilhjalmur Stefansson, author and explorer, for encouragement and assistance; to librarians at Bowdoin College, Dartmouth College, Library of Congress, National Archives, National Geographic Society, and Navy Department Library for help with the earlier book that carried over into this one; and to Paul Brooks of Houghton Mifflin Company for his interest.

A man who was as devoted to his diary as Peary delineates his character in his daily entries. I have quoted liberally from these diaries and from private letters, with the aim of portraying Peary as the man he was, and not merely as a hero.

JOHN EDWARD WEEMS

Foreword

FEW GREAT EXPLORERS have been subjected to such a spate of criticism and doubt as Robert Edwin Peary was following his great journey to the North Pole in 1909. Even after distinguished geographical societies had examined all the evidence and declared their complete confidence in his success, many questions were still being asked.

On my first visit to New York after Mt. Everest in 1953, I can remember listening with astonishment as some members of the Explorers Club energetically debated the topic, although the hero they were talking about was long since dead.

I had not read widely about Peary. My heroes were more from the Antarctic—Scott, Amundsen, Shackleton, and Byrd. But I took it for granted that Peary was the first man to set foot on the North Pole and as such was a great explorer. Now I was learning that maybe Dr. Frederick A. Cook had gotten there first. I heard criticism of Peary that focused on his incredible determination, his ambition, even his arrogance, while Cook was regarded as agreeable, cooperative, and not at all aggressive. Cook seemed too good to be true, and this, alas, is probably a fair summing up of his character.

Robert Edwin Peary was not a relaxed and easy person, and this is clearly brought out in John Edwards Weems's book. Even as a child Peary was unusually independent and ambitious. He frequently demonstrated a desire for his own company but also had the ability to excel socially when he so desired. His academic ability was considerable and he succeeded in most endeavors, motivated by an unwavering determination to be the equal of any man. But at times I feel he must have been a most uncomfortable friend. I have known many great explorers and adventurers but few with the single fundamental motivation that so clearly drove Peary. As he wrote in a letter to his mother at the age of 24, "I would like to acquire a name which would be an 'open sesame' to circles of culture and refinement anywhere, a name which would make my mother proud and which would make me feel that I was the peer of anyone I might meet." Such an attitude is rather terrifying to a person such as myself who only wanted to climb a mountain to prove that I could do it, and who was well aware that there was a multitude of people with greater skills and abilities than I possessed.

But no one could doubt Peary's incredible courage and determination and his motivation despite every defeat to return and battle again and again until success was achieved. His choice of companions did not always seem infallible and he was clearly a hard taskmaster, but Peary was well ahead of his time in having as his main supporter a man of completely different racial origin—the black American, Matthew Henson.

The story of Robert Edwin Peary is one of unrelenting determination and a final triumph. But in many ways it is also a sad story. For although he had faithful supporters, he had many enemies too. Even in success he was allowed few moments of pleasure and satisfaction and instead had to fight for his name and honor. Perhaps he wondered at times if all his great sacrifices had really been worth the effort. But indeed at last he did achieve a name that will never be forgotten.

SIR EDMUND HILLARY
January 1988
New Delhi, India

Introduction

THE MORNING OF April 2, 1909, was superb for traveling by dog sledge across the icy expanse of the frozen Arctic Ocean. A hard wind blew fiercely from the north, but a clear sky and a temperature of 25 degrees below zero heralded good progress. A celestial navigation reading the day before had put Robert Peary's position at 87 degrees, 46 minutes, 49 seconds North—about 133 miles from the North Pole. After seven previous Arctic expeditions, the first commencing in 1886, this would be his final assault.

That morning, Peary began walking northward alone. Curiously, the quality of the desolate, blindingly white icescape before him seemed to remind him of his first days of exploration in Greenland: the appearance of the ice fields, the brilliant blue sky, the piercing, unrelenting wind. A man often thinks of the very beginning of his work, Peary mused, when he feels it is nearing its end.

"This was to be the time for which I had reserved all my energies," Peary would write, "the time for which I had worked for twenty-two years, for which I had lived the simple life and trained as for a race. In spite of my years, I felt fit for the demands of the coming days." From the distance came yells and the cracks of rawhide whips. Matthew Henson, Peary's black assistant for two decades, and four Eskimos drove their forty dogs and five sledges forward to rejoin their leader.

Four days later, on April 6, 1909, at the age of fifty-two, Peary became the first human to reach 90 degrees North—the North

Pole. It was a goal upon which his entire life had focused since he had mentioned it in a letter to his mother written in his youth.

From the moment that he reached the Pole, controversy surrounded Peary. It began with the simultaneous claim of polar attainment by Dr. Frederick A. Cook, a surgeon and explorer of questionable ethics. Ever since then, critics of Peary have come and gone, and come again. For instance, experts have used computers in analyzing navigational data to disprove or re-verify Peary's claim of reaching the Pole. In the early years of the century, Peary was criticized by many racially prejudiced Americans for choosing Henson, a black man, as his assistant. Recent criticism has made a full swing, with Henson supporters claiming that Peary abandoned his devoted assistant after the polar attainment, and that Henson deserves more fitting acknowledgment.

It is unfortunate that people were not more appreciative of Henson. But it should be noted that Peary was well aware that his long-term friendship with and reliance upon Henson alienated and angered many Americans of that more racially prejudiced era. This resentment may have even helped fuel the temporary popular support of Cook and his questionable polar claim, which brought Peary deep sorrow and humiliation. Nevertheless, Peary's remark about Henson, "I could not do without him," resounds as ultimate praise of any assistant, regardless of racial origins.

Today, Peary is still in the news. Both he and Henson had fathered sons with Eskimo women during one of their Arctic expeditions. This rumor was mentioned only in whispers for many years and was finally documented, in regard to Peary, upon the first publication of this book. The visit of these two 80-year-old, half-Eskimo sons, Karree Peary and Ahnahkaq Henson, with their American kin received national attention in the summer of 1987 and has spawned renewed interest in Peary, Henson, and polar exploration.

My research for this biography began in 1961, when I was given sole and unrestricted access to Peary's truly voluminous collection of private papers. Until that point, this wealth of material had been unavailable for more than 50 years due in part to the various controversies just described. Despite all that has been said of Peary since the publication of the original edition, the biography need not change. The essential, lasting, and important story remains the same. Above and beyond all other considerations, Peary's endeavors stand as a fitting testimony to the undeniable will of the human spirit to pursue and realize a lifelong dream.

In those pioneering days of Arctic exploration, Peary and his men had only their own ingenuity to keep them alive: no high-tech insulated clothing to prevent frostbite, no radio or satellite communication with the rest of the world, and no aircraft for evacuation or for making deliveries of food or medical supplies. The group did not even have sufficient goggles to screen out wind or to filter out the blinding ultraviolet rays that shower down upon the polar extremes.

Today's Arctic is not nearly so unknown, lonesome, or forbidding as it was in Peary's day. As a matter of course, submarines make their way under the ice to the North Pole, and airliners fly overhead. Scientists study the Arctic and Antarctic to learn more about polar effects on weather, the availability of natural resources, and, more ominously, each area's potential strategic military use. Adventurers, researchers, military personnel, and others —both men and women—travel in relative comfort in planes, helicopters, and snowmobiles over the barren ice toward 90 degrees North. Recently one noted group of adventurers retraced the old North Pole route by the dog sledge method, a nostalgic reenactment of the seemingly ancient days from which Peary carved his fame.

The world becomes smaller and smaller in modern times. But in Peary's persistence and pioneering indomitability one gains insight into a fundamental reality of human existence. It is rarely easy to be first in anything.

JOHN EDWARD WEEMS
January 1988

Part I

PREPARATION

Youth

Early education

College life

First job

Naval commission

Chapter 1

"I DON'T WANT to live and die without accomplishing anything or without being known beyond a narrow circle of friends," Robert Edwin Peary wrote his mother when he was twenty-four years old. "I would like to acquire a name which would be an 'open sesame' to circles of culture and refinement anywhere, a name which would make my mother proud and which would make me feel that I was the peer of anyone I might meet." [1]

To understand Robert Peary and his long, agonizing struggle in the Arctic for attainment of the previously unseen North Pole, one must realize at the outset the extent and the background of his ambition and desire for fame. Only a tremendous craving, conceived and nurtured in his youth, could have flowered later into an obsession sufficiently intense to push him forward against apparently insurmountable obstacles, forward when most men would have quit. On one expedition, before he had even landed his men and supplies, his leg was broken in a painful shipboard accident, but he was later disembarked, strapped to a board, and after a condensed period of convalescence continued his work. On another expedition most of his toes had to be amputated after he had frozen his feet, but he was up and exploring again as soon as he could be, even though frequent bumps against jagged ice left his stumps bloody and aching at the end of a day's march.

Peary's craving for fame was originally motivated by a rather defensive attitude, by a youthful smarting under the stigma of being a "poor relation," although this feeling moderated quickly after he had reached manhood. Though his original motivation was largely thus centered, his later exploits broadened to benefit many others besides himself: Peary was the first to reach a pole of the earth, rolling back a shroud from much of the world's surface; first to realize the actual size of the Arctic Ocean, where submarines now operate; first to speak realistically of the future value to his country of the Arctic regions — all this at a time when, as in the space age, conquering new worlds meant prestige for the nation whose representative accomplished it. Despite his many feats, however, Peary generally regarded the opening fifty-two years of his life as being comprised of one failure after another, and considering the goal he had set for himself one must agree with his stern assessment. Paradoxically, however, his final success, when it did come, actually seemed to be more of a climactic tragedy; for his most notable achievement, the one that won him the enduring fame he had yearned for when young, became muddled by a ridiculous controversy that caused him and his family boundless grief and that probably shortened his life.

His youthful desire for fame, and for the money that he expected to follow, stemmed from a humble origin and from a peculiar childhood spent with his mother, a widow of modest finances who doted on her only child. Certain unfortunate facets of this early environment, and of his heritage, arrayed themselves against Robert Peary, who at birth appeared destined to be a nonentity.

He was born in Cresson, Pennsylvania, May 6th, 1856, when the storm clouds of civil war were looming darker and larger — but without people like the Pearys ever really realizing the portent, for none of them possessed much of an education, even for that day. None of Robert Peary's immediate ancestors attended college, and only his great-grandmother, Martha Beacham of Maine, could boast of any significant lineage; she was the granddaughter of an English nobleman, Lord Beacham.[2] Most of Peary's forebears, especially on his father's side, were God-fearing New England merchants, none of whom became very wealthy, but most of whom were gifted with sufficient practical sense to make their way, by dogged labor, in business.

That was, in fact, the reason for Robert Peary's birth in Pennsylvania rather than in Maine, where most of his family had resided for generations. His father, Charles Nutter Peary, and his mother, the former Mary Webster Wiley, after their marriage about 1854 had moved with Charles Peary's brothers to the gently rolling, heavily wooded Allegheny country of southwestern Pennsylvania, there to seek, with youthful enthusiasm, a bountiful future in the shook trade — the manufacture of staves and headings for barrels, most of which went to the West Indies and were returned to the United States brimming with molasses or rum. Cresson, located on the virtual summit of the green Alleghenies, was ideally suited for providing the lumber.

The house in which Robert Peary was born lay near the fork of two historic roads — an old state turnpike between Philadelphia and Pittsburgh, and the Loretto Plank Road, chartered in 1851. Surrounding the house was a forest of beech, oak, and hemlock, and verdant masses of wild crabapples, rhododendrons, and vines. It was an idyllic location for a couple in love.

The soft sweetness of this new marriage and the eager hopes for a substantial future were shattered suddenly: Mary Wiley Peary, who never enjoyed vigorous health, became ill before her son's birth and was not able to sit up thereafter until his first birthday.[3] Within two years, in January of 1859, her husband also fell ill — so seriously ill, with pneumonia, that he was forced to seek the expensive professional advice of physicians in Pittsburgh, eighty miles away. From his residence in Gallitzin, a town near Cresson to which the Pearys had moved, Charles Peary described his symptoms, by mail and with clinical unemotion, to Doctors C. M. Fitch and J. W. Sykes.[4] His condition, instead of improving, grew worse. In late January his doctors wrote:

> We regret to learn that you are no better. . . . Give cherry balsam in doses of two teaspoonsful and use inhaling fluid every three hours. . . . Take a hot footbath . . . and bathe at night with salt, brandy, and lemon juice as directed in the printed directions for night sweats. Enclosed for you some cough pills.[5]

Still Charles Peary failed to improve, and within a week he was dead, at the age of thirty. Mourners besides his brothers and his young widow were few, but a local newspaper in its obituary commented favorably on his regular church attendance and concluded:

> Much might be said of him, but we forbear. He was a good man, and he died in peace, leaving an affectionate wife and an only child to mourn their loss.[6]

"Bertie" — as his mother was to call him, to his later pain, for most of the rest of his life — was not even three when his father died, and he could scarcely be described as a mourner. Many years later Robert Peary was to recall his most vivid memory of the months in Gallitzin: watching trains disappear into a railroad tunnel through the mountains near his home and waiting anxiously for the plumes of smoke to reappear on the other side.[7] Of his father he recalled virtually nothing, but within a few years Bert, a rambunctious boy being reared more like a girl by his loving mother, would come to miss the counsel, companionship, and masculinity of a father.

After Charles Peary's death his inconsolable widow immediately packed the family possessions, dressed her son in his finest suit, and with him left for her native Maine, taking the body of her husband home for burial in Brown Hill Cemetery in South Portland. Her relatives-by-marriage in Pennsylvania could not understand why she refused to stay there; they urged this alternative upon her, but she apparently never considered it. Before her husband's death her first duty had been to him, beyond question; now, without him, she would return to the country they had come from, there to rear the child. In retrospect nothing else should have been expected of this demure, retiring woman of simple, conventional, and sometimes blindly provincial nineteenth-century loyalties.

Mary Wiley Peary did not remarry, apparently never considering this possibility either. She had bound herself to a Peary, had consummated the union with an irrevocability that not even death could alter, and she would remain a Peary for the rest of her life. She would devote herself, financed by a twelve-thousand-dollar estate left her, to the auburn-haired, blue-eyed youngster.

She also refused to change her name in another way. Sometime after Charles Peary's death his brothers surrendered to the many individuals who, through ignorance, insisted on spelling the name P-e-r-r-y; the brothers adopted it. Mary Peary vehemently rejected this compromise; she retained the traditional spelling, as well as the pronunciation *pēr'i,* which rhymes with cheery. The name was said to have been an Americanization of the French *Pierre,* which would substantiate Peary family claims of Gallic ancestry.

On Cape Elizabeth — near Portland — where the young mother and her son took up residence, her firmness of purpose evolved into a doting attitude that evoked occasional rebellion from her son. With an insensitivity that was to become characteristic in her relations with him she brought Bertie up almost like a girl, teaching him the handwork practiced by genteel young ladies of that generation and sending him out to play wearing a bonnet to protect his fair skin from sunburn. Bert Peary's acquaintances were quick to notice these peculiarities — and a lisp that he was able later to subdue only by grim effort, and even this failed sometimes when he became excited. All these characteristics left him open to the charge of being a sissy; and to prove otherwise he often had to fight.[8] When Bertie came home scratched and bruised, his clothes soiled and torn, his mother would look at him confusedly, not knowing what to say. Once she wrote in her faint, fragile script, on a piece of paper Robert Peary later found and preserved with his own papers: "We mothers never know what path across the wilderness of life our little ones may have to tread." She never really understood the path or her son, although these early taunts and the resulting fights seem to have accounted for at least part of his desire, expressed later, to be the equal of anyone he met.

Neither could Mary Peary understand why Bertie should have been full of mischief, even when not taunted. He shattered glass windows with stones to hear the tinkling sound, tripped his feeble Grandfather Wiley to see him fall, frightened little girls with a variety of mean tricks, uttered man-sized oaths not learned at home — and sometimes uttered them when the minister was a guest in the house.

One such incident became a Peary family legend. The minister was present for supper one evening when another diner began relating the news of a shipwreck off Cape Elizabeth. The vessel had been loaded with cutlery, and the overly imaginative speaker declared, "The entire beach from Cape Elizabeth to Portland Head is ankle-deep in forks, spoons, and carving knives." Robert, who had been listening with adult attentiveness, exclaimed, "Good God!" Then he noticed the array of grim faces turned toward him, stiffened in his chair, and slid under the table out of sight.[9]

No program that Mary Peary could devise improved Bert's behavior very much. Once she persuaded him to pledge himself to the "Cold Water Legion," which won for young Robert a certificate stating that he had promised to abstain from "Spiritous and Malt Liquors, Wine and Cider" and from the use of tobacco and profane language. Even before that she had enrolled him in Sunday school, where she supervised his attendance — and, of course, she attended church regularly herself, because she had sincere religious convictions.

Although her son's life failed to become any saintlier, the Sunday-morning activity possibly served to mark his life considerably by exposing him to the lure of the Arctic. In his papers is preserved a copy of a mass-published Sunday school newspaper, picturing in a fanciful sketch four Eskimo boys playing a game resembling baseball. The text elaborated:

> The dress of these little ball players is very unlike ours, and so is their play place, for it is away among the ice mountains of the . . . north. Dr. [Elisha Kent] Kane, in his voyage to the Arctic regions, once saw the scene represented in the picture. Each boy had a rib of a walrus for a stick and they were contending to drive a ball, made of bone, up a bank of frozen snow.[10]

The writer then described Dr. Kane's work in the Arctic; and one can visualize six-year-old Robert Peary, whose curiosity was already blossoming, studying the drawing and asking his mother to read and reread the story. Perhaps significantly it is the only copy of that Sunday school newspaper preserved in the Peary Papers, which contain hundreds of thousands of items ranging from Arctic diaries to receipts for minor purchases.

In the absence of any reformative spark generated by Sunday school Mary Peary turned to Santa Claus, but with similar lack of success. At Christmas of 1862 Robert's gift was accompanied by this note, in his mother's handwriting, which was frail for so young a woman:

My Dear Boy:

I hope you will be pleased with what I have brought you this year. I have had so many little boys to visit, that I could not give you as much as I did last year. And the wind blows so hard that it is very difficult for me to get round with such a lot of presents as I have to carry. I hope you will be very good after this, much better than you have been the last year. Always do as your mother tells you, and you will surely be right. I will now bid you goodnight for my fingers are very cold. I have a long way to go yet before I can rest.

Santa Clause [*sic*].[11]

Eventually Mary Peary sent her boy away for his early education. She disenrolled him from his first school, a red building near their Cape Elizabeth home, and paid precious dollars to install him in a succession of schools in Gorham, Topsham, Bethel, Bridgton — all in Maine. The location depended on her whereabouts; she insisted that he be near her. She was not with him constantly, however, and this proved to be beneficial for both mother and son: Mrs. Peary enjoyed a respite from watching over an unpredictable boy, and Bert learned a bit more about life. From Topsham he wrote his mother:

I was very glad to hear from you and intended to write before but I have been putting it off for I have had such good times playing with the boys in the gymnasium and out on the baseball ground. . . .[12]

From Gorham he wrote that he had a new roommate whom he liked, Samuel Delano from Bath, Maine, and that the other boys were playing tricks on him, sticking pins in his chair for him to sit on. "But I guess they won't after a while," he added.[13]

A week later he wrote that he was enjoying winter activities common to all Gorham boys:

We have had splendid times snowballing the last two or three days. We have made two snow forts out on the field and we go out every day and have a regular snowball. This afternoon we are going to bathe. We bathe in the schoolroom every fortnight.[14]

Robert's school work ranged from good to excellent; he matured; and his curiosity became remarkable for a boy so young. Often, on free afternoons, he would obtain permission from his teachers to take hikes off the school premises, and he would revel in these new sights. Always he shared his experiences with his mother, writing her enthusiastic, detailed descriptions of what he saw; for despite his occasional rebellions his devotion to his mother had the deep roots often typical of an only child.

First I went as far as the railroad and as the snow had been melting for several days I found a good sized waterfall. I sat down by the side of it and sat there quite a while. After I had sat there as long as I wanted to I got up and went to the monument and Town House. There are on the monument about fifty names of citizens of Gorham who have been killed in the late war. The monument was erected by the Hon. Toppan Robie, who is the richest man in Gorham. It is about fifteen or twenty feet high. It is made of granite rock for about two and a half feet above the surface of the ground. The rest of it is made of marble and it has a carved eagle on the top.[15]

Although Bert was seeing more of the world and mingling with more of the people in it, he never lost an innate desire for the privacy of his early childhood. Significantly, these hikes were usually taken alone; and once, while he was in Gorham, he wrote his mother, ". . . Some of us changed rooms according to the desire of us all and I got a little room by myself and I like it very much." [16] Young Robert Peary, though socializing more, was retaining his identity and acquiring a self-reliance that was later to become a notable facet of his personality.

Once, in these early years, he was tramping about the country-side — this time with a friend, Ned Reynolds — when the two boys located a hawk's nest high in the top of a tree. Both had long desired to possess hawk eggs, and Bert quickly shed his coat and scrambled up the tree, disregarding the joint danger of an attack by the parent birds and of a painful fall. He returned with three eggs, handed one to Ned, and declared he felt he had earned the right to the other two — a claim that his friend did not feel like disputing.

In March, 1870, Robert Peary entered Portland High School, one term behind the rest of the class. Despite this handicap, he was able to make up the work missed, and by June 29th, when the term ended, his scholarship mark was 3.97 of a possible 4.

During his high school years his mother bought a two-story house on Oxford Street, where they lived together. Robert had a room on the second floor, just above the front door, and there his friends were enthusiastically received — except when he was in a mood for privacy or when he was studying. Although he acquired several close friends in high school, he never lost a reticence that was to set him apart, however slightly at times, from others.

Loneliness, in varying degrees, was to be another characteristic of his life. In his youth there were times when he felt isolated; then, for security, he clung more closely to his mother, looking at the world with the eyes of a stranger, and with a stranger's apprehension.

Once, while he was in high school, his mother had one of her frequent sick spells. The day, a Sunday, had been quiet and pleasantly normal until then. Robert had attended Sunday school and church in the morning, then, after a big dinner, had read in Dickens' *Little Dorrit* and still later had composed two verses for submission to his high school paper. He recorded in his diary his ensuing fright and his sense of desolation:

About nine o'clock as mother got up to go to bed she suddenly became very weak and cold on her left side so she could not walk. It scared me very much, but she laid on my bed and I chafed her hands and feet till she recovered and I then got the pistol in case of emergency.

The next day he added:

I was so anxious last night I did not get to sleep till nearly twelve and woke up a little past four. I started for mother's room, trembling, but was relieved to find her better. I then dressed and sat in a chair by the fire dozing until six, when I started the other fire and did the chores.[17]

Just before the fall term of 1870 Robert himself became seriously ill with what was called "slow fever" — no doubt typhoid. For weeks during his long convalescence he could only try to stifle his restlessness and lie quietly on a sofa. During this agonizing period he read a good deal, and he was especially fascinated by the natural history books that his mother brought him in a frantic effort to amuse and interest him.

By the following January he was well enough to accompany two of his relatives on a trip into the South, where he hoped to find the sunshine and fresh air recommended by his doctor. Life out-of-doors in North Carolina, South Carolina, and Georgia brought him back to robustness; again he was the blue-eyed, auburn-haired teen-ager — tall, slender, agile — who was becoming known as "a good companion" by acquaintances. His youthful enthusiasms, his continuing interests in many subjects, his warm optimism, and his cool self-reliance made him a popular boy among contemporaries of intelligence, Northern or Southern. At this time in life he made friends easily, a characteristic that was to change, to some extent, years later, after misfortune and failure had made him less communicative.

During his Southern tour Robert observed birds and collected geological specimens, and he recorded his experiences in a carefully kept diary. Always he was a discerning observer. At Raleigh, North Carolina, he "found that it was a city of about 10,000 inhabitants though it covers as much ground as a northern city of 40,000."

The principal buildings are the Governor's Palace at one [end] and the capitol at the other end of the main street. The former is built of brick and the latter of granite. It has four wings, an entrance in each. The east and west have a portico and in front of the south a bronze statue of Washington, a state library, and a geological museum. Shade trees . . .[18]

Two days later:

Left Charlotte this morning at half past eight for Columbia, South Carolina. Arrived at 3:15. Prettiest city I've seen. Streets wide, made at right angles, and trees on both sides and middle. Does not look as pretty as before the war. Sherman burned 1,400 houses. Many of the ruins left now.[19]

Three months later, near the end of his tour, he visited Charleston, South Carolina, and saw Fort Sumter, then left for New York at noon on April 11th, 1871. Later that day he wrote in his diary:

. . . traveled all the afternoon through dense cypress swamps where the water abounds in snakes and the dense underbrush is almost impassable. The trees of these swamps are cover[ed with] a parasite known as Spanish moss which hangs from the trees in long festoons some thirty feet in length.

Finally, with the Southern tour ended, Robert wrote in his diary a climactic line: "Resolved not to exaggerate." [20]
Although Robert Peary had been a Yankee visitor in a region

only a few years removed from Sherman's ravaging march, he had made friends. After he returned to Maine one of them wrote him:

. . . Your old friends in Aiken [South Carolina] have not forgotten you. We missed you a great deal when you went away, for you came in like a ray of sunshine with your bright, happy face. Walter, I think, missed you most of any of us. He used to say, "Oh, I do wish Mr. Peary was here." He took a beautiful rose one day, filled the top of it with pepper and took it to Emma, looking very innocent, and asked her to smell it. She did so and almost sneezed the top of her head off. When Mr. Ashley came in she told him of it, thinking he would scold Walter, but he laughed immoderately. Emma very indignantly turned to Walter and said, "Yes, Mr. Peary learnt you that, I know. . . ." [21]

Bert returned to Portland High School in April, 1871, and in three months he had made up the year's work. Again he finished with his class. Whenever he assigned himself a difficult task his energy seemed boundless, and he could never content himself to lag behind others.

Robert Peary's junior year in high school marked a turning point in his life. For the first time he began the term with his class and completed the entire year without an extended absence. His interests, which had been growing, broadened — sufficiently to include one of the heart, a girl known only as "Em" in diaries and letters of those high school days. Further, he became an acknowledged leader among his classmates. His outdoor activity, begun mainly for health, increased; he and two or three close friends enjoyed frequent tramps through Maine woods, sailings on nearby Casco Bay, and explorations of remote areas that had not yet been trampled.

During these days Bert explored Eagle Island, in Casco Bay,

and determined to own it some day. He became an expert taxidermist and enough of an authority on birds to be invited to address the Portland Museum of Natural History while he was still in high school. He practiced declamation, at which he became proficient despite his handicapping lisp, and he wrote — both prose and poetry. Once he prepared a humorous piece about Adam and Eve that his teacher read to the class and later had published in the school newspaper. "When I came to school this morning," Peary gloated, "I found that my piece had created more excitement than I had expected." [22]

About this time Bert's enthusiasm for partaking of what few cultural activities the small city of Portland offered led him frequently to the public library and to most of the lectures and concerts scheduled locally. These programs he attended with Em or his mother or any one of several close boyhood chums — but usually with Em, when her mother gave permission.

Always he was eager to better himself, whether in the classroom or out. Often he recorded in his diary suggestions that he had heard and liked, such as these:

Rules for talking:
Tell the truth.
Do not talk about your own affairs.
Confess ignorance.
Talk to the person who is talking to you.
Never underrate your interlocutor.
Be brief.
Rules for writing:
Know what you are going to say.
Say it.
Use your own language.
A short word is better than a long one.
The fewer words the better.
Cut it to pieces.

How to read:

There are a few books it is necessary for every intelligent person to have read, i.e., the *Bible*, the history of his country, general facts of the history of England, most of Shakespeare's plays. He should also possess a knowledge of geography or have an atlas.

Rules:

Do not try to read everything.

Do not read too much at a time.

Stop when you are tired.

In some way make a careful review of what he reads.[23]

Also at this time his interests were molded for a later career as an explorer. In a school essay dated in 1872 he wrote:

My studies are numerous and varied, though if I were asked what they were and should answer without thinking I should be likely to say, "Vergil, chemistry, and moral science." To be sure, these are my studies at the present time, but there are others to which these are merely preparatory. And the most of these come under the head of the study of nature, and this is the grandest study in God's world. It is the study adapted to all ages, all races, and all intellects. A child can learn its outward lessons as shown in the animal and vegetable world around us, while there are secrets deeply hidden which would have fully occupied the mighty brains of such men as Cuvier [and] Linnaeus. . . .

The study of nature is a never-failing source of happiness to the earnest seeker after wisdom. Nature does not repell [*sic*] the student with monotony but shows a new side of her character every time we turn to her. And she has solace and amusement for every mood and phase of the human mind. The more she is studyed [*sic*] also, the more she entices you with glimpses of hidden treasures to study farther.

The phrase, "Eyes and No Eyes," applies here, for one who

keeps his eyes and ears open will see and hear things which another person would never dream of. As for instance, suppose you have taken a short walk across the fields with a friend some pleasant morning. You see the larks and the bobolinks busily engaged in building their nests, you see the numerous communities of insects engaged in the labors and cares of their short lives, and all around you notice the abundance of exuberant life. Your friend, walking by your side, sees nothing of this, and wonders what you can find to amuse yourself with. I pity such persons, for they lose much of the enjoyment of this life.[24]

Another time he wrote:

Without [self-reliance] no one can hope for very great success in any undertaking, for finding that one cannot trust himself, people will soon cease to trust him, although he may be competent in every other respect.[25]

Robert Peary had not reached his sixteenth birthday when he wrote these observations, which seem rather advanced for one so young. In another respect, however, he was a typical boy: he pursued his interest in "Em," an intriguing girl who continued to be only a nickname in his diaries.

January 14. . . . We were going sliding this evening and I made another attempt to induce Em to go, but she had a bad cold and could not.

January 16. I have bought tickets to Anna Dickinson's lecture tonight. Mother not being able to go I started in time to invite Em. . . . At last she yielded to my persuasions and got ready. It was very slippery. Consequently she clung to me closer than usual which, of course, was pleasant to me. . . . Going home it was more slippery than ever, which was good for me. Lewis Street was especially slow, and after crawling along at a snail's pace and dancing about till we got to the corner she let go my arm and said she would try it alone. However, I took her arm, which was all the better. In this way we gained the steps and then said goodnight.

February 1. . . . I am going to see how she would take it if I should kiss her one of these evenings.

February 16. [Em] thought sliding was splendid. I did not believe in all pulling the sled up so I took the sled myself, gave Em my arm and let the rest walk on before. In this manner we reached the top. . . . We went down again, almost tipping over this time. Coming up I let Charlie take the sled and Em and I took the sidewalk. She was enthusiastic over the sport and said she was sorry she had never tried it before. . . . The next time I took the sled and in this way we passed the time until 10:30. We went home. . . . Going, I asked for a kiss. Of course, she refused but it was not a very decided one, and I am going to take one some evening.[26]

Bert found his "Em" difficult indeed to corner. She was an independent girl — coy beyond her years — who alternately charmed him with her good looks and with her singing ("Leaf by Leaf the Roses Fall," "The Haunted Stream," and other pieces), and rebuffed him with slighting remarks that were especially galling to a person as sensitive as he. Once he recorded:

[Em] said she didn't like it because her [school] rank in deportment was below mine, which meant, I thought, considerable. I shall endeavor to show her next term that I am not so much of a dunce as she might think.[27]

Through it all Bert remained outwardly imperturbable, however, confining whatever agony he suffered to these brief, often-questioning sentences in his diary. The ebbs and flows of young romance did not affect his friendships with other boys. Nor did it retard his scholarship. He graduated from Portland High School June 25, 1873, and he was one of the speakers on the program

His topic was "Nature's Mysteries," which at that time included an unanswered question about what man would find at the top of the world, the North Pole, if he should ever reach that remote place.

Robert Peary thus graduated not only from high school but from a boyhood that had been marked by maturing, particularly after gaining a measure of freedom from the domination of his mother. Perhaps at this time he was given a reward beyond his own feeling of accomplishment: in a pocket of his diary for that year is this printed verse:

> Love! Joy!
> How it thrilled me
> Pleasure sweet
> Lillie kissed me.

> Far away from me thou art,
> Another lover claims thee,
> But fondly I remember this.
> Sweet Lillie kissed me.[28]

One wonders whether Robert Peary had indeed ascertained how "she would take it if I should kiss her one of these evenings," and whether perhaps "Em" ought not to have been substituted for "Lillie."

Chapter 2

SOMETIMES Robert Peary lagged behind his own restless spirit, although it was to carry him to many new places; for he always wanted to be going, seeing. Sometimes, in new surroundings, exuberance and optimism became clouded by a melancholy, by a longing for days when he had known much happiness.

This became true at Bowdoin College, where he enrolled in the late summer of 1873. During his final year of high school he had determined to attend college, reasoning that it would be a way of broadening his horizon. In his last high school year he had devoted himself even more intensely to his studies and had applied for the Brown Memorial Scholarship at Bowdoin. When he learned that he had won it he sold his collection of mounted birds for enough cash to buy his books, and he embarked on a four-year college course.

His mother insisted on moving with him to Brunswick, although it was only twenty-three miles from Portland. This was against the advice of dismayed relatives who suggested as diplomatically as possible that perhaps it was time for Bertie to be allowed to hack out his own path.

"I am going to college," Mary Peary reiterated, in her way that left no doubt about her determination.[1] She and her son occupied rooms on the second floor of a boarding house on Lincoln Street, "the prettiest street I ever saw," Bert — as he was now known to his friends — wrote in his 1873 diary.

It is bordered on each side by a thick row of oaks and maples. The drooping branches of these as they spread over the way form a tremulous green roof which [when you look] down the street from either end seems almost level with your head. Looking down from Maine Street the view is closed by a green and gently sloping hill on the edge of town.

Melancholy overtook Robert Peary in the next paragraph. He had found his place in the four years at Portland High School, and now he longed for those recent but vanished days with a feeling that he was to experience perhaps more often than he ever admitted outside the pages of his diary:

But for all that it is so lonesome, oh so lonesome, here that I don't know what to do with myself. All the faces are strange and I seem to be in a distant country.[2]

Nevertheless, Bowdoin College was a good choice for a boy who loved nature. The verdure of Maine rolled across the Bowdoin campus; and one mile away lay the cold, dark Androscoggin River and, a few miles to the eastward, Casco Bay.

Bowdoin College had been incorporated in 1794, when Maine was part of Massachusetts. Among its graduates were Nathaniel Hawthorne and Henry Wadsworth Longfellow, both of the class of 1825. Robert Peary delighted in reciting poetry, and Longfellow was a favorite. Years afterward Peary's college classmates were to remember that he could put great feeling into Longfellow's "My Lost Youth" and especially into the line, "A boy's will is the wind's will."

At Bowdoin Peary met a teacher of civil engineering who was to exert a major influence on his life — Professor George Leonard Vose, who was forty-two and still youthfully energetic when Peary met him. Vose, a native New Englander, made enemies by his straightforward talk and by a continuing war on sham and pretense, but he could generate enthusiasm in his students through these same qualities — and through his extensive civil engineering experience: he had worked for railroads at a time of their great expansion. Vose drove his students hard, and he was able to illustrate his classroom work with practical examples from his own experience. Altogether, Vose's background made him a teacher who could be admired by a group of young men, and Bert, who had missed the guidance of a wise father, soon recognized the professor's quality.

Nevertheless, the first year or two were rather unpleasant. Bert Peary was removed from his classmates not only by a reticence which became more pronounced around strangers, but also by living with his mother off campus. He disliked Brunswick ("the dullest hole that ever was")[3] and found it especially frustrating for a shopper ("I had to go to every gentlemen's furnishings store in town to get a pair of No. 8 brown kids and to every dry goods store for three yards of green barége").[4] Even his fascination with nature that first autumn tended to become bogged down in the depths of his gloom:

> In our trees all the leaves have turned bright yellow, and while those on the tops of the trees have fallen, those on the lower branches still remain, changing the emerald street of summer into a royal passage arched and paved with glittering gold. The rustle of the leaves as they reach the earth seems as full of sorrow and lament . . . as a human sigh. . . .[5]

One classmate, George A. Holbrook, later said of Peary and his early years in college, "I do not think the fellows knew him much except in the casual way of a pleasant morning greeting. . . . He seemed to be by himself, going on long tramps, hunting and fishing, mounting the specimens he obtained. He was always hale and hearty, laughing at the cold we felt so much. I never heard of his forming any particular friendships . . . though in the scientific department he may have done so."[6]

Worse, Bert's mother, never robust, suffered another one of her frequent sicknesses, and Bert, already dejected, felt certain she would die. This was an event he felt he could not cope with; for despite his mother's continuing efforts to manage his life he realized she was motivated by her love for him. He reciprocated this love; later he was to be known for the trait of standing by those who stood by him.

Furthermore, his mother was actually all he had in the world, an insecurity that led him, subconsciously or not, to yearnings for belonging — but not necessarily following — and to firm loyalties to the organizations that accepted him. He observed his mother's frailness, and he wrote:

> Mother is so weak she can hardly walk. If she gets through this she will probably be better but — it makes me dizzy to think of it — I don't believe she ever will. I have seen this coming a long time and knew that it was waiting for me down the path, but now that it seems so near I can't bear it any better. She may live a few months, but I do not think she will ever see the summer. Then follows a weary, lonely path for me. Oh, you who have always had a father and a mother can but faintly imagine what it will be. No one to go to [when] in trouble. No home. Nothing but strangers. In a word, to be alone in its deepest, dullest sense of agony.[7]

Then gradually, came brighter days. His mother recovered, although she continued to have occasional ailments of varying seriousness for the rest of her life. Furthermore, time brought Bert Peary a sense of belonging, an easy feeling in what was no longer "a distant country" peopled by strangers; and he became more deeply involved in his studies, especially in his junior year.

Professor Vose's civil engineering class was largely responsible for Bert's adjustment to and integration into Bowdoin College. The class was small enough so that the members knew each other personally; the subject was one that fascinated Peary; and the teacher was a natural leader of students. The civil engineering course eventually nourished strong roots for Robert Peary at Bowdoin.

Later, one member of Peary's class was to recall that Vose, who enjoyed informal gab sessions with his students, often brought up the subject of how man might reach the North Pole — he suggested a system of caches for traveling parties — "but no one knew that Peary was any more interested in it than any of the rest." [8]

Vose was a teacher who had little sympathy for any student not trying his best. For the student who did try, however, Vose always had warm praise. Bert soon became identified as such a student. He wrote to a friend:

Tuesday afternoon Professor Vose gave us a problem in graphical statics. . . . It was something new which he himself had not worked out. We were to have it the next day, and as it looked similar to a number of others we had had, I supposed we could work it out in about half an hour, and went home and finished figuring strains on a bridge. I went back to the drawing room a little before dark and found the boys had been working at it all afternoon and could make nothing of it. In the time I had before dark I reached the same result. The next morning Professor Vose took hold of it with us. The rest of the boys worked on it till noon then left it disgusted. The professor and I worked on it all day with no result. The next day we worked till noon, then he had his lecture to look over in the afternoon, so I got half a day's start on him. The next day, Friday, we went at it again and worked all day. At night I got it, obtaining the most perfect result. I tried all the tests and checks possible and then showed it to him. He took it home to look over and brought it back the next morning saying it was the best piece of work that had been done in the department since it was founded. I tell you I was as happy a boy as you often see. I was completely rewarded for my labor.[9]

College work eventually occupied so much time that Bert had no more leisure time for gloomy thoughts. He did have moments of introspection, however — mostly limited to entries in his diary and to occasional letters. Ten days after his nineteenth birthday he wrote:

I have been thinking lately that I am getting to be almost a man, and though you may laugh at me, even now I can see that I have got beyond the days of boyhood when there is no care or anything of the kind and all you have to do is enjoy yourself and indulge in a pleasant dream of the future semi-occasionally. As long as I was eighteen I didn't think anything about this, eighteen sounds so young, but nineteen — there seems to be a long distance between the two.

I have thought more of the future this spring than I ever did before. It seems as if I had waked just as the flowers have, and now instead of the future seeming distant and indistinct, it seems to be right before me in a sharply defined, tangible form. I have asked myself a thousand questions, which only time can answer. Where shall I be in ten years, in twenty years? Shall I be alive or dead, fortunate or unfortunate, shall I be trudging along in the narrow tracks many men make for themselves or shall I be known outside the circle of my acquaintances? All these [thoughts] and many more present themselves to me whenever I have a chance to think. Shall I ever in the years to come think of my college days and the night I sat writing to you? [10]

In the days immediately ahead Bert certainly thought only rarely of that night. He studied long hours: "The past week since Monday I have worked from five in the morning until eight at night, which makes a pretty fair day's work." [11] He competed in athletics: "I have been pulling on the class crew for the past two weeks and yesterday we won the class race." [12] He had charge of arrangements for the annual Ivy Day class program: "I had a thousand and one little things to attend to, which kept me traveling incessantly. . . . Then someone in the class discovered that we had no curator for Ivy Day . . . and I was elected. This added another mite to my business." [13] He continued his work in taxidermy: "Thursday night I didn't get to bed until past eleven and Friday morning I got up at half past four and skinned a loon and a fishhawk before breakfast." [14]

Bert Peary became known as a student with abundant energy, which he continued to pour into any activity that attracted him. His summer vacations, for instance, were as intense as the class work. One year, 1876, he went to the Philadelphia Centennial, where he tramped himself into daily exhaustion taking in the sights. "I haven't seen enough to give you any idea," he wrote a friend, "still I have seen so much that I shouldn't know where to begin to tell you about it." [15]

Another year he and several friends spent part of the summer on Haskell's Island, off the Maine coast. The boat trip there would scarcely have been considered vacation by most people, but it was a rugged journey that Peary loved — and it was of the type that conditioned him for a career of exploration.

It was so foggy that we couldn't see from one end of the boat to the other, and all we had to guide us was the sound of the surf on the surrounding shores. We kept on pulling, thinking everything was all right, until the skipper and his son began to dispute about where we were, and then we began to suspect that all was not all right. We still kept on pulling until we heard the breakers dead ahead. The skipper then sheered off, putting them on one side, but in a moment we heard them dead ahead again and fearfully near. We immediately stopped rowing and endeavored to find out where we were. The skipper, after listening a while and allowing the boat to drift in until we could feel the churning of the breakers, in order if possible to get a glimpse of the shore, came to the conclusion that we were outside. This wasn't very pleasant, for although there was no danger we had no anchor and would be obliged to lay on our oars all night, keeping within sound of the breakers and still looking out that we didn't get caught in them. To add to the anticipated comforts of the night, it commenced to rain and for a few moments it seemed as if it would swamp the boat. It rained . . . then stopped almost as suddenly as it commenced, and almost at the same instant a light shone out on our starboard bow and we knew at once where we were. We had rowed to the opposite side of the island, and now we had to follow the coast round to the other side. When we finally landed it was half past eleven, and wet was no name for our condition.[16]

In his last two or three years at Bowdoin Bert Peary became known as a young man who relished competition when he felt he had a chance, a characteristic that stayed with him. He never was much of a gambler, however; he needed to be sure of having a good chance at victory before announcing his intention of trying.

Always a good student, he naturally yearned to be top man in his class. He observed, however, that to gain such an honor at Bowdoin he would have to surpass the effort of a remarkable classmate who pored over his books most of every day and far into the night. Bert concluded that to outrank that particular student he would have to give up all extracurricular activities and concentrate solely on studying, and even then he might not win. The decision for him was not difficult: he wanted more out of his college education than a textbook knowledge; so he contented himself, for once, with striving for second place, and he held that position all four years.[17]

Bert Peary put the same devotion into all his activities. Years later a classmate, George W. Tillson of La Grange, Illinois, remembered a visit to Peary's residence. For a few minutes Peary was occupied elsewhere, and he asked Tillson to wait in a room which held most of his mounted birds, including, Tillson recalled, fifteen or twenty Arctic owls mounted in different positions. "As I walked around looking at them the head of one turned around, following me with its look. This one was alive, but the others were so naturally placed that I did not see the difference." [18]

As he had done in high school, Bert Peary took advantage of local activities to improve himself where he was lacking. At the end of his second year he was chosen to compete in the sophomore prize declamation. He did not "entertain any hopes" of winning, he wrote in his 1875 diary. "I shall not even try for it as I know it is useless. Speaking is not my forte. I shall probably go up on the stage and declaim just to gain more confidence but that's all."

Although he never liked to enter into competition when he felt he was beaten beforehand, neither was he one to be left far behind any time. Once Peary and four civil engineering classmates accompanied Professor Vose to Bailey Island, just off the coast, on a ten-day field trip to make a simulated railroad survey.

> One morning . . . on a dare, two of the boys went in swimming for a few minutes. The water was cold as anyone must know who has been in it in May on the Maine coast, but when they came out they both declared it was fine. . . . Towards night Peary came into the room where the rest of the boys were and said, "Say, I don't see that this water is so warm as you fellows say." He had been down and tried it. [19]

Athletic events were exhilarating to Peary, who was wiry — and stronger than he looked. During his sophomore year he won a baseball-throwing contest, and he recorded it exuberantly in his 1875 diary:

I had two of the best throwers at college . . . against me, and no one had any idea that I should do anything. As it happened my turn came last, and after they had thrown [three times each] and only reached 306 feet I was pretty confident that I shouldn't come out last. While I took my place to throw some of the boys laughed at me a little and told me I'd better not throw if I couldn't do anything better than that. . . . I didn't say anything but picked up the ball and threw it the first time. . . . The wind took the ball and carried it to one side so that it went only about 290 feet. The second time it did the same thing, only it went further, but the third time I made full allowance for the wind and the ball struck the track 316 feet distant. . . . There were a good many surprised looks when it was announced who had won and what the distance thrown was. I overheard one of the fellows telling another that he didn't see where I kept all my throw, that it didn't look as if I could do it.

The following year Peary decided against accepting a place on the class crew. He had studied his own teammates and the opposition, and had concluded that his class did not stand much chance. The race proved him right:

The time made by the sophomore crew was eighteen minutes fifty-six seconds, our crew coming in twenty-five seconds later. . . . You see, my philosophy was correct. If I had pulled this year it would have taken the shine off my former laurels.[20]

Obviously Peary never was much of a team man. Neither was he a student who accepted without question what his teachers gave him; he enjoyed working classroom problems his own way. Once his civil engineering teacher, Vose, assigned him to examine a nearby railroad bridge, which Vose considered unsafe, and to make a report on it. Bert spent three days observing and sketching the bridge alone, then turned in his report, describing various

weak points. Later, despite Professor Vose's warnings to the railroad company, the bridge collapsed, at the very points Peary had
described as weak.

Another time:

Vose sent us out to level in order to see how well we could do
it. We leveled out a mile and back and made an error of only
1/1000 of a foot, wherein Vose was very pleased. When we
came back in the middle of the day we stopped at the depot a
few minutes to watch a gang of men who were raising the track.
When we were watching, the roadmaster [who had seen the
equipment] came up and wanted us to grade off the track and
make it even. This was something that neither of us had ever
seen done or read anything about and I said I'd tell him we
couldn't do it when I thought he'd consider us a pretty sort of
men to be working on the road and not know how to grade, so
I winked to Jim and asked him whether he thought we could
spare the time. He looked meditative for a while and then said
that he guessed we could manage it, as it wasn't much of a job
and wouldn't take us long. We told the man we would do it,
but we would have to go to the office and get some more tools.
With this excuse to gain time we went down to the office and
went to work on the problem. We dug out two or three ways of
doing it and selected the one we thought would be most convenient. We then went back to the depot and went to work.

Whenever the roadmaster came by we would talk in a learned
manner about the correction necessary on account of the presence of heavy freights and the consequent change of level, and
various other abstruse subjects, so that the old fellow got the
idea that it was nothing at all for us to do, when in reality it was
something which at first we hadn't the slightest idea how it was
to be done. The best of it was, however, that we hit upon the
very method that is used in practice, and the next day Vose,
who was about the depot, saw the stakes and told us that when
we had the time we had better go and look at that work as it

was very well done and we could take it as a pattern for any work of that kind that we might have to do. We told him then who it was who did it, and he was so proud of it that his wife told me he had told every person he saw about it.[21]

Robert Peary's senior year at Bowdoin was the happiest of the four. He was well acquainted on the campus; his studies were coming easier; he knew his way around. He still lived off campus, but he was enjoying this too.

I've got my room fitted up. Mother and I have been two weeks making the curtains and lamerquins and one or two little things. Just think of that. But the result fully repays the labor, I think. The curtains are of a soft glossy buff-tinted material just having enough [fullness] to fall in graceful folds any way you can arrange it. In the evening by reflected light they are a red-gold color and give that tone to all the light that enters the room. My room is fixed now so that without actually looking out the window you couldn't tell whether it was stormy or pleasant. Inside it is sunny all the time. I think my room the . . . pleasantest in college.[22]

During the winter of his senior year Peary "went into company more and made more acquaintances than in all three previous years."[23] Many winter evenings he spent bobsledding over a favorite one-mile course, either with his Bowdoin classmates or "with a lady," and became acquainted with most of the girls in Brunswick.

Peary's steadiest girl friend during his four years at Bowdoin, however, was a young lady in Portland, Mary Kilby, no doubt the "Em" of his high school days; she had grown out of that nickname into "May," which is how Bert usually addressed her now.[24] He saw her often during his college days, enjoying the week-end hike from Brunswick to Portland and back.

Some of his most confiding letters went to Mary Kilby. One of them was mailed on his twenty-first birthday, about a month before his graduation from Bowdoin.

Today, as you observe above, is the sixth of May, 1877, and consequently yours truly is twenty-one years old. I suppose I should feel my importance, and above all I suppose it is customary on such occasions to make hosts of good resolutions. Strange to say, however, I have done neither. In regard to the first, I don't know what the reason is, but in regard to the second, I didn't make any resolutions because I shall have plenty to do between now and commencement without having a lot of resolutions to break, which I believe is also part of the customary performance. The only way in which I have celebrated has been by indulging in vague wonderings whether the contest with the world will be harder than the contest with the college. Will it prove too much for me? Whether in ten years from now I shall be in Maine, in Patagonia, in Sweden, or in Australia, or whether it will all be a blank to me then. It seems almost an impossibility to me how anyone, as some of our farmers do, can look forward to living their lives out in the same place and doing the same things their fathers and grandfathers did before them.

Today as I think of what the world is and that I have my life before me, nothing seems impossible. I wish that as in the story books some fairy might place the mirror of my life before me and tell me to look at whatever scene I wished. Yet if I could do so, I could hardly say but I should close my eyes and refuse to look. How many have wished and wondered about the mysterious future as I do, and yet if the curtain were permitted to be drawn aside, would shrink from doing it for fear of gazing upon rugged rocks and yawning graves in place of the velvety paths they wish for.[25]

About the same time, Robert Peary wrote the class ode, which showed — as Peary was always to show — that curious daydreaming mixture of nostalgia and ambitious hope.

Listen, old oak,
Aid I invoke,
Aid from thy sylvan heart.
Hush thy soft sighs,
Bend from the skies,
Teach me one song ere we part.
Teach me those mystical murmuring strains,
Born of the sunshine, the wind and the rains,
Give me thy restless wild essence of life;
Let my verse thrill like an army's wild strife.
Softly, O, friend,
This is the end.
End of our college days.
Fleeting so fast,
Here is the last,
Gilded by sunset rays.
Down on the meadows at evening tide,
Noiseless and spectral the river-mists glide.
Up from the campus and halls as we gaze
Float the white wraiths of collegiate days.
Now with a sigh
Whisper good-by,
Bowdoin, fair Eastern queen.
Treasure her gems,
Opaline gems,
Lucent with astral sheen.
Let their keen gleaming our young brows enshrine,
They shall the stars of the morning outshine.
Led by their clear light again and again,
We will be rulers and kings among men.

To Peary, being a "king among men" had, of course, already become an obsession; and what was his idea of a "king among men"? He gave an indication in this rough draft of an essay written at the end of his senior year:

To the Ancients the story of Atlantis remained a story, but the minds of later ages, urged by the curiosity and progressive spirit born of the growth of the world, have striven to reach the Atlantis of their dreams, and have endeavored to force their way through the sea of ignorance, of superstition, and incredulity, which separated them from their ideal. Some have succeeded, and the labors of the heretic Galileo, of the insane Columbus, of Newton, and the rest, have blessed the world. . . .

Robert Peary's days at Bowdoin had been good ones, after he had put down roots. He had measured up to his own high standards; his confidence and his optimism were back in their normal balance. He had been taken into a social fraternity, Delta Kappa Epsilon, and because of his excellent classroom work he had been elected to the honorary fraternity Phi Beta Kappa. All this made parting from college days and friends more difficult, and though he would be saying good-by frequently in years to come, this never came easily for Peary. While at Bowdoin he had recorded his feelings on this subject, in his 1876 diary.

If I am to say good-by to someone for a long time, I never want to say it in the daytime. It is too real. It is much better said under the enchantment which night always breathes upon everything, when the dusk may help a tell-tale face to hide too great emotion, when the shadow of a dream is over all, half persuading you that you are merely saying, "Goodnight" and not "Good-by," keeping from you all the meaning of good-by until time and sleep and the light of another day enable you to face the fact.

Chapter 3

ROBERT PEARY chose Fryeburg, Maine, to begin his climb up life's ladder, and he could scarcely have picked a less likely place for his purpose: Fryeburg was a typically quiet New England village near the New Hampshire border, and though it had certain attractions, its citizens rarely needed the services of a recent graduate in civil engineering.

Nevertheless, Fryeburg became a pleasant place for Peary and his mother, who moved into a newly built two-story house that they called "the house of three gables." From Peary's second-floor room he could look eastward to a range of low, hazy mountains, and southwestward — across a grassy field and then dense woods — to Stark's Mountain, a steep, tree-covered rise.

Getting moved in was a chore, but when it was completed Peary found little to keep him occupied. Then this young man who had been known in college for his boundless energy slipped into another paradox: he slept a good deal — ten hours or so a night, with a nap in the afternoon. "It seems as if I could sleep all the time," he wrote Mary Kilby.[1] Eventually came the longing for the place he had just left:

> Last night I went to bed . . . homesick. Homesick for my college course, for my class, for those years I shall never live again. I commenced to look over my college papers for data to

answer inquiries by a member of [the class of] '78 who has my place as chairman of the executive committee, and the result was that I pored over them till eleven or after. . . . I think sometimes that I have no feeling at all, for I can leave places and people in whose company I have been daily for years without a thought of regret, even though I know I may never return, then some little thing will turn my thoughts back, and I can hardly endure the pain of my desire to see the old scenes and faces once more. I find every year proof of my conclusion that I am a creature of pulsations, of ebbs and flows. I know I am in many things mentally and physically, and I think I am in everything.[2]

In Fryeburg Peary at first had no interests to occupy his time profitably — no interests to keep him awake and too busy to indulge in thoughts of college days. His civil engineering skills lay dormant; and Peary never was a creature who could be happy when he felt his time was being wasted. Inevitably he compared Fryeburg with the place he had just left, and though he had once called Brunswick "the dullest hole that ever was" he now forgot such epithets. Fryeburg was an even smaller town, one with a more rural atmosphere, and more gossipy than Brunswick.

I went to [church] this morning and there wasn't a pleasant thing about it. Not a nice fitting coat, not a becoming bonnet, not a fresh graceful dress in the whole audience. The seats were uncushioned and uncomfortable, the preacher had on dirty cuffs and spoke through his nose, and the leader in singing started one hymn so high he couldn't go on with it and had to commence over again — and another so high that but two could follow it through. I don't think I shall go there again right away. I expect the people here will think we are an awful family. The first Sunday I was away mother went to the Swedenborgian church and . . . next to the Congregationalist, and today I went to the Methodist. They have made up enough stories about us already with no foundation. I don't know what they will do with such startling facts as these. . . . I want to act just as bad as I know how. As for the scenery here, there are no two days in which the mountains are alike.[3]

Peary never could dismiss nature from his mind for long, and he reveled in the beauty of Fryeburg before he came to appreciate its people. The summer storms that swept the woods close by his house fascinated him, and he enjoyed watching from an upstairs window while vivid lightning flashes, enormous claps of thunder, and, finally, heavy rain sent wildlife to cover and bowed the trees in seeming obeisance. During one such storm "lightning made kindling wood of two large pines within an eighth of a mile of the house":

It played a curious freak trick with one. It took about twelve feet of the trunk of it, commencing a few feet above the ground, and stove it into splinters, sticking them vertically into the ground in a circle of about twenty-foot radius. One splinter about eight feet long and four inches in diameter was stuck into the ground as straight as any person could have done it. . . . This makes the fifth tree that has been struck within two minutes' walk of the house. There is a verse of Whittier's which I guess I will never forget. It has been so thoroughly rained into me:

> For weeks the clouds had raked the hills
> And vexed the vales with raining,
> And all the woods were sad with mist,
> And all the brooks complaining.

At first merely the ghost of it flitted through my head, then I got the first line, then a day or so later it came to me who wrote it. Whereupon I found it in a volume of Whittier. It is about as appropriate as anything I have seen lately.[4]

With virtually no civil engineering work available Peary occupied himself in other ways. His most profitable business was taxidermy; he mounted small birds — robins, for instance — for $1.50 each, and larger birds — crows, ducks, hawks — for from $1.75 to $2.25. When local residents saw the quality of his work orders poured in. He also gained local renown as a horseman. Many summer evenings he passed in riding and in breaking some of the animals.

Peary's paradoxes carried over into his recreational pursuits. He could enjoy breaking temperamental horses and making rugged camping trips, and he could cherish with the same devotion trips onto nearby Stark's Mountain to gather "sylvan treasures" — dainty ferns and delicate mosses, lichens, evergreens, leaves, and vines. "I can't begin to describe the treasures on that hill," Peary wrote. "I never knew there were such 'rarest mosses that ever were seen, orange and russet and emerald green,' I find something new every time I go." [5]

Peary left some especially vivid description of Fryeburg scenes, since he had plenty of time to write.

> There is one thing I have noticed this fall that I never observed before. The sides of the mountains now are all splashed with patches and streaks and spots of crimson and yellow relieved by the darker green of the pines and firs, and no matter how clear the day or how cloudless the sky, the mountains have the effect of being flecked with cloud shadows. Then again, no matter how dark and stormy the day, if you can get a glimpse of the mountains you can hardly persuade yourself that an August sun is not shining there, and that the clouds will not break away in a little while. [6]

This and many other letters went to his sweetheart of Portland High School days, Mary Kilby, whom he had begun calling "May" and now, occasionally, "Mamie." They were engaged to be married, and waiting, apparently, only on Peary's establishment in his chosen profession. During his days at Fryeburg Peary traveled occasionally to Portland to visit her, and once she visited Fryeburg for a week to see him. Peary took rooms for her at the local hotel and was careful to observe all the proprieties, which were both numerous and rigid in nineteenth-century Fryeburg; yet he felt moved to write her after she had returned to Portland, ". . . I have as yet heard no remarks about you." [7]

Despite this engagement, Peary began to appear frequently in such society as Fryeburg offered, and he was a popular escort among the town's young ladies. Eventually, as was usually the case with him, Peary made many friends easily, after a rather slow start.

In Fryeburg he deliberately set out on another self-improvement program.

> I am trying an experiment now. You know I always was a great case for that. I am testing my ability to make myself agreeable. I find no trouble at all with the little folks. They come to me at once. With the young folks I have to exert myself more, and with some of the old folks, I can't as yet break the crust of their unsociability and old-fogyism; however, I mean to try, as I should like to gain that attractive personality that when I was with a person, they would always have to like me whether they wanted to or not. [8]

Peary succeeded in making himself popular, at least among the younger set. He rode up on Jockey Cap, a round-topped granite rise overlooking the village, with six-year-old May Barrows in his arms, her hair streaming and she laughing with excitement. He rigged a chair-on-skates for an ailing young lady, Clara Mason, who otherwise would have had to stay home from a notable skating party. He climbed Chocorua Mountain with a young man who taught at Fryeburg Academy. At dances he was sometimes careful to seek out partners not well endowed with beauty, although this was not always the case.

Eventually, too, he managed to keep busy, studying German and mathematics when not engaged in taxidermy or in breaking colts or in other financially profitable ventures. In 1878 he was appointed justice of the peace of Oxford County, with authority "to make out deeds and other documents and marry folks."

All the while, he deliberately practiced civil engineering, although most of his work at this time was indeed practice in the true sense of the word. In the absence of much profitable employment in his profession he determined to keep up the work anyway, and in desperation he turned to an exhausting project: mapping the village of Fryeburg, entirely for his own satisfaction.

His forenoons were reserved for this, and often he spent the entire day at it. Without assistance he trotted off distances, and in the evenings, although exhausted from the day's activity, he did the figuring on this work. Finally he was ready to begin the drawing, and he devoted long evening hours to its completion in his best style.

As it happened, the project proved to be profitable after all. Soon after Peary had completed the drawing he noticed, in the Fryeburg post office, a poster soliciting applications for employment as draftsman with the Coast and Geodetic Survey in Washington. By this time Peary had begun to despair of any future in Fryeburg, had tired of the round of "sociables" he attended, had become restless again.

Four new men were to be chosen for the Coast and Geodetic Survey. Their salary was to be ten dollars a week during a six-month trial period. This should have been scarcely tempting to a man of Peary's restless spirit, but under the circumstances the possibility had all the look of Opportunity, and Peary applied. As a sample of his work he sent the map of Fryeburg. After a time he was notified of his acceptance, and he wrote his sweetheart May in Portland:

> . . . I hardly know whether I feel . . . pleased or not at the numerous congratulatory letters I have received this week, a dozen, I believe, between Sunday and Thursday night when your letter came. . . . They are all so glad I am going away . . . and in most of them I can detect an undertone of the same feeling which I have expressed to you, that I have been out of college nearly two years and have done nothing yet, and it is about time that I was doing something. I saw by the paper that [Al] Burton [a classmate at Bowdoin] was one of the elect, also, and then got a letter from him. I am glad he is going not only on account of his company, but because I think I shall work better, for I should hate terribly to go at the end of six months and have him stay.[9]

Once the decision had been made Peary was eager to leave, and he chafed under a delay that lengthened to weeks, then months. "I don't know of anything that would please me more than to know that I was to start for Washington tomorrow morning," he wrote May on March 30th. "I am not very docile under restraint and I am getting sick of this constant surveillance."

In June, finally, he could begin packing. On July 4th he left Fryeburg, and that night he was in Portland for three more days of good-bys, to friends, relatives, and May. On July 7th, in a renewed spirit of adventure, he left by boat for Boston and New York, sleeping long hours, once observing a "very sweet girl's face," and reading a novel in the saloon "to the music of the band," which he had discovered "gives an intensity to every thought of the author." He arrived in Washington by train early in the evening of July 9th, ready for new challenges.

The next morning he and his Bowdoin friend Al Burton reported for work at the Coast Survey Building. Together with four other young men who had been accepted for trial employment they were ushered into the superintendent's office, where they met the head of the organization. "He took our names and where we hailed from," Peary wrote, "and then we were passed down from one to another till we reached the chief of the drawing department. He showed us specimens of work done there, assigned us to our rooms and tables, and ordered us to report at nine o'clock the next morning for duty." [10]

Peary was excited by his new surroundings, eager to begin work, elated by the opportunity for advancement. The working conditions were ideal: the Coast Survey Building was located on New Jersey Avenue, the brow of Capitol Hill, the highest ground in Washington, and every breath of wind seemed to waft through Peary's office. Furthermore, the room was located on the north side of the building, away from the sun, and was always shady. Washington's summer heat, which Peary had dreaded, was not unbearable after all.

The hours were easy, too: nine to four Monday through Friday, and nine to three on Saturday. One hour, from twelve to one, was allowed for lunch. No one was permitted to leave the building in that period, but Peary found that during the last part of the lunch hour, after he had eaten the light lunch he invariably brought, he could rest and even nap briefly.

Peary and his friend Al Burton had taken rooms at 405 East Capitol Street, between Fourth and Fifth. They occupied the entire second floor: a large study with three windows, fronting the street; a spacious hallway; and, in the back, an expansive sleeping room with one large window. Downstairs, the board was excellent.

Peary fell into a comfortable routine of work, relaxation, and self-improvement — routine with which he nevertheless could not be content for many months. Only the uncertainty of the future perhaps kept the routine from becoming a rut for him; Peary was on trial for six months, and he would be selected or rejected for permanent employ in competition with his fellow trainees. This surely occupied his mind: he had determined to be one of those selected for retention.

The forty-dollar salary monthly got him by all right, and he could even spare a dollar bill out of the very first earnings to wrap in a piece of paper, label it as his "first earnings under Uncle Sam," and, with a typical touch of sentimentality, lay it away among his keepsakes, which included theater ticket stubs, newspaper clippings, pressed flowers, and numerous other mementos.

After a few months, however, the office work indeed began to pall. For several weeks in a row Peary was given a job of practice lettering, which soon became monotonous because, after a while, there was no chance for steady improvement — "Then, being practice, you don't have anything to show at the end of the week." [11]

He despaired of his work. Some days he would be satisfied with it; then everything would go wrong, and his work seemed to him to be the worst of the lot. Typically he began fretting about the inaction, and about the lack of social contacts in Washington, which also left his mind free to dwell on the happy times remembered of the place he had just left. Fryeburg, despite its lack of promise of any future, had been pleasant.

One evening . . . just before sunset the sky and air looked so much as they used to on the lakes that glorious free winter in the woods that it made me homesick for the rest of the day. These moments of irresistible longing for the freedom of the open air do not come to me quite as often as usual, but they come with increased force every time, and some day they will get away with me and I shall wreck the traces.[12]

The time devoted to such monotonous tasks as practice lettering opened the door a crack to his old longing for fame and the
desire to see strange lands. Peary read an article somewhere
about the proposed "Inter-oceanic Ship Canal" project to provide
a faster passage from the Atlantic to the Pacific oceans, and he
evidently spent nights dreaming of himself as another de Lesseps.
At the office one day Peary devoted some of his practice lettering
to the canal, printing notes on the subject. Mr. Bright, Peary's
department head, noticed them, and with understanding remarkable for a bureaucrat helped Peary cultivate his interest: the following day Bright summoned Peary into his office, showed him an
English map of the isthmus, and gave him a half-day leave of
absence to see what there was on the subject in the Library of
Congress.

This sparked an enthusiasm in Peary. Not only did he devour
everything he could find on the subject in the Library of Congress; he also began browsing in the secondhand bookshops after
working hours, and within a few weeks he had spent ten dollars
on books and documents.

Still, the office work was competitive, and Peary had determined to be a winner. He disciplined himself about the canal
project, not allowing his interest in it to affect his chances for job
selection at the end of six months. Furthermore, as the summer
waned and autumn came on, the cooler weather also lifted his
spirits in regard to his present situation. One day late in October,
when all government employees were given a half-holiday to attend the National Fair, Peary took advantage of the time off, and
of the crisp, cool day, to hike into Maryland. Five or six miles
away from the city, "the fields and woods are cut up by paths as
completely as any sheep pasture, and you can go in any direction
you please." Such freedom was exhilarating to Peary, and a week
later he hadn't "gotten over the . . . effects of it." [13]

Freedom might have been one reason for his breaking the long-standing engagement with Mary Kilby, although he never mentioned this possibility in his diaries or letters. Toward the end of the year 1879, seeing the pointlessness of continuing the engagement, he asked May to "release" him. After much castigation she did so, and he exulted in his diary, "I enter the new year . . . free of an engagement which for the last year has been like a nightmare to me. The past is dead. Vive la future!" [14]

Two weeks later Peary and his Bowdoin friend Al Burton learned that they, and two others from among the trainees, had been chosen for permanent employment at the Coast Survey. Peary, who ranked first, took a two-week leave of absence for a victorious journey to Portland and Brunswick, where he joyously reported the news in person to his mother and to several of his college professors, including his admired Professor Vose. By the second of February he was back in Washington, but he remarked in his diary for that month that he spent much time reading editorials and articles on the proposed canal, and that he was making notes for future use.

For another year and a half Peary stayed with the Coast Survey, living pretty much the life as before his acceptance for permanent employment as draftsman. Occasionally he brought his mother to Washington for extended visits; he always enjoyed her company, and his social contacts in Washington were still pitifully few. He joined an athletic club and began visiting the natatorium every day for a swim of as long as one mile — or a hundred feet underwater. He hiked, attended performances at Ford's Theater and elsewhere, heard a lecture on "The Gods" by Robert Ingersoll, who disappointed him. He enrolled in a dancing class to make himself "a first-class dancer if possible, and I think it is." He bought Eagle Island in Casco Bay, a bit of wilderness that had lured him since boyhood, when he had camped there. His eye was, however, on the main chance, and at this time he was certain the proposed canal in Central America was his opportunity. A few months after his selection for permanent employment he wrote to his mother:

I want to have a good long talk with you on a subject that I have been thinking of for a long time, and that is in regard to going to the isthmus. I want to discuss the pros and cons with you. This and questions of a similar nature I have been thinking of a great deal the past year, and it is this which has made you think I was souring and perhaps sad. I have got to the point where years do not have leaden feet, and I feel as if I must do something before too many of them slip by. What good will fame or a name do me if it comes when I am an old man? I want to have some years to enjoy it in, and then, my mother, I want you to have some pleasure from it. Here I am twenty-four years old and what have I done, what am I doing, or what am I in the way of doing? Nothing. It will not be long before I am thirty and if I remain here I may be drawing two-thousand as a drafts-man, a machine, working so many hours a day and known only on the payroll of the department. When I think of these things it makes me so restless that I can hardly keep quiet. I feel my-self already thirty or forty years old with nothing accomplished, and I feel a feverish desire to do something at once. What think you, mother, is it the restlessness of ambition which spurs men on to be in front of their fellows, or is it an ineffective uneasiness productive only of unrest to its unfortunate posses-sor? Thinking of all these things and wondering what I could do, it has seemed to me that there are more opportunities for a lasting fame to be obtained on the little strip of land called the isthmus, in area about half as large as the State of Maine, than anywhere else on the globe.

Many men have made themselves world known by looking forward, seeing something sure to be of importance in the fu-ture, making the subject thoroughly their own, and then when the right moment came, stepping forward as the chief or only authority on the subject. . . .

The short time I have been here has widened my horizon vastly, and among the many striving for fame or fortune or both, I feel myself overmastered by a resistless desire to do something. . . .

The engineer does not attempt to change the course of Nature — he simply conforms to her and by his skill enables her at the same time she is following her laws, to aid him. There are men who are capable of becoming machines and there are men who can do nothing unless permitted to do it [on] their own, and the world has need of both. If it was a case of daily bread with me it would be different, but I do not strive for money, but for fame, though money as a secondary consideration would be no objection.[15]

For two weeks Peary impatiently awaited a reply, and when it came his mother virtually ignored "the canal question," as he wrote in his diary.[16] Peary composed another letter immediately, asking for a firm answer. For four more days, in a late-summer heat wave with discomfort compounded by mosquitoes and by a boil on his right cheek, Peary labored through seemingly interminable days at the office and tossed through intolerable nights. Finally his mother's answer came. It was no, and Peary wrote in his diary, "I bow to her wishes though it may change my entire life." [17]

For a while Peary was filled with a melancholy, although he did not let this show at the office. His dream was shattered; he seemed destined to be chained to a desk by day and bound to a middle-class home by night. One afternoon after work, a short time earlier, Peary had sat at his desk in his new apartment, 9 B Street N.W., had observed out the window the liquid light of a cloudless afternoon, had heard the sound of a train commencing its journey from Washington. Entranced, Peary had written, "[It] fills me with an intense longing to go with it, out to the unknown golden country beyond, out among the rolling hills through the light-flooded valleys, so beautiful because so distant, so enticing because so unknown." [18] Now there was only the desk by day, and by night the lonely apartment. For a year this was so, but in fancy, at least, Peary became an observer of new places, a hearer of new sounds. Frequently, in evenings after work, his desire for fame — for exploration — showed itself to be an obsession that was not to be denied by any woman or man, including Peary himself. One evening he mused and wrote:

I never come under these glorious influences of Nature, the sound of a rushing stream, the dash of waves, the [sigh] of the wind in deep green boughs, or a glorious landscape losing itself in the distant sunshine, but my thoughts turn to those first few views which have turned themselves into the eye of Columbus, Cortez, Livingstone, . . . Balboa, De Soto, and all the host of travelers and explorers. And sometimes I can feel something of the thrill and blended aroma of all such first views since the world was in its infancy. Do you know I have stood upon the summit of a mountain after a long day's climb through woods and over rocks and, looking toward the setting sun, have given my imagination full sway until I know I have felt something of that same thrill that Cortez felt when at the close of that beautiful spring day he gained the summit of the last range of mountains that lay between him and the city of the Aztecs and, looking westward, saw the valley nestling in the rays of the sun and the mysterious city glistening in the midst of its surrounding lakes.

And as for Balboa, one moment such as that when, bidding his followers halt, alone he climbed the last rock upon that "peak in Darien," and saw beyond the tree tops the flashing waves of that great mysterious ocean, was worth years of ordinary life. Just think of the life of the travelers in an unknown country or on an unknown sea.

Then think of the nights and their thoughts of the morrow — what will it bring? Some new strange sight, the realization of some wild dream — or will it bring disappointment, disaster and perhaps death? . . .

Then there is the constant expectation of some new strange sight. You struggle on with feverish anxiety to see what is beyond this mountain or that turn in a river, or if you are sailing on some unknown sea you rack your imagination to fill the unknown region just beyond the misty horizon, and then when you least expect it, some glorious sunlit island, more beautiful than pen or brush can paint, some emerald shore, or wild rugged coast, bursts on your sight and then you go to work wondering what mysteries lie beyond the beautiful shores, what secrets the distant mountains are guarding and the distant valleys hiding in their unknown depths. Tis a glorious life but, ah me! the poetry of the world in this respect is rapidly fading. I am glad that my lot is cast upon the world now rather than later when there will be no new places, when every spot will have felt the pressure of man's foot, and earth and air, and fire and water, the grand old primal elements and all that is in them, will be abject slaves. . . .[19]

In mid-1881 Peary heard of another opportunity: the possibility of appointment as a civil engineer in the United States Navy. To a deskbound draftsman in the Coast Survey this sounded like a chance for action, and he wrote the Navy Department for details. On July 21st he had their answer — they were selecting six civil engineers for naval service — and he took the afternoon off for a physical examination, which the Navy required in advance, and for a personal follow-up visit to the Navy Department itself. When Peary became interested in a project he always threw his whole being into it. To take the naval examinations he turned down a late, unexpected chance to go to Mexico as draftsman at $125 a month, a job he likely would have jumped at a few months earlier. Also characteristically, however, he had earlier asked around Washington, at the Coast Survey and at the Navy Department, if there were any use for him to try for the naval appointment. His chief concern was whether influence would aid in the appointments. If so, he would not try, because — as he said — he had no influential friends. Once assured that influence would not count — examinations would — he knuckled down for the attempt. Again characteristically, however, he told no more persons than were necessary, not even his mother. Peary never wanted people to know he had failed. He had to get a leave of absence for the tests; so he notified the Coast Survey.

On August 12th, a Friday, the mental examinations for the appointments began. They lasted ten days, and each evening Peary returned home tired and discouraged, only to arise the next morning and "go at it again, determined to see it through." [20] He studied every spare moment.

On the last day, after the last question, he felt sure he had failed. He attached a note to the last examination paper:

> My professional experience has been so entirely in the field, reconnaissance and railroad work principally, and thus so largely topographical and so slightly mechanical, leaving me in ignorance of architectural details except as far as strains on roof trusses or a side issue of strains in bridges, that had I known the direction the examination was to take I should not have attempted to compete, yet once started it was against my principles to back out, even though I saw that all the chances of gaining one of the prizes were against me.
>
> I have a little personal pride, however, lest the board should think I am utterly ignorant, and submit a few specimens to show that I can do some things and that I have a habit of doing things well and thoroughly. The mountain profile is part of three made from different points, in leisure hours while running a transit in that region. Each profile includes about 120 degrees of the horizon. . . .[21]

Two months later he learned that he had been appointed a civil engineer in the United States Navy — by reading it in the Wash-

ington *Star*. He resigned at the Coast Survey, where — he recorded — several colleagues were quite envious. He bought uni-
forms and left again on a triumphal trip to Maine.

Back in Washington, he could gloat. He seemed well on his
way to position, perhaps even to fame. He wrote his mother:

> It's different from the Coast Survey. I am "boss" instead of
> "bossed," have a room of my own, messenger, clerk, and drafts-
> man. Have over a hundred men under my control. But the
> thing which I have a good deal of to do and for which I possess
> peculiar qualifications is signing my name. It is fun writing
> letters when you only have to write your name. The uniqueness
> of my signature has been remarked by the commodore com-
> manding the yard. More business than the renowned "man on
> the town [.]"
>
> > Hastily,
> > Bert[22]

All this was important to Peary. He was determined to be infe-
rior to no man and obligated to no one; he constantly repeated
this resolution in diaries and in letters to his mother:

> You know "our family" do not like to be under obligations to
> anyone. . . .[23]
>
> . . . I don't know whether it is my fortune or misfortune, or
> whether it is the sign of an ignoble spirit, but I cannot bear to
> associate with people, who, age and advantages being equal,
> are my superiors. I must be the peer or superior of those about
> me to be comfortable, not that I care to show my superiority,
> simply to know it myself.
>
> Consequently I rarely go out but what I return feeling the
> touch of the spur. . . .
>
> I have thought out . . . what I want to be like at thirty or
> thirty-five at the latest.
>
> Tall, erect, broad-shouldered, full-chested, tough, wiry-

limbed, clear-eyed, full-mustached, clear-browed complexion, a dead shot, a powerful, tireless swimmer, a first-class rider, a skillful boxer and fencer, perfectly at home in any company, yet always bearing with me an indefinable atmosphere of the wildness and freedom of the woods and mountains, master of German, Spanish, and French, and as a specialty (all these things being mere accomplishments) a knowledge of the Isthmus equaled by no man living. . . .[24]

Part II

EARLY EXPERIENCE

Nicaraguan canal survey

First Greenland visit

Chapter 4

NAVAL SERVICE was, at first, a glamorous way of life to Robert Peary. The social calls required by naval etiquette inspired him; they offered delightful relief from his old Washington life of near-solitude, when he was an outsider looking in. To mingle then he had been forced to use his own ingenuity and charm — in a city where there was much competition in these fields. A draftsman at the Coast Survey did not stand much chance. Now, Lieutenant Peary was expected to mix socially, and he reveled in the feeling of new importance. He savored the title "lieutenant," although he was soon to discover that most graduates of the Naval Academy did not think the title really belonged to him. Officers like Peary were civil engineers first — "civil engineer" was, in fact, Peary's official title — and whatever rank these mavericks held in the Navy was of secondary consideration, a means only of establishing relative rank, as the Navy called it. Few of the Naval Academy line officers, however, held much regard for any equivalence of the two commissions. As sea-going officers potentially capable of commanding ships they were really the commissioned Navy; civil engineers and other staff officers taken from civilian life were regarded as somewhere between them and the enlisted men in authority — and, frankly, a good boatswain's mate was more "Navy" to them than some of the staff officers.

If Peary noticed this feeling on the part of his fellow officers and was annoyed by it he gave no indication at this time. He was delighted when his mother saluted him in a letter with "My Dear Lieutenant"; and when he wrote her to say that he would be unable to visit in Maine on New Year's Day, 1882, it was with obvious pride that he explained, "I find that social and official considerations render it very desirable, in fact almost absolutely necessary, that I be in Washington on New Year's Day." [1] Peary was also elated to receive a letter from Professor Vose that began, "My distinguished old boy."

Altogether, Peary's future seemed assured by this latest development, and though he was always slow to talk about a new position for fear something would happen to cause him to regret his words, he entered into naval service without doubts. "Everything I get nowadays is money," he gloated in a letter to his mother. "Have $32.90 for you . . ." [2] "Worry not over any little things, for you know your days of worrying are past, but possess yourself in calmness and the belief that money and your boy will make everything come smooth." [3]

His first naval assignment was as assistant to A. G. Menocal, a naval civil engineer who had gained some fame as an authority on the proposed interoceanic canal, having been chief engineer for privately financed expeditions to Nicaragua in 1872–1874 and in 1874–1875. Peary's interest in the canal had become known to Menocal and was, in fact, the reason for Peary's assignment: Menocal had asked for him. The two men struck up a mutual admiration that was to last for several years.

Then, early in 1882, Peary received his first important assignment from the Bureau of Yards and Docks of the Navy Department: to oversee the building of a new iron pier at the U. S. Naval Station at Key West, Florida. Key West was at that time an important coal and stores depot for ships of the Atlantic Squadron, but its pier was outdated and almost useless. Congress appropriated thirty thousand dollars for a replacement. The job might have sounded routine, particularly since Peary himself was to be

only an inspector — a representative of the Navy Department —
and was not to be responsible for the actual construction; a nationally known builder from New York, Alf P. Boller Company,
had that responsibility. Nevertheless, Peary, in typical fashion,
read all the letters and reports on the project, and he studied maps
and charts of Key West. After familiarizing himself thoroughly
with the forthcoming work he traveled to Pennsylvania, to inspect
the ironwork that was to be shipped to Key West for the pier; then
he went to Jacksonville, Florida, for a close look at the lumber to
be used.

At Jacksonville he had plenty of free time — enough for a boat
trip up the Saint Johns river. During the day a stiff breeze from
the east ruffled the water; and from his vantage point — at the
extreme bow, with a rope finder for a cushion, the rail for a foot-
rest, and the anchor davit for a backrest — he gazed meditatively
at the wooded green banks. Despite this joy, something was lacking.

> Ah, if this were only an unknown river on whose bosom I was
> floating southward; if this breeze only blew from unknown
> forests across the river to unknown forests; if that distant,
> dreamy, hazy point only had something which no man had seen
> before, how I would study each tree and question each wave
> and cloud. But when book after book has been written and the
> same thing said over and over, when wise men and fools have
> gabbled about the sights, I lose all interest other than the enjoy-
> ment of the moment.[4]

Peary arrived by steamer at Key West on the morning of April
19th to find the weather "decidedly warm." Warm also described
the antagonism that greeted the young lieutenant, from both the
commanding officer of the station, Lieutenant Commander J. K.
Winn, an Annapolis man, and the builder of the pier, who was
having troubles that Peary thought he could clear up. Altogether,

the time at Key West was to be one of the loneliest periods in Peary's life. There he was — without official support, at least locally, and as yet an untried officer, commissioned directly from civilian life — daring to tell a nationally known builder that his pier construction was all wrong.

Furthermore, Peary had to overcome the effects of a severe illness. On the third of June, while still awaiting arrival of some of the building materials, Peary awoke with a searing headache and a severe backache. He reported at the office, but soon returned to his quarters and turned in. That afternoon a doctor examined him and diagnosed the dread — yet prevalent — yellow fever. Peary was given "two hours sweat," then some calomel, and was ordered to stay in bed. He wrote in his diary:

> June 4. Hot oppressive day and innumerable mosquitos. Slept none last night but my head stopped aching after the calomel operated. Have been tossing back and forth all day.
> June 5. Another sleepless, restless night, the mosquitos almost unbearable, it being almost impossible to keep them out of the bar. Today my stomach went wrong and have been in agony all day. Half crazy this afternoon. Not until 10 P.M. did the doctor succeed in relieving me, though he was with me nearly every hour.[5]

For almost another week Peary tossed feverishly in his bed. Then, on the morning of June 12th, he got up and, though still weak and "yellow-eyed," visited the old wharf, which he found covered with newly arrived lumber. Actual construction now began, and Peary was faced with another ordeal; but, characteristically, he took time to write his mother — about the last trial:

> My Dear Mother;
> I have only a few minutes to write you in but have some good news for you. If you have been and still are worrying about my

being here through the summer and getting the yellow fever you may rest perfectly quiet from this time on, for I have been through the ordeal, and by making myself very small and crowding close to the wall succeeded in speeding past "yellow jack's" outstretched claws and now am just as secure here as I would be at the North Pole.[6]

Within a few days Peary had returned to his routine, and now came the other ordeal. Two days after Peary had contracted yellow fever most of the building materials had arrived, and Winn had assumed the responsibility for accepting them. Winn and Peary later disagreed not only on the quality of the materials, but on the advisability of starting work in that season: Winn wanted to wait — in fact, he was in favor of canceling the contract altogether. When the Navy Department disagreed, Winn felt rebuffed. He asked for a transfer, which was disapproved. In frustration he vented his feelings on the young lieutenant whom he felt to be incapable and decidedly un-Navy.

With admirable self-control Peary devoted himself to the pier, restricting his brooding about Winn's actions to diary entries and to an occasional letter. Peary, however, now aroused the wrath of the contractor, who had run into the problem that Peary thought he could solve. At the construction site of the new iron pier the bottom was covered with a tangled mass of junk that had slipped into the water from past years and had shoaled the bottom to a depth of fifteen feet. Bricks, coal, a quantity of telegraph wire, and other matter covered the bottom, and yet the constructor was trying to sink iron pilings by using water jets designed to remove the sand, then allowing the pilings to sink into place by gravity. With the bottom so fouled, however, water jets could not do the job. Divers were sent down for a look, but Peary was dissatisfied with their reports and he dived to see for himself. Then he notified the Bureau of Yards and Docks that blasting was necessary, and he improvised his own method: he rigged a torpedo with a powder-filled pickle bottle and with this device was able to blow a hole three feet in diameter in the layer of coal. Before he had gone further, however, the Bureau instructed him to cease blasting, reasoning that it endangered the workers' safety. Morale collapsed; the workers, who had come from Northern states, were anxious to get away because of the danger of yellow fever. The equipment was inadequate, and the foreman in charge of the job was incapable of getting the work completed. With construction getting nowhere, Peary assumed responsibility for suspending it, on July 8th, in a letter to Winn:

> To sum up, the plant and the men, however efficient they might be in a northern climate under conditions similar to those under which the recent large iron piers have been constructed, are not so under the extra requirements in this case, and they cannot or will not work as the government has a right to expect. Under the clause of the contract especially covering this state of affairs, I shall assume the responsibility of suspending the work tonight until further instructions from the bureau.[7]

The contractor was furious at this slap; he threatened to sue Peary. Winn himself was no more sympathetic: he was quoted as saying that Peary was conceited, and that Peary could not handle men.

No doubt Winn hoped that Peary's drastic action in suspending work would backfire on him, but it did not. Civil engineer officers in the Bureau of Yards and Docks had come to know the young lieutenant well enough to trust him, and they recalled him to Washington to discuss the situation personally. After he had made an exhaustive report he returned to Key West, with orders to finish the job on his own. The original contract was canceled, but the threatened lawsuit died — apparently because the builder figured he would only lose more face by going to court. At Key

West, Peary's superior officers also exhibited a change of heart.
Peary wrote:

> I am inclined to think that my friend the commandant had a
> good-sized flea put in his ear while in Washington, as now it is,
> "Would you like this, Mr. Peary? Would you like that, Mr.
> Peary?" and, "Order just what you like, Mr. Peary, and your
> orders will be obeyed as if they were mine." [8]

In January, 1883, Peary again began work on the pier. This
time he had permission to do it his way — to use explosives. Addi-
tionally, he designed or adapted his own equipment: water jets,
traveler derrick, excavator, ten-ton crane. Three months later
Peary triumphantly notified the bureau, "Last pier is down. All
iron work is completed." Four days later the pier was ready for
use. Its total cost was twenty-seven thousand dollars, a saving of
three thousand dollars out of the money allotted for it. Peary returned to Washington exultantly; he had proved himself against
formidable obstacles on his first important naval assignment, and
he was more urbane, more knowledgeable about Navy life, and, if
possible, more confident.

For the next year and a half, however, Peary sank back into a
dreary routine of unchallenging Navy work, broken only by an
unsuccessful application to the government of Siam, made on
Menocal's recommendation, for some special work to be done in
that country, and by a warming friendship with a radiant young
woman, Josephine Diebitsch, the daughter of a scholar attached
to the staff of the Smithsonian Institution. Peary had met her in
1882 at Marini's, a popular dancing place in Washington, and he
had found her unforgettable.

Then, toward the end of 1884, Peary met with the opportunity
he had been hoping for and preparing for: a treaty with Nicaragua had been negotiated, and Peary was ordered to report for

duty in connection with the interoceanic canal survey. Again, his friend Menocal was responsible for this assignment; Menocal was to be in charge of the work, and he had asked for Peary.

With characteristic enthusiasm Peary began an intensive program of reading on Nicaragua. He had already become acquainted with the country, and particularly with the proposed canal, through his earlier reading, which he had continued in his spare time. Now, however, he wrapped himself in the work: he studied Spanish and the geography of Nicaragua, and the people, customs, animal life, plant life.

Through his reading Peary realized the difficulty of the assignment before he ever set foot in Nicaragua: he would be expected to survey a canal route — and to explore, actually — in snake- and insect-infested swamps and jungles, with half-civilized natives for companions. None of this shook his confidence. He knew his ability, he had good health, and he knew he had endurance, both physical and mental. In 1882 he had proudly written his mother that he could walk a mile in thirteen minutes "with the level on my shoulder, and keep it up, too." [9] A year before that he had mused on mental endurance, writing out his thoughts in pencil on a piece of paper that he saved:

Taking it for granted that in situations requiring great powers of endurance and capabilities for resisting hunger, thirst, exposure, and fatigue, as in Strain's expedition, an intelligent educated man will hold out longer than an ordinary one, and that it is will power that does it, the superiority of mind over matter, in what way does this will power act? Is it a direct, conscious, painful exertion of the will, saying to the body "you shall not give up," "you must keep on," "I will make you," just as one suppresses a groan when hurt, or forces himself to work when ill or suffering, conscious every moment of pain, able to suppress the groan, or continue the work only by constant effort; or is it the indirect effect of hope, of thoughts of fame, etc., as the result of success, lifting him away from present pain, rendering him partially unconscious of it, and helping him through severest hardships? Or is it that an educated man knows better how to husband his resources so that every particle of force, of stamina, of life itself shall tell in the bitter struggle? Or is it all of these combined? [10]

Now Peary would have a chance to find out for himself more about endurance. On December 15th the Navy secretary signed his orders to report to Menocal five days later in New York City, there to take passage on the Pacific Mail Steamer *Colon*.

Outbound from New York the steamer sailed through snapping cold seas into the Gulf Stream, where winter vanished overnight. On Christmas Day, when the *Colon* (which the romantic Peary could not miss observing was the Spanish name for Columbus) passed San Salvador, Peary wrote his mother a letter:

. . . This morning, awakening at 6:00, I pushed the blinds aside and seeing preparations for a gorgeous sunrise went back to my bunk, leaving the blinds wide open, to watch the pageant. From crimson to gold, from gold to vivid yellow-white, and there was the magic light full in my face. When I came on deck the stay sails were set, and a little later the square sails, and then full dress. The steamer went ploughing along before the "trades." We met and passed two steamers going in and at 4:00 P.M. San Salvador, or Watling's Island, hove in sight in the [southwest], and later the sun set behind it, bringing out the long low shore with its detached keys and two or three rounded prominences in purple relief against the yellow sky. Birthplace of the New World, land which first gladdened the eyes of Columbus, purple against the yellow sunset as it was nearly four hundred years ago when it smiled a welcome to the man whose fame can be equaled only by him who shall one day stand with 360 degrees of longitude beneath his motionless foot, and for whom East and West shall have vanished; the discoverer of the North Pole.[11]

In Nicaragua the job would be to look closely at the eastern
section of the proposed canal. Menocal believed that a shorter
route could be found, by sloshing around the swamps and jungles
in the vicinity of the San Juan and adjacent rivers. Field work
began on January 23rd. Only four men had come from the United
States — Menocal, the chief engineer; Chambers, in charge of
base camp; Bransford, the doctor; and Peary, who as pioneer and
transitman would do most of the sloshing.

The area of swamps and jungles through which Peary's party
later traveled had not been penetrated before even by rubber
hunters, but any glee at looking upon comparatively new land was
surely dulled for Peary by the work: cutting lanes, with machetes,
through impenetrable underbrush — "scarcely a place where fifty
feet could be gained without cutting or clearing away a log
or lifting the boats over one; . . . all the men and myself as well,
constantly [in water] to our knees and waists and even necks, cutting, lifting, pulling, pushing, swimming." [12]

Minor frustrations troubled him too. Once his party broke the
only axe it had, and after that, for the rest of the day, the men had
to chop their way with hatchets. Sometimes, too, the natives,
hungry and tired, quarreled at night, and it was up to Peary to
pacify them — which he was always able to do, because he was a
leader who was not above work himself. His diary is full of entries describing conditions: ". . . From here to camp a hard pull.
The men walking in water and dragging the boats after them, myself working with the men, singing with them, yelling at them,
and at the last moment giving them a drink of gin all around,
which brought them yelling into camp at 6:05 P.M., though everyone was thoroughly wet and tired, having been in the water over
ten hours." [13]

After three horrible months the work was over. If Peary was no
nearer the fame he sought, he certainly had, at least, further prepared himself for its calling in the future. Primarily because of

his sloshing through swamps and forest at the risk of his life — and he stayed in the field an extra week, at his own request, to finish the job — the proposed canal had been shortened by more than sixteen miles, which was estimated then to mean a potential saving of seventeen million dollars to the United States. Although the information would never be used, and the money would never be saved, Peary's work nevertheless remained a fact, as did his superior's praise for a job well done. In typically dry Navy language, which disallowed the hardships from even being imagined, Menocal said, "This information was mainly obtained through the untiring energy, skill, and devotion to duty of Civil Engineer Peary, who, under the discomforts and hardships endured through many rainy days in the field, and many nights with only a few palm leaves for shelter and a rubber blanket thrown over a pile of palm leaves for a bed, and scanty rations, never flinched while there was work to be done." [14]

Chapter 5

ROUTINE NAVY DUTY, after the excitement and hardship of Nicaragua, left Robert Peary with time on his hands and a good deal of unused energy. Some of this surplus he again spent on browsing in Washington bookstores. Years later, at a dinner honoring George W. Goethals, the engineer who was at that time engaged in building the Panama Canal, Peary reminisced:

> After [the Nicaraguan] survey had been completed and the report made to the government, the matter of the canal at Nicaragua seemed to lag. I had no occupation for my leisure hours and, prowling about a Washington second-hand bookstore one evening, found a fugitive pamphlet containing an account of Baron Nordenskjold's "Exploration of Interior Greenland." [1]

Peary's interest in Arctic exploration actually had never waned; it had lain dormant, of necessity, while he was in Nicaragua. Throughout his papers one sees clippings and notes on the Arctic compiled during all the eighties, including the years when he was involved in the Nicaraguan project. Furthermore, Peary's interest was centered not only on Arctic exploration, but on the North Pole. Other writers on Peary, including the two previous major biographers, Green and Hobbs, speculated that he had entertained no thought of trying for the North Pole attainment until after several years of Arctic work. It is true that he did not seriously attempt to reach the North Pole until after severely testing his theories and equipment in the Arctic; but Peary's personal papers indicate that long before he first visited the Arctic he had dreamed of being the first man to reach the North Pole. Peary's early written references to the North Pole were no accident: in casting about for a way to fame, he had definitely imagined himself "the discoverer of the North Pole." His exhaustive preparation and planning and his steadfast work toward reaching that goal, which finally came twenty-three years after his first visit to Greenland, make one of the most amazing stories of dogged persistence ever recorded. If ever a man regulated his life — planned it, controlled it, was himself its master — Peary did.

Nordenskjold's pamphlet on the exploration of the interior of Greenland rekindled Peary's interest in the Arctic, which actually had been first aroused when, as a child, he had read the stories of the Arctic explorer Elisha Kent Kane in front of a flickering fire while, outside the house, a Maine blizzard howled. As was typical of Peary, when he again became interested in the Arctic he began reading everything he could find on the subject. He devoted a good deal of time to studying first-person accounts of men who had already explored in the area, and with a remarkable keenness of intellect he made up his mind, even before ever visiting the Arctic, how he would improve on their methods. His ability in mechanics, his training as a civil engineer, and his experience in the field in Nicaragua, where spontaneous problems demanded instantaneous solutions, helped give him the perception to carry this out.

On October 13th, 1885, only six months after returning from Nicaragua, Peary wrote himself a memorandum, after having read numerous books by Arctic explorers.

The time has arrived now for an entire change in the expeditionary organization of Arctic research parties. The old method of large parties and several ships has been run into the ground and almost every American authority at least is beginning to see the necessity of a new departure. The English with true John Bull obstinacy still stick to the old plan. The new plan of a small party depending largely on native assistance, inaugurated by Schwatka, deserves to be recorded as the American plan, and another successful expedition will make it permanently such and put us far ahead in the race. Noting the opinion of various Artic authorities it is interesting to observe that almost without exception those who are not biased by having failed themselves, and thus being as it were compelled in self-defense to assert that because their antiquated plan had failed no other could succeed, are leaning more or less to the side of small parties.[2]

Peary showed himself as a perceptive reader and an original thinker, even before going north. Along with this same memorandum are other notes, among them a speculation to the effect that an Arctic winter, if properly prepared for, might not be so unbearable as "legends" said. Peary wrote down a guess that life might even be enjoyable there, provided one adopted the native manner of living. This theory Peary later proved valid; and it was the adaptation to Eskimo life and the utilization of Eskimos that distinguished Peary's eight expeditons to the Arctic and made possible his attainment of the North Pole — after two decades of frustration and failures. This choice Peary made after wide reading, but before he had gone north the first time. Many years later, another Arctic explorer, Vilhjalmur Stefansson, would write a book on his experiences in proving the same theory, in *The Friendly Arctic* (1921). Stefansson, however, credited Peary with being the first Arctic explorer to incorporate this thinking into his planning.

There, in Peary's 1885 diary, are other notes the hopeful explorer-to-be wrote out. They are lucid and detailed; they were written, obviously, after some hard thought on the subject. Some of Peary's notes referred to the uncertainty of ice and atmospheric conditions in Arctic regions, as shown by the writings of Hayes, Hall, Nares, Greely, Parry, and other earlier explorers. In other notes Peary reminded himself to "look up the various drifts of Arctic parties upon ice floes . . ."; to have made a "model of sledges and model of complete depot . . ."; "to have pemmican prepared with spices, etc., in addition to the currants, making it something like deviled ham. . . ."

Longer notes, all in the same diary, were filled with amazing detail, enlightened speculation, and resolutions:

The physical makeup of the party should in all respects take pattern after the physical structure of a tough hardy man. There should be one head and but one, the body should be [small], compact, homogeneous, accustomed to cold and hardship, without an ounce of superfluous weight, and under absolute control of the head, which as with a man should accompany the body on all occasions.

Following this analogy, one intelligent white man would represent the head, two other white men selected solely for their courage, determination, physical strength, and devotion to the leader would represent the arms, and the driver and natives the body and legs. The presence of women an absolute necessity to render the men contented; farther than this they are in many respects as useful as men, and are nearly if not quite their equals in strength and endurance.

Finally the head should be absolutely free and independent, free to risk his own life and his companions, in the dark of some supreme moment, which holds within its short grasp utter success and utter failure. . . .

The whole history of attempts at colonization under circumstances of hardships and strange and untried dangers shows that though the results *may* be failure with women it is *sure* to be without them. It is asking too much of masculine human nature to expect it to remain in an Arctic climate enduring constant hardship, without one relieving feature. Feminine companionship not only causes greater contentment, but as a matter of both mental and physical health and the retention of the top notch of manhood it is a necessity.

. . . If colonization is to be a success in polar regions let white men take with them native wives, then from that union may spring a race combining the hardiness of the mothers with the intelligence and energy of the fathers. Such a race would surely reach the Pole if their fathers did not succeed in doing it.

In all expeditions where women have taken part they have been of as much or more assistance than the men, notably in Hall's explorations, and I am not sure but what a party of which the larger properties were women would be best.

. . .

I propose to make the passage up Smith Sound as far as Thank God Harbor or farther, as well beaten and marked and as safe as a Siberian post road, by building permanent stone huts or stations at convenient distances which shall always contain supplies and always offer shelter. Then even if I fail I shall have left permanent assistance to my successors.

. . .

Such an expedition [as Peary has written about throughout these memoranda] can when the moment arrives shoot forward to the Pole like a ball from a cannon. Suppose the ice breaks up, then take the chances of getting ashore. Even if the floe passes down the Sound there will be depots of supplies all along so that whenever the shore is reached there will be safety.

. . .

Smith Sound is preeminently the American route. Almost the entire shores from Cape Sabine and Cairn Point north on both sides have been mapped by our expeditions and now we are farthest north on this same road. Let the English, the Germans, the Austrians have the Spitzbergen and Franz Josef and all the other routes, but let us stick to Smith Sound. . . .

. . .

I do not believe in a perennial open polar sea, neither do I believe in a paleocrystic sea, but I do believe that the unknown sea is like Kane Basin or Smith Sound. . . .

. . .

There is the same wild, fierce poetry and grandeur in the work that there is in the Norse Sagas, and it can be prosecuted with the same dash and daring that filled the old Vikings, and with the same dazzling yellow midnight sunlight flashing from every step as shone upon their sails, and tipped their lance heads.

. . .

. . . [It] is evident that the chances which an expedition of one season now and another a dozen or more years later have of striking a favorable season are small. . . . The only way is to lie in wait at some favorable point and watch season after season ready to take advantage of a favorable one, and believe me, there will come that season when the fortunate man waiting on the verge of the unknown region can speed away to the Pole. . . .

. . .

. . . Finally, to the patient waiter and the persistent devil all things come round in time, and I will be both. I will stake my life on the throw of that favorable season and with two companions, a Danish or half-breed driver and interpreter, and three natives and their wives will settle down and live there on the shore of the Northern ocean till the secret is wrested from the ice or I leave my life.

There it was: Peary's credo, hopes, and intentions all contained in handwritten memoranda in the 1885 diary. It was a sort of personal bible. In it Peary left no doubt that attainment of the North Pole was to be his life's goal, and any other Arctic exploration was to be secondary — preparation for the primary objective. Neither of Peary's two major biographers, Green or Hobbs, was aware that Peary had set such a goal so early in life; at least neither mentioned it. Peary himself certainly never would have publicized this fact: as reticent as he always was concerning his hopes and plans, he kept strictly to himself these dreams as outlined in his memoranda. For four centuries men had been striving to reach Peary's objective, and they had failed — many tragically, with great loss of life in the expeditions. Now here was a young naval officer, with little money, no outside support as yet, and no firsthand observation of the Arctic reaches, who was presuming to second-guess the illustrious, daring, and knowledgeable explorers of four hundred years.

Amazingly, he called virtually every shot. These memoranda could almost stand as an outline of the next twenty-four years of Peary's life; for almost all of his guesses proved to be good ones, and few of his plans required permanent major overhauling. When, finally, he succeeded, he did it pretty much as he had said he would in 1885. Peary, however, could not possibly have foreseen the difficulties, the harrowing escapes, and the heartaches that would be his for the next twenty-four years.

The vicissitudes were soon to begin. After Peary had completed a good deal of his Arctic reading and after he had written out for himself his method of reaching the North Pole, nothing was going to keep him from traveling northward. A short leave — six months — from the Navy was relatively easy to obtain; although a good many of Peary's colleagues thought he was foolish to go into such a treacherous region which was well known for claiming so many lives of curious men who ventured into it.

Money was more difficult to obtain, but he cleared the barrier by getting a five-hundred-dollar loan from his mother, who was even less understanding about the trip than Peary's fellow officers, but also a good deal more indulgent than were they. The money was not much, but neither were Peary's immediate goals — not at least, in comparison to his long-range objectives. On this first trip to Greenland Peary hoped to get some information about whether Greenland was an island or a continent; he wanted to find out the nature and the extent of the icecap, which at that time no one had ever traversed; and to learn whether it might be used to penetrate far northward; and he wanted to test some of his own ideas for Arctic equipment. Not a word did Peary say about the North Pole.

At the last minute Peary tried to get his leave of absence revoked in favor of orders "to special duty with the [American] Geographical Society," which had taken some interest in his journey, but the Navy secretary, W. C. Whitney, replied negatively and somewhat scornfully that "the service upon which you are about to engage can in no sense be considered naval duty." [3] It was the first of many rebuffs from the Navy, although Peary always contended that the service had every obligation to look upon exploration with sympathy and understanding.

Deciding what equipment to take was a problem, regardless of Peary's copious notes on Arctic plans. In the end he did much of the deciding by hunch, but he devoted considerable thought to a sledge, the most important item. It would have to be large and sturdy, to carry all of his provisions across deep snow; yet it must be light, he knew, because he would have to drag it himself. Finally, he decided on a toboggan-like sledge, turned up at the bow to ride over drifts, that could carry two hundred pounds. It was named *Sweetheart* in honor of Jo Diebitsch, even though Peary continued to have doubts about the wisdom of marriage.

As to my regard for [Jo], I think so, I do not know. That she loves me I know, that she can make me happy I think; that she would hamper me less than any woman I have met or am likely to meet I am confident. Still I shrink from voluntarily chaining

myself; and hate to submit my last fairest dream to the cold
light of prosaic daily life.⁴

For now, however, his dream was in no immediate danger. He
took passage to Saint John's, Newfoundland, there to find a whaler
to take him to Greenland. Peary chose the *Eagle*, which sailed on
May 22nd. He was given Captain Jackman's cabin; passengers on
these whalers were a rarity. From Sydney, Nova Scotia, four days
later Peary wrote a last letter to his mother; then the *Eagle*
headed north.

Thursday, May 27, 1886 — The day has been perfect, warm
and clear, and the wind just right to take us up the gulf, but it
has been wasted. At any other time I should have enjoyed the
scene with the low blue hills of the island in the distance, but I
am too impatient to reach that northern region which holds my
future name, to enjoy anything and have paced the bridge all
day.⁵

The trip was not a pleasure cruise. Peary observed everything:
handling of the sails and handling of the ship in ice — "a constant
slowing, then stopping, then going ahead again of the engines accompanied by the grinding, quivering shock of the vessel in ram-
ming the ice, a continual rattling of the tiller chains as the helm is
shifted port, starboard, then port again . . . and a constant shout
from the officer on the foc'sle or the foretop as he conns the vessel." ⁶ And he listened to the captain: "[He] says the heaviest
swell never penetrates the pack more than fifteen miles, and
whalers sometimes run into the edge of the ice to get away from
the heavy sea outside." ⁷

All the while Peary was mentally cataloging every bit of information he thus obtained, for future use in "that northern region
which holds my future name." Though such a statement as this
was, at this time, no more than sheer speculation by a young man

given to daydreaming, there was no doubt that the Far North was
an elixir to Peary:

> Monday, June 7, 1886 — Only a ripple on the water through
> which the old *Eagle* swam as steadily and as gracefully as a
> swan. Just dipping enough to peer beneath the bank of cloud,
> the golden sun stopped thrice his breadth above the sparkling
> sea and then began his upward climb. Truly this midnight sun,
> this Arctic circle has given me a glorious reception, even if it
> was somewhat delayed. This morning when I came on deck the
> same clear serene sky hung above the sparkling sea, and dead
> ahead lay the brown, snow-capped, snow-streaked cliffs of Disco
> Island.[8]

At Godhavn on Disco Bay, Peary encountered unexpected difficulty: a Danish government official at first refused him permission to proceed with his short exploration of the icecap — said, in
fact, that he could not even remain in Godhavn. Peary gave the
official's children some of the fresh oranges he had brought with
him, however, and he turned on some of his practiced charm, and
the official capitulated. Peary moved his equipment ashore and
took a room in the governor's house.

> Sunday, July 25th, 1886 . . . Have spent the day lying on the
> ground under my [mosquito] bar in the shadow of a great boul-
> der, dreaming and listening to reports from the ice to the north
> of us.[9]

From Disco Peary went farther north, to Ritenbenk, by native
boat. This settlement, located near the edge of the inland ice,
seemed to Peary to be better suited as a jump-off point. Certainly
it was a fortunate choice in another respect: at Ritenbenk Peary
met an energetic blue-eyed Danish youth, Christian Maigaard,
who listened with enthusiasm to Peary's plans for traveling over
the inland ice and insisted upon accompanying him. Sledging

alone across the interior ice would have been, at best, dreadfully lonely — and, at worst, perhaps fatal. Peary was soon to realize how lonely it was traveling across the Greenland ice — "an Arctic Sahara, in comparison with which the African Sahara is insignificant. For on this frozen Sahara of inner Greenland occurs no form of life, animal or vegetable; no fragment of rock, no grain of sand is visible. The traveler across its frozen wastes . . . sees . . . but three things in the world, namely, the infinite expanse of the frozen plain, the infinite dome of the cold blue sky, and the cold white sun — nothing but these. The traveler . . . across this frozen desert knows that at no time during his journey are the highest rocks of the mountain summits below him nearer than from one thousand to five thousand feet down through the mighty blanket of snow." [10]

This awesome icecap stretches across interior Greenland to a length of fifteen hundred miles and a width of nine hundred miles. Around its rough edges are deep blue crevasses often hidden by snow bridges that are sometimes firm enough to support a man and his sledge — and sometimes not. Even before arriving at this formidable barrier, however, there was another one to be surmounted: Peary had to find a way to get his equipment up the almost-perpendicular edge, to the floor of the icecap. This work required three days of reconnaissance, hard climbing, hacking, and lifting. Finally Peary and Maigaard had succeeded in lugging their equipment to an altitude of three thousand feet above the sea and were eagerly contemplating a beginning in earnest, when the vicious Greenland weather proved still another obstacle. First they were enveloped in a dense fog that seemed to submerge them; then a hard sleet set in, forcing them to halt and to take shelter in the lee of their sledges. The sleet changed to thick snow, however, driven before gale-force winds blowing from out of the inscrutable interior. After a few hours the drift had buried them, and the weather looked even more forbidding. Ominous,

heavy clouds foretold an even greater storm; so Peary and Maigaard gathered up their most valuable equipment and crept down
off the icecap to their tent below, where they waited out the raging blizzard. Four days later, on July 5th, they were able to begin
all over again. Under a new blue sky Peary and his companion
retraced their steps, dug out their equipment, and again started
inland.

Then came the crevasses. Under a new mask of snow, they
were particularly hazardous. Peary and Maigaard were forced to
test every step before they made it, but even this safeguard was
not a sure method of traversing the danger area. Suddenly Peary
felt the snow crumbling slowly beneath his feet and instantly realized that he had walked into a crevasse. He yelled, grabbed for
the rapidly disappearing snowy surface across which he had been
feeling his way and scrambled back up to a firm footing, while, in
the black depth below, huge cakes of ice and snow from the
broken bridge smashed into fragments on blue ice, tinkling "like
the chimes of silver bells." [11]

As they inched forward the crevasses disappeared — only to
give way to a new danger: ponds of glacier water covered with ice
of varying thickness. Into one of these Maigaard fell. The water
depth was only five feet, and Peary was able to pull him out
quickly; but even before this rescue was accomplished Maigaard's
clothing had frozen stiff. Hurriedly Peary made camp, lit the
stove, and helped to thaw out his chilled companion.

Every minute brought other vicissitudes. One constant source
of aggravation was the ever-present brilliant sun, reflecting from
the interminable, glistening white surface. Peary discovered that
it was as eye-searing in clear weather as the sun of any southern
latitude. "A man placed in the center of the 'great ice,' in mid-
summer, with no means of protecting his eyes," Peary wrote later,
"would be as completely helpless at the end of a day as a blind
kitten. The traveler upon the 'great ice' must keep his eyes con-

stantly protected by goggles of heavy smoked glass, and even with
this we frequently, when in camp and trying to sleep, were
obliged to protect our eyes still further by a strip of fur tied across
them to exclude the light which would otherwise penetrate the
closed lids." [12] At other times, on this trip, Peary and Maigaard
wielded the snow saw to cut blocks of hard snow from the surface.
These they arranged into a three-wall structure and stretched a
rubber blanket over the top to keep out the awful rays of the sun.

> In clear weather, the traveler upon this white waste sees but
> the snow, the sky, the sun. In cloudy weather, even these dis-
> appear. Many a time I have found myself traveling in gray
> space, feeling the snow beneath my snowshoes but unable to
> see it. No sun, no sky, no snow, no horizon — absolutely noth-
> ing that the eye could rest upon. . . . My feet and snowshoes
> were sharp and clear as silhouettes, and I was sensible of contact
> with the snow at every step, yet as far as my eyes gave me evi-
> dence to the contrary, I was walking upon nothing. . . . The
> strain, both physical and mental, of this blindness with wide-
> open eyes was such that after a time I would be obliged to stop
> until the passing of the fog, or formation of higher clouds, gave
> me something to keep the course by.[13]

Day after day they pressed forward, anxious to travel a significant distance onto the icecap. Almost continually they were
whipped by an annoying wind blowing into their faces. Occasionally they were wrapped in a white blanket of fog. Sometimes
they were again stopped by screaming Arctic gales — once for two
days. But by the 19th of July the weather had cleared, enabling
Peary to get a sunsight showing that he and Maigaard had penetrated the icecap to a point about one hundred miles from where
they had begun the trip. At this time, Peary figured, they were
7525 feet above sea level. The snow beneath them was like granu-
lated sugar, to a depth of at least six feet.

At this point, with six days' provisions left, Peary decided to turn back. "The sky above was flawless blue, the crimson sun in one direction, the yellow moon opposite, and the plain on which we traveled spread with diamond dust," Peary wrote later, with obvious affection for the scene and an implied reluctance to leave it. Years earlier he had written of his longing to see places no other man had seen; now he had fulfilled that desire. His journey onto the ice, brief though it was, represented the deepest penetration of the icecap made at that time, and attainment of the greatest elevation. For the first time man had reached the real interior plateau of unchanging snow, and had determined the characteristics of the inland ice, from its edge to its interior.

On the return trip the wind proved to be friendly. Blowing into their backs, it seemed to shove them homeward; and it soon gave them an idea for increasing their speed still further. They lashed together their two sledges, arranging them side by side. Then they rigged a sail for this improvisation, and had to hurry to keep up with the strange vehicle, which was comparatively light because many provisions had been used.

Before long another improvement suggested itself. Peary and Maigaard rigged a rudder by lashing a hatchet to the end of a snow skate, then took places on their respective sledges to await results.

From midnight till five A.M. we sped along, taking levels at the speed of a fast walk, and dashing rapidly down the incline, the hatchet rudder working admirably. Then a group of enormous snow-covered crevasses sprang across our path and the land, Noursoak and Disco dark and half shrouded in haze, leaped up from behind the white expanse below us with a suddenness that was absolutely startling. The crevasses, the most magnificent ones we had seen, were many of them fifty feet wide, and the group was about half a mile across. As a rule, they were covered by snow arches, though in several places these had fallen in. The snow arches being apparently strong, we rushed the sledges over, taking flying steps and half supporting ourselves on the yard of the catamaran, as the wind and the impetus of our run hurried us across. The edges of all the openings into these huge chasms had an overhanging lip of snow, making it impossible to approach them to sound or look down. We could only get hasty glimpses into them as we passed over the snow arches, and these showed that their ragged blue walls, hung with giant icicles and frostwork of fantastic patterns, descended into depths of blue-black night.

Beyond the crevasses the descent was very rapid, and, jumping on the sledges again, we began an exciting run. The wind, straining the sail till it threatened to tear it from the mast, and the rapid descent together, drove us down the frozen slope with a breathless rush which only those who have been on a toboggan can understand, our supple catamaran gliding over the snow and rising and falling to every inequality with sinewy ease and grace.

There are two who will not soon forget that glorious dash down the slope of the eternal ice in the crisp air and rosy light of that arctic summer morning.[14]

Later, two nearly fatal accidents made the descent even more memorable. While working the lashed sledges over a snow bridge, Maigaard pushing and Peary pulling, Peary was horrified to see the surface give way beneath Maigaard, but before he sank out of sight the man was able to grab the rear of the sledge and hang on. This additional weight almost wrenched the bow out of Peary's hands, but he quickly flung himself onto the front section, and his weight anchored the sledge on the very edge of the chasm, so that Maigaard could pull himself up to safety on it.

Peary's turn came not long afterward, when he slipped and fell into a churning glacier stream. The water appeared to be carrying him past stark walls of blue ice toward a quick death when his spiked shoes caught on some ice, quite by accident. This gave

Maigaard time to reach out a sturdy arm and to help Peary clamber out.

The close escapes left Peary undaunted. While he waited for the *Eagle* to carry him back, he was still able to daydream about his future in this region and to muse on its charm.

> Sunday, August 29, 1886 — There is no bluer, softer, fairer, brighter summer sea in all the tropics than this Sea of Baffin and this Bay of Disco on such a sunlit August afternoon, as yesterday, to one lying on a mossy shelf on the cliffs eight hundred or nine hundred feet above the water. Pale blue, distant mountains gird the bay, icebergs fleck the sapphire waters, the murmur of the sea comes faintly to the ear, and everything, blue sea, white bergs, brown and red cliffs, and emerald moss and grass-grown slopes, are bathed in brilliant sunshine.[15]

Less placid was the trip back; the *Eagle* ran into a vicious storm that seemed to provide a fitting climax for what most persons except Peary would have considered a harrowing journey. The little ship pitched, rolled, twisted, and heaved; it shrieked, groaned, and wailed. Peary had to hold himself in his bunk to keep from hurtling out along with the contents of his locker. Peary mused, "If an artist could only personify and transfer to canvas the action of the *Eagle* during the night in some such subject as a damned soul, both fame and fortune would be his." [16]

Back in the United States, Peary was welcomed by his relieved, but still perplexed, mother, and by some friends in the Navy — including A. G. Menocal — most of whom voiced their hope that Peary would not again try such a foolhardy trip. Peary was elected to membership in the American Society for the Advancement of Science, and he was invited to talk about his trip at his Bowdoin class reunion. The invitation was extended by George Little, the student to whom Peary had conceded first-place academic standing in the class of '77; and Peary must have smiled at the great respect expressed in Little's invitation.

This was, however, only the beginning of his quest for fame. Already he was badgering his mother for her approval of another trip to Greenland, in a Danish ship by way of Copenhagen, where he might have the United States minister present him to the king of Denmark.[17] To his mother he implored further:

My last trip has brought my name before the world; my next will give me a standing in the world. . . . The trip means to me, my mother, first an enduring name and honor, second, certainty of being retained in the Navy even in case of adverse legislation in regard to the Civil Engineer Corps, third, social advancement, for with the prestige of my summer's work, and the assistance of friends whom I have made this winter, I will next winter be one of the foremost in the highest circles in the capital, and make powerful friends with whom I can shape my future instead of letting it come as it will. . . . Remember, mother, I *must* have fame, and I cannot reconcile myself to years of commonplace drudgery and a name late in life when I see an opportunity to gain it now and sip the delicious draught while yet I have youth and strength and capacity to enjoy it to the utmost. And I am not entirely selfish, mother. I want my fame *now* while you too can enjoy it. . . .[18]

On Cape Elizabeth, Mrs. Peary read her son's letter with little sympathy and some self-pity.

If fame is dearer to you than anything else, [she replied], what am I to say [?] I think if you should look at the matter calmly and dispassionately you would be less enthusiastic — such fame is dearly bought.

I am only one year older than when you first talked of going to Greenland, but I feel as if I was ten. I do not care to repeat the last summer's experience. There, I am too dizzy to write more.

Mother

Chapter 6

In April of 1887 a group of American businessmen formed the Maritime Canal Company, an organization that was to make a new, and final, survey of the proposed Nicaraguan canal route. Once again the veteran A. G. Menocal was chosen to be chief engineer, and he selected Peary to be second in command. Navy leave was arranged without difficulty.

Peary devoted himself to the venture with typical intensity, and for the moment at least he put the Arctic out of his mind. Here was real opportunity, he thought, to win fame — a greater opportunity than during his last Nicaraguan work. This time he was to be in full charge of the surveying work, and he was to be in command of the party that sailed from New York. Under him would be about forty-five engineers and some hundred laborers, many of who were to be recruited during a stop at Jamaica. With him when he left New York was a Negro manservant whom he had met in Washington, D. C., and who would later accompany him to the Arctic — Matthew Henson.

Typically, Peary refrained from spreading the news of his imminent selection as subchief of the survey until it had become a fact. "I could not write to you . . . about these things," he told his mother, "until everything was settled, because it meant so much to me. Even now I cannot write of all it means for the future; we will talk of that later. For the present it means that during the next year I shall have a salary from the company and from the government of $6,600[1] and that from the moment our steamer leaves New York, I shall be in command of a party of 150 men."[2]

Peary's mother never shared his enthusiasm for these adventures, despite the possibility of fame and the certainty of some money coming in. Earlier he had intimated to her his desire to return to Nicaragua, and she had written this letter, dripping self-pity:

From my childhood I was not strong, less so since your birth. In my weakness and loneliness I have tried hard and earnestly to do what I thought was best for you. I do not tell you this to excite you but that you may judge me more leniently or justly. Now I cannot have your unhappiness laid at my door. Leave me entirely out of the question and do what you think will give you sunshine and happiness. The sudden though not unexpected announcement of your intentions wrung from me a cry of pain — It shall not happen again. All the clothes that you brought home I have put in as good order as my strength and ability would admit. You have only to say what else I can do to assist your preparations. If I have caused you the loss of a night's sleep you will forgive

Mother[3]

For this trip there were to be further complications, which heretofore Peary had avoided. However reluctant he was to anchor himself, the attraction of Josephine Diebitsch was getting to be overpowering. "If she does not love me with her whole heart," he mused in a letter to his mother, "then she is a most consummate and consistent actress. I shall take the risk and within the week shall ask her to wear my ring." Then an upsurge of practicality overtook him, and he added, "I shall not think of marriage, however, until after my return from Nicaragua."[4] Accompanying

Peary as a member of the expedition was Jo's brother, Emil Dieb-itsch.

Peary always experienced a feeling of relief when finally bound for a destination: bonds were broken; he was free at last, if only for a while, and he determined to make these months count before he returned to the everyday drudgery. Furthermore, a reporter from the New York *Herald* sailed with the Nicaraguan party, to report from the field on its accomplishments. ". . . If you sub-scribe to the *Herald*," Peary wrote his mother proudly, "you will get all [the reporter's] letters and the telegraphic news." [5]

On the last day of November, 1887, Peary's Nicaraguan party departed New York in the chartered steamer *Hondo* and later plowed into rough seas which were portentous. The weather was not stormy, however, and the winds were favorable; and within a week the *Hondo* had arrived in sunny Jamaica, where Peary en-gaged for expedition work fifty men, "young and strong looking," and seven cooks.

Peary was exuberant. Faraway places always fascinated him, even when viewed from close up: he always left his depressions — at least at this point of his career — in the workaday "drag and load" back home. He feasted on the glory and grandeur of the Jamaica landscape: green mountains, purple valleys, the golden light; he breathed in the sea wind; he "really lived again."

From Port Morant, Jamaica, the *Hondo* sailed on December 6th on the last leg of the journey. En route, Peary made good use of the captain's cabin, which he had all to himself. With the seas smoother now, he spent much of the day reclining on the "berth," thinking out last-minute plans, catnapping, and summoning his clerk, a shorthand writer to whom he dictated expedition plans. The clerk wrote out the plans for Peary, and this heightened his luxuriant feeling: he was always pleased to have someone else do his writing for him. Even Peary's usual sea-voyage trouble with constipation was absent this time. He was feeling "first rate"; and in musing on expedition orders he was acquiring valuable experience for his Arctic future, although this must have been far from his mind as he relaxed in his cabin.

Peary tried to foresee every eventuality the expedition might face. In his orders, which were to be read and understood by every leader of a group of men, he stated exactly what survey work was expected and how to do it; he outlined medical instructions in great detail — for both avoiding and treating ailments and injuries — utilizing the knowledge acquired from his previous Nicaraguan experience; he explained meticulously the discipline he expected his subordinate leaders to enforce.

Typical of Peary's detailed forethinking is this instruction regarding routine:

Your daily routine will be as follows:

Cooks must be called and coffee and hardtack served to the party so that all hands may be ready to start at 6:30 A.M. You will *invariably* have coffee served to the officers of your party in their *mosquito bars before rising.* You will take with you on the line a cold lunch or breakfast consisting of canned meat and hardtack as per the ration schedule. You will stop work for a half hour at 11 A.M. for this lunch and will then continue work until half past four when you will return to camp for dinner.

It is recommended that the officers on arriving in camp shall take a small dose, (1 or 1½) ounces of spirits, and you will then see that each officer removes his working clothes *immediately,* takes a thorough bath and rubdown, and puts on his thick flannel sleeping suit. By this time the cook will have your dinner on the table. Before leaving Greytown satisfy yourself by personal inspection and report to me if each officer of your party is provided with a suitable mosquito bar and a heavy flannel or merino sleeping suit and socks. In the location of your camp you will endeavor in all cases where practicable to have it pitched on the bank of a stream in some dry-land place and you will pitch the officer's tents upstream from those of the men. You will have the brush and the trees in and about the space occupied by the tent thoroughly cleaned away in such a manner as to bare the ground and give the sun free access to the tents and their surroundings. Sanitary conveniences for the men must be placed on the stream below their quarters and all refuse from the camp will invariably be carried and thrown into the stream at that point. No offal or refuse of any kind whatever must be allowed to remain or to accumulate in or near the camp.

You will keep a minute private journal of each day's doings, which journal will, upon the completion of your work, be turned over to me for the records of the expedition.

You will treat all visitors to your camp with courtesy; at the same time you will not furnish information in regard to the survey to anyone without sanction from headquarters. . . .

You must be especially careful in your treatment of your Nicaraguan employees. While docile and willing to work almost without exception, they are not accustomed to profanity or personal chastisement or abuse, and you and the officers in your party will endeavor by a proper combination of firmness and kindness to control and direct them without recourse to either of the above means. You will doubtless find it advisable to select one suitable man both from your Jamaica laborers and also from your Nicaraguan laborers who from his intelligence and energy will command the respect of the others. . . .

You will make it an invariable rule that every man of your force shall as soon as he arrives in camp at night deposit his machete in your tent where it will remain until it is issued to him in the morning as he starts to work. . . .

The *Hondo* arrived at Greytown December 9th: Peary scribbled a hasty 29-word note to his mother to go back on the same steamer, then began spending the energy he had stored during his days of lolling in his bunk in the captain's cabin. For nineteen days he hurried from dawn until late at night, in Greytown, selecting and evaluating his men and getting them ready to go into the field, and, later, "in the woods" himself, with his two native assistants, helping with the work. And for all nineteen days the rain poured down, almost continually, drenching everyone. Only at night, usually, was Peary snug while he was "in the woods" — after he had taken a quick warm bath, between downpours; hurried into his "sleeping suit"; gulped a cup of the steaming hot coffee that one of the men had managed to brew in some nearby sheltered place; and crawled into his warm, dry "bed," set up by one of his men beneath a rubber-blanket roof and inside a mosquito bar. After that nothing could disturb him.

". . . It began again and all night the rain fell through the big trees," Peary once wrote, "while I lay in my warm clothes under the fleecy folds of the roomy bar, comfortable as if in my room at home." [6]

After the first three weeks he knew his men: he had already acquired a competence at judging them quickly, and he had no sympathy for malingerers. His orders regarding discipline called for a fine of fifty cents from any man who was not ready for a day's work when the roll was called at 6:30 A.M. From the field he returned thirteen Nicaraguans to the Greytown agent who had corralled them, with a written declaration that they were men "who either from the result of sickness or inherent worthlessness have in no case done a single day's work since joining the expedition."

I do not know what were the terms of the agreement with them, but I trust there is nothing in it providing for return transportation at the expense of the company when discharged for cause. They have been fed and taken care of by the company for one month and have given absolutely no equipment for it. [7]

After four weeks Peary had a respite from the work. The canal company had instructed him to call on the president of Nicaragua as soon as feasible, and on January 19th he arrived in Managua, accompanied by the *Herald* reporter and a *New York Times* man. For three days he had "a picnic." He had two audiences with the president, and he went to a glittering official ball attended by most of the prominent people of the capital. This was the social life that Peary craved, and he was ecstatic. From Managua he wrote his mother, ". . . No matter how hard the day's work, how wet or tired I may be, at night I think to myself, 'I am lifting myself'; 'I am writing my name before the world.' . . . It is glorious work . . . to feel that every stroke counts for yourself, that the credit will not be absorbed by someone else, but it is spoiling me for any future drudgery in the service. They will have to give me something special or give me up." [8]

Peary wrote the letter in his room, before a broad, open door facing a sun-drenched balcony. He reflected on what the winter day would be like in frigid Maine, and he felt doubly exhilarated, although he was often uncomfortable in hot weather elsewhere. This was superb: outside, a cool trade wind rippled the surface of the Lake of Managua, rustled the palms nearby and the curtains in his room, and gently fanned his face. Still, he was no cooler than he had been — and after considerable effort — in Washington, but there was satisfaction and comfort in his present situation: his work had much compensation and seemed to offer a great future; he was in society on his own, being received by presidents; he was seeing new places and people.

The sky, he reflected, looked like the sky of Italy — where he had never been, but Peary was a romantic — or of Greenland.[9] Across a square from where he sat a military band played waltz music. In leisurely situations like these Peary indulged in reverie, and he did now. He never allowed his daydreams to encroach on a necessary day's work, however, and on the following day Peary commenced his trip back to reality, into "the woods," where new problems soon presented themselves for solution.

> Tuesday night the steamer brought letters [to Peary at Camp Carazol on the San Juan River] from Greytown, informing me of the return of Mr. [J. W.] Pethard, chief of Party No. 1, in a state of utter intoxication. Though I had but one man at headquarters capable of handling a paddle I started downriver at daylight the next morning and arrived at Greytown late in the afternoon. After investigating matters I discharged Mr. Pethard and began straightening out the affairs of the party.[10]

Pethard had been drunk once before, but Peary had declined to discharge him then, reasoning that he would give a second chance to both the man ("thinking that once over his spree he would be in condition to work") and to the canal company (which had not "received . . . return for its month's advance").[11]

Two weeks later another chief of party, a man whose acute despondency had caused the expedition doctor to advise the man to resign, shot the doctor and killed himself. With a feeling of both weariness and annoyance, Peary conducted an investigation, authorized funeral expenses for the dead man, and saw to medical care for the doctor, who lived. Peary was finding that responsibility brought its burdens, that the last Nicaraguan expedition was play compared to this one. He wrote:

> . . . Strange as it may seem I find my tent at headquarters the last place in which I like to be. The woods with their opportunities for studying and planning without interruption are my refuge. I have had more than one disagreeable experience and shall be fortunate if I have no more. One of my chiefs of party developed into a crazy and irresponsible drunkard, disgraced himself and indirectly the expedition, and put me to great annoyance and anxiety even after I had discharged him.[12]

Another became crazy with suicidal tendencies, attempted his own life several times, and finally, in spite of all precautions, shot one of the doctors, though not fatally, and killed himself. . . . Sometimes I think I shall be foolish if I ever allow myself to engage in any such work again, then I think of the name. . . .[13]

A little more than two months later, on his thirty-second birthday, Peary wrote his mother:

. . . I am not as heavy as I was when I was here last time because anxiety and responsibility have kept me down, but I am much heavier than when I left New York, and I have been well. I shall be willing, however, when the time comes to come home, June 1st, I expect. I shall be indispensable to the Canal Company after this trip and can make my own terms. At the same time am making myself known, as you see by the *Herald*. I am 32 today . . . and I hope you are satisfied with my progress. I am as far along as I dreamed eleven years ago when I left college, and I have prospects ahead of me beyond what I dreamed. I have now a firmer grip upon this canal matter than even Menocal himself, because in addition to his knowledge of the general scope of the work, I have a personal knowledge of every foot of the ground. . . . I have learned more in regard to my abilities in the past five months than in all my previous life.[14]

During the seven months that Peary was in Nicaragua — with six land parties, one hydrographic party, and two boring parties — the proposed canal was relocated and, under Peary's direction four thousand miles of lines were surveyed by transit and level, virtually all of this in extremely difficult terrain. Indeed he did make himself invaluable to the company, and certainly he forged for himself qualities in handling men and expeditions that would prove vital in the future.

His work, however, came to nothing. In 1889 the canal company made him an offer that he concluded was insufficient for acceptance, and in June of 1902 a government commission appointed to decide between the proposed Nicaraguan and Panamanian routes for a canal reversed a previous decision in favor of Nicaragua, and chose Panama. Peary, however, always believed that, in time, two isthmian canals would be required, and that eventually a canal through Nicaragua would be built.[15]

During the summer he finished his Nicaraguan work and returned to the United States. On August 6th he wrote Josephine Diebitsch impatiently, from New York, "Let me see if there is anything for me to obtain except the minister, the license, and the ring? . . . By the way, what kind of a ring?" Methodically, he scouted for a honeymoon site and chose the Octagonal Hotel in Seabright, New Jersey. On Saturday, August 11th, he married his spirited, rosy-cheeked fiancée in Washington and took her to Seabright. Peary's mother accompanied her son and his bride on their honeymoon.

That fall, after completing the last of the canal paperwork, Peary was ordered to duty at the New York Naval Shipyard, and he seemed to settle into a routine life. If the naval duty was uninteresting, his bride certainly was not; and for a time she was the Nicaragua, the Greenland of his life.

They found rooms on Madison Avenue; then, dissatisfied, looked further and moved "just around the corner on 32nd . . . the other side of Fifth Avenue" for twenty-three dollars a week. Their new home seemed cozier and more homelike to Jo, and the boarding table was "so much better than the one on Madison." Peary had a considerable distance to travel to the shipyard; otherwise, their location was idyllic — as would be almost any location to newlyweds. They went to the theater; they quarreled, laughingly, over economizing — she was for, he against; they took long walks in Central Park on Sundays and shorter ones elsewhere on week nights.

Robert Peary devoted himself to his bride. "Bert puts the [Nicaraguan] Canal aside," she wrote to his mother, "and devotes the whole time to me, and if he is as happy as I am then we must be the happiest people in the world." [16]

In time, however, the other yearning returned. The longing for fame still had its hold on Peary.

Part III

SEASONING

First serious Greenland

expeditions (1891–1892

and 1893–1895)

Summer expeditions

(1896 and 1897)

Chapter 7

ARCTIC EXPLORATION had never been far from Peary's thoughts, even in the steaming heat of Central America. Now, with the Nicaragua opportunity fading, he looked northward again. The quickest possible feat there, Peary felt, was a crossing of the Greenland icecap. This was the plan that he had been mulling over ever since his visit two years earlier. He had proposed two routes for himself: one, a southerly route across a narrow part of Greenland, in the general area he and Maigaard had explored in 1886; the other, a much more demanding traverse to the north, venturing diagonally onto the icecap in a northeasterly direction. Peary thought the latter course might also show whether or not Greenland was an island. At that time its northeastern section was a blank area on all maps, and some persons guessed that Greenland might extend all the way to the North Pole.

Six weeks after his marriage, Peary's dream of being the first man to cross the icecap crumbled into unalterable reality: on September 22nd news came that the Norwegian explorer Fridtjof Nansen had crossed the icecap at the narrow southern part. Peary heard about this and returned home that day looking "as if he had just seen someone die." [1]

Later, in a letter to his mother, he brooded about getting beaten:

> . . . I bought Nansen's book while in New York recently and we have been reading it. It is a pretentious affair in two thick

volumes, with numerous illustrations and maps. The original
material in it is, however, hardly greater than I obtained four
years ago. . . .

Nansen profited much by my experience, and frequently refers to me in the book. His maps show my work and he named a
mountain after me and gives a picture of it.[2]

Peary's resilience soon became evident. If he was not destined
to be the first man to cross the icecap, he could at least be the
explorer who contributed some even more significant knowledge,
by following his proposed route into the blank area of northeast
Greenland.

As the weeks, months — years — went by, this seemed to be another dream — another one that might be dashed any day. Peary
was careful to attend to his Navy duties, but without his initial
enthusiasm.

In 1890 he was stationed at League Island Navy Yard; that fall
he and Jo rented front rooms on the third floor of an apartment at
4118 Elm Avenue in Philadelphia. The building overlooked Fairmount Park and stood directly in front of the site of the main
building of the Centennial Exhibition that Peary remembered so
well from his visit fourteen years earlier.

They had settled down for "a comfortable, economical winter,"
as Peary wrote. Their rent was twenty-four dollars a month; his
ride to work, on steam cars, took only seven minutes. He left at
8:30 A.M., taking downstairs with him the night's accumulation of
ashes, and returned at 4:30 P.M., carrying up coal and kindling
wood. It was a cozy time for a couple still in the bliss of new
marriage; and across the street was Fairmount Park — at their disposal for a stroll or, when the day was bright enough, for a
bundled-up sun bath. Despite the somber Philadelphia winter, Jo
noted, her husband kept well and was handsomer than ever, "if
you can imagine such a thing." Apparently they had no cares;
they seemed perfectly happy. Some tenant neighbors with an ob-

vious small-town nosiness thought it would be "nice," Jo heard, if they had a baby — "evidently they are anxious that we should have care." [3]

During that same year, however, Peary himself admitted to being in low spirits several times. These admissions were limited, as they usually were, to pages in his diaries, to discussions with Jo, to letters to his mother. Peary's idea of manliness precluded his confiding private woes to an outsider. Furthermore, with his excessive sensitivity, Peary was not a likely confessor of moods to anyone else anyway; reticence about these private matters certainly was not likely to boomerang in a brutal society and thus to compound his dejection — as might talking freely about his feelings. Peary was, of course, vulnerable to hurt, although some critics, and some admirers as well, were later to say, fitting it to their own use, that Peary was a rather cold man who was impervious to criticism. He certainly never showed these characteristics in his private writings.

At this time Peary's depressions were due to the passage of some two years without furthering of his primary ambition. "I consider it a matter of importance," he wrote his mother, "not to let myself drop out of sight." [4] He continued to read books on Arctic exploration, bought at secondhand bookstores on nineteenth-century Navy pay, and he mulled over his proposed plan to travel into northeast Greenland. He yearned to put wings on his plans, but the zealous exploring he now intended would require more than a five-hundred-dollar loan from his mother.

Restless, he began writing letters to geographic and natural-science societies across the country, soliciting contributions. The ensuing lack of support was dismaying — doubly so to a sensitive man. This was not all due to apathy, however; much of it evolved from acute recollection of certain recent Arctic tragedies — and particularly of two: the DeLong expedition, which had left the United States in 1879 in the *Jeannette* to attack the Arctic by way of the Bering Sea only to be caught, instead, in vicious pack ice which héld the ship securely for two years before crushing it and claiming the lives of all except one boatload of survivors; and the Greely expedition of thirty-three men, which departed from the United States in 1881 to set up a research station in the Far North, became the collective victim of sundry mistakes and disasters, and returned two years later counting only six survivors — some of whom might have owed their lives to cannibalism in the Arctic, said gossips.

Even Peary's home town did not proffer much hope. To William Wood, president of the Portland Society of Natural History, Peary had addressed a request for three thousand dollars, reminding Wood that he, Peary, was "a Portland boy," recalling for Wood his earlier trip to Greenland, and asserting his desire "to return and conquer some of the secrets of the mysterious interior." [5] The Portland group did not have money for sponsoring Peary's second Arctic journey, however — not even for passage on a whaler, a means of transportation Peary was currently considering. He turned elsewhere for contributions.

Meanwhile, however, the geographical department of Brooklyn Institute had fed Peary a spoonful of encouragement by sponsoring a lecture on his first visit to Greenland. It brought him out of his doldrums, at least for a while: "It has made me feel as if I might yet make myself known and felt outside of my present narrow routine circle." [6] Furthermore, it suggested another way of arousing interest and raising money: by lecturing. His Brooklyn talk was sufficiently well received to send him home with a gleam of fresh hope. He would work on the speech and enlarge on the illustrations.

Last week I took my sledge and fur costume to the photographer and had three new slides made; another slide that I am having made is of Maigaard, and several of the slides that you saw I am having colored. Altogether by the time that my slides are ready for the lecture they will be doubled in interest and completeness compared with what they were when I lectured in Brooklyn.

Then I am brushing up my elocution and declaiming every evening before the glass and all that sort of funny business which you can remember.

I intend to make the lecture a success, and who knows? Perhaps I may have discovered my vocation, and shall give Stoddard pangs of jealousy.[7]

Whoever it might be with whom Peary put himself in competition, either seriously or half-jestingly, he had to assert his superiority — had to know it himself — and it is to Peary's invariable credit that he expected to push himself ceaselessly to attain this superiority. He never desired it, not even later, as fulsome applause from hero-worshipers or as a wilted concession from those less strong-minded than he was. Now he worked on his lectures with a vigor that was to bring its greatest reward in future years.

During the winter of 1890–1891 moral and financial backing finally appeared for Peary's proposed reconnaissance of northeast Greenland: the American Geographical Society, the Brooklyn Institute, and the Philadelphia Academy of Natural Sciences all voted their support of the expedition, which helped Peary get a leave of absence from the Navy. About ten thousand dollars was raised, a considerable part of it from several scientists and other individuals who were given passages north in return for their contributions.

One of the individuals was John Verhoeff, a twenty-five-year-old bachelor outdoorsman whose most notable claim, by his own estimate, was a swim in 1890 across Oregon's Willamette River and back in sixteen and a half minutes — with the water temperature at 44.5 degrees Fahrenheit. Peary suspected young Verhoeff of being something of a thrill seeker, but another of Verhoeff's claims was inescapable: the young man had some money, and he was willing to contribute two thousand dollars of it to the expedition. Peary's decision, under the circumstances, was unavoidable, but he was careful to warn Verhoeff:

> . . . Your contribution, generous as it is, cannot entitle you to any share in the management or control of the expedition.
> This must in the very nature of the case rest absolutely with me. . . .[8]

Peary was ready to tell even the Federal Government the same thing, but he never had to. In a letter to a Bowdoin College professor Peary stated:

> I have not asked, nor would I accept government aid unless it were given entirely without conditions or restrictions, which would not be done. Neither do I care to spend several years getting such aid through Congress. If I can raise the money this winter I want to start next spring [1891].[9]

In the same letter he elaborated on his plans:

> My party will be small, not over six in any event. This I believe absolutely essential to success.
> . . . The vital feature of my project, which marks it as a distinctly new departure in Arctic work, and as I believe renders success a certainty, is that I propose to attack Greenland from the *inside*, across the uninterrupted snow which shrouds the inland ice.
> . . . In the higher latitude of Whale Sound the zone of crevasses and ragged ice which I was obliged to cross in the latitude of Disco Bay, before I reached the unbroken snow field of the interior, will be eliminated, and I can step from the mountains about Whale Sound, directly upon the unchanging snow surface.

To another person he explained:

Once my idea is grasped of exploring Greenland from the *inside*, from the smooth serene heights of the interior ice, instead of from the outside, through grinding ice fields and along a ragged coast, it will be seen how effective it is.

It is like exploring an atoll around the margin of the placid central lagoon, instead of along the outer shore, through reefs and breakers.[10]

This is the earliest hint of a characteristic that Peary was later to claim, with pride, as a quality that distinguished his expeditions from others: he advocated doing things the easiest way, if there was a choice. Although Peary would have agreed with all other Arctic explorers that "easy" is a hard word to use in the Far North, it was his contention that life and exploration in the Arctic need not be so miserable as some earlier explorers had made it. Later Peary was to prove to his own satisfaction that his preconception was well founded, and as his experience grew, so did the strength of the idea. Peary determined to adapt to the land, to live like the Eskimos. Any other effort would not only be insufficient but also foolhardy. Years later Peary was to say, "The more dramatic the expedition, the less efficient the leader," [11] and he was drawing on his philosophy of the Arctic: it could be a friendly place if a man knew how to blend into the environment. Some of the terrible Arctic tragedies that had awed the public could have been prevented, Peary contended, had the expedition leaders chosen to accept the geography rather than to fight it.

Peary's plan for attacking Greenland from the inside drew favorable comment from some leading authorities. The hard thought that went into it impressed the president of the American Geographical Society, Judge Charles P. Daly, who wrote Peary:

. . . I especially approve of the small number of persons that are to compose the expedition. The sufferings, privations, and ultimate lack of success heretofore in many expeditions for geographical explorations have been due to the fact that the number composing the expedition has been too large. . . .

An accurate knowledge of Greenland is very desirable. I was never impressed by [the German geographer] Petermann's theory that it was a continent stretching across the North Pole, but am, and for years have been, inclined to believe, for reasons geological and geographical, that the land in the immediate region of the Pole is an archipelago, and that Greenland will prove to be an island.[12]

From George L. Vose, Peary's civil engineering professor at Bowdoin, came a request: "If you have a spare photograph of yourself I should like to see how old you are growing, before you have been frozen and thawed again." [13]

Peary's leave of absence from the Navy was granted, and he hurried his final planning. One plan shocked the nation: Peary announced that his wife Jo would accompany him as a member of the main expedition, which was to number seven persons in all. Jo would thus become the first white woman to endure the harsh Arctic winter, and a good many Americans were fearful that she might not survive it. They urged Peary to leave her at home, but their pleadings were unsuccessful. Jo was as eager to make the trip as was her husband.

Five other persons comprised the main expedition: Eivind Astrup, an athletic Norwegian; Dr. Frederick A. Cook, a genial man who was to be surgeon and ethnologist; Langdon Gibson, ornithologist and chief hunter; Matthew Henson, Peary's Negro manservant; and John Verhoeff, the Willamette River swimmer who was named as mineralogist and meteorologist. Accompanying the expedition, but only for the summer, were nine scientists from the Philadelphia Academy of Natural Sciences, led by Dr. Angelo Heilprin. They were to return with the ship after depositing Peary and his small party in Greenland.

On the 6th of June, 1891, this North Greenland Expedition sailed for the Far North in the barkentine *Kite,* a sealer of 280 tons commanded by Captain Richard Pike. A crowd of friends and curious sightseers covered the end of the pier at the foot of Baltic Street in Brooklyn, which was the site of Peary's departure. The friends were there to say good-by and perhaps, some thought, farewell; but many of the sightseers were there to gawk at this relatively unknown man who had the temerity to take his wife and five other persons into the obscurity of the Arctic — and for what reason? To these people the unmapped areas of the earth's surface posed no challenge, pricked no conscience, stirred no emotion whatsoever. Let it stay that way. There was change enough, anyway, in this nineteenth century, with new steam transportation, great industrial development, fresh and dangerous vices, problems with the new generation.

At five o'clock in the limpid late-spring afternoon the *Kite,* with auxilary steam power, pulled into the stream and was saluted by nearby ferry boats and steamers. The little vessel puffed under the Brooklyn Bridge, was dwarfed by it, and chugged on up the East River, where it met a fleet of Long Island Sound steamers whose passengers crowded the decks to wave handkerchiefs. Night fell as the little *Kite* entered the sound; the next morning at eight o'clock when Peary came on deck he saw Montauk Point abeam. Sails were shaken out, to take advantage of a light southwest breeze, and the North Greenland Expedition, for whatever future lay ahead, was on its way.

As was always the case, Peary was elated to be at sea and to be free, at last, from the rush of last-minute worries. From a stopover at Sydney he wrote his mother:

> At first as things came round in my favor I could hardly realize the meaning of it, but now I feel that all is written in the irrevocable book that I have been selected for this work and shall be upheld or carried safely and successfully through.[14]

Then the *Kite* headed northward again, and the closer Peary got to Greenland, the more ecstatic he became. It was as if he were going home. His exhilaration became evident in the pages of his diary:

Tonight an exquisite sunset, the sea like glass, reflecting the yellow and rose-tinted glories of the western sky, the Labrador coast purple as amethyst, strange fantastic bits of ice floating softly all about us, a subdued murmur from the edge of the pack as the ice cakes rise and fall with the gentle swell. . . .[15]

The following morning the *Kite* plowed into ice, which became more and more compacted and, after six hours, stopped further advance by the vessel. "Steam was run down," Peary wrote in his diary. "Everyone, Jo included, got out on the ice and took a promenade."

That event heralded further vicissitudes. A gale shrieked over topside decks, flinging almost solid sheets of cold rain before it, pounding the ship, churning the seas, and making life "a burden" for occupants of the tiny staterooms. Then came clear weather — then more ice.

Peary and his wife enjoyed watching from the bow while the *Kite* forced a passage:

Great masses of ice were thrust to one side. Sometimes a piece was split from a large floe and wedged under a larger floe, . . . the commotion causing the ice in the immediate vicinity to fairly boil. Then we would run against an extra solid floe that would not move when the *Kite* struck it, but let it ride right up on it and then gradually slide off and along the edge until it struck a weak place. Then the floe would be shivered, just as you would shiver a sheet of taffy when you strike it a sharp, hard blow. The pieces would be whirled against and on top of other pieces, crashing and splashing about until it seemed as though the ice must be as thick again as it was before the breakup, but the good old *Kite* just pushed them to one side, leaving them groaning and creaking in the distance at having been disturbed.[16]

The *Kite* called at Godhavn, on Disco Bay, on June 30th, and Peary exposed his wife to the lure of Greenland that had taken hold of him in 1886. They climbed the steep brown cliffs overlooking the settlement and sapphirine Disco Bay, alternately stepping over colorful wildflowers, ankle deep, walking across snowdrifts, then leaving footprints in moss "so soft and beautiful" — moss of all shades of green and red. During the climb they halted at every mountain stream, "tumbling down in every little gully," stooped down to drink, and thought it the best water they had ever tasted. Finally, from atop the cliffs overlooking the bay, they lingered for a long look: far below them, the tiny settlement of Godhavn and, beyond, blue Disco, thickly studded with icebergs that resembled a fleet of sailboats. A blue mist shrouded the brown cliffs lying in the shadows, providing a striking contrast to the radiant icebergs beyond, gleaming in dazzling sunlight.

After several calls on the Danish governor, the *Kite* sailed northward again on July 2nd — into stubborn ice that threatened to prove particularly frustrating: Peary hoped by July 15th to reach Whale Sound, there to offload his supplies and equipment and set up his Greenland headquarters.

Nine days later Captain Pike was still lobbing his ship at the ice, when, again, all progress stopped because of heavy fog. Then, late in the afternoon of a raw Saturday, July 11th, the curtain gradually lifted and the *Kite* began moving again. Peary anxiously gave the vessel mental thrusts forward toward clear water ahead that, said the mate, could be seen from the crow's nest.

Peary and his wife bundled up in warm clothing and went forward to the bow, their favorite ice-watching station. There, for about an hour, they peered over the side of the ship, fascinated by the exciting scene below: the *Kite* was slicing through a large area of rotten ice as if it were butter. The chill began to penetrate their clothing, however, and they retreated to their tiny stateroom to warm up. Peary could not stay in the room for long periods, and soon he and Jo were topside again, this time on the bridge.

The *Kite* was backing away from heavy ice ahead when Peary stepped behind the wheelhouse to look astern. At that instant the rudder struck a large cake of ice, jerking the wheel from the hands of the two helmsmen, who were thrown some distance across the deck, and forcing the iron tiller against the wheelhouse where Peary stood. Before he could realize what was happening, the tiller had broken his right leg just above the ankle. He thought he heard it snap. Instantly he knew he had been seriously hurt, and though he might have visualized more dreams crashing around him at that moment, he did not fall to the deck. His voice was calm as he asked one of the helmsmen to summon the doctors on board — Sharp and Cook.

Jo had not seen the accident, but when she noticed the helmsman hurry behind the wheelhouse she realized something had happened to her husband, and she rushed to see what the trouble was. She found Peary standing on one foot, "looking pale as death," and heard him say, "Don't be frightened, dearest. I have hurt my leg." [17]

Sharp and Gibson carried him below to his stateroom, discovered they could not squeeze him in, and in desperation laid him on a table in the cabin, where his leg was set and put in splints. A bed was improvised for him on a long seat across the head of the cabin, and there he lay, "cold as ice," but seared with pain that was unrelieved even after one of the doctors had given him a giant shot of whisky, and in doubt again about the future. Peary was never blessed with good luck; he had to fight for what he got, but he could retain a sense of humor. When his wife asked him what she might do to make his leg more comfortable he replied, "Oh, my dear, pack it in ice until someone can shoot it!" [18]

Only doses of morphine allowed Peary to get any rest for the first few days, and even then it was fitful. Worse, he began to have doubts about the activity above him. He had determined to continue with the expedition, but he feared someone would try to turn the ship back; so he had a compass installed nearby, to keep an eye on the course.

> The first day [his wife noted] everyone was very considerate, but the novelty wore off and now [they] rush in and out of the cabin at all hours of the day or night, and he is being disturbed constantly. He is just as good and patient as it is possible to be under the circumstances.[19]

As the days went by Peary's mental distress became as acute as his physical pain. Hearing activity on deck, he could only guess what might be happening. Once, five days after the accident, the watch on deck sighted a huge white bear with black snout, black eyes, and black toes advancing toward the ice-besieged ship. Eleven rifles roared almost simultaneously. The only knowledge Peary had of the occurrence was an immediate description from Jo, who then noticed her husband look longingly toward the deck and heard him murmur, "Oh, my, I wish I could be there." [20] After that she developed a primitive method of letting him glance at occurrences on deck: "Whenever anything particularly striking or pretty appeared I was called by someone on deck and with my hand glass I went upstairs, opened the transom over Bert's head, and succeeded in giving him a faint idea of how things looked by tipping the mirror." [21]

Peary's fears about the demand to turn back proved valid. With the *Kite* encountering more ice and further delay, and with the expedition leader helpless on his back in the cabin, one of the

Philadelphia scientists began to work up sentiment for returning home at once instead of going on to Whale Sound. Peary could, he reasoned, set up his headquarters at some point farther south if he still wanted to remain in Greenland for a year. Jo reported on his plotting:

He has not said a word to Bert about it but talks to members of our party and tries to intimidate them. He also talked with Captain Pike, even asking him to turn back, but the captain replied, "It is for the lieutenant [Peary] to give the order." I cannot lose the impression [the man] made first upon me. In spite of his being exceedingly nice to me I think he deals in an underhanded way and have told Bert to look out for him.[22]

Later:

[He] tried to convince me that it was my duty to take Mr. Peary home whether he wished it or not. He even said we better go home now when we had a good excuse than to stop a year at Whale Sound and then return unsuccessful, as he was positive we would.[23]

Finally:

[The man] at last summoned up courage enough to say to Bert today, "Well, Lieutenant, I am afraid we will have to change our course," to which Bert replied over the top of a novel, "Oh, we have a few more days time." This is the first time [the man] has mentioned the subject to Bert, although he has talked with all the members of our party and tried to frighten them into going back.[24]

Toward the end of July the *Kite* finally struggled into Whale Sound, and unloading commenced. On July 27th Peary was strapped to a board, lowered from the *Kite* into a boat, and rowed ashore to a tent that had been erected for him and his wife. It was located just in back of a house already under construction by the other expedition members, and at a site most favorable for raising low spirits. Nearby rippled a freshet; overhead cried flocks of little auks, the Arctic diving birds; from cold blue Whale Sound in the distance came an occasional crash and thunder of a sundering berg, which whipped the mirrorlike surface of the water into gentle undulations; and, along shore, the mosses showed a purplish hue, as if in their autumn foliage. That night a school of white whales "puffed and grunted" near the beach in front of the tent.

Two days later the *Kite* sailed for home, leaving the seven members of Peary's expedition ashore in these remote surroundings. Their snug headquarters house, named Red Cliff after the lichen-covered heights that overlooked it, had been nearly completed — and under the supervision of Peary, who oversaw the construction from his tent. Peary had drawn plans for it the winter before, basing them on requirements he had formulated after his broad Arctic reading.

He had decided on a small, compact house, one with only two rooms: a small one for him and his wife, a large one for the other five men. One large stove, set below the floor level in a pit lined with stones, heated the whole house; and as a further safeguard against fire, one man was always on watch.

The building was twenty-one feet long, twelve feet wide, eight feet high. Outside was a covering of tar paper, excellent for keeping out drafts, and entirely surrounding the house was a wall of turf and stones, topped with boxes of provisions arranged in rows. From them Jo, who was cook and dietitian for the expedition, could select her canned goods for the day's meals. Connecting this wall to the main house was a canvas roof, providing additional warmth as well as a space for stowing snow-laden fur garments outside the house.[25]

Impatiently, Peary began exercising his leg, putting pressure on his foot more and more often. Five weeks after the accident he noted that his recovery was "coming along well" — and he had plaudits for Dr. Cook, who had taken good care of him — but he mourned the valuable time lost. Six and a half weeks later he was still inactive:

. . . During the forenoon and early afternoon my . . . leg feels hot and full and uncomfortable, then it gets numb and does not bother me any more. When I take off the wraps at night the foot is the size of three, and foot and leg nearly devoid of sensation. The next morning the swelling is nearly gone but returns very soon after I get up.[26]

Autumn came on — a large supply of fresh meat was obtained by hunters — then winter neared, when a cold darkness would engulf Red Cliff, and blizzards would leave the house buried in snow. Peary spent the time arranging for an immigration of Eskimo families to the vicinity, dispatching his inexperienced men to the icecap in an unsuccessful attempt to lay down a series of caches for the spring work, studying the men, mulling over his plans for the long journey across the inland ice, and eternally testing his equipment. Two of his men proved to be extremely questionable. Of one, whose name has been deleted at the request of the Peary family, he observed:

. . . I have a strong suspicion that either from laziness or cowardice the idea of going on this inland ice trip makes [him] sick to his stomach, but it is too late to change now.[27] . . .

Am disappointed in this man, . . . next to the strongest in the party, yet the laziest and biggest eater; in fact, his voracious appetite is the cause of his present indisposition. He is said to have remarked that the inland ice trip next spring would be hell.[28]

The major disappointment was John Verhoeff, the expedition mineralogist, meteorologist, contributor of two thousand dollars, and winter swimmer of the Willamette River. Verhoeff proved to be not only a thrill seeker but also an independent soul who would not be bridled — just the sort of man who should have stayed away from Peary, or, in fact, from the leader of any serious exploring expedition.

Once, after Peary had reprimanded Verhoeff for venturing away from Red Cliff House to a distance greater than the five-hundred-yard limit Peary thought safe in the winter, Verhoeff pouted for days afterward and wrote in his diary, "I think the . . . rule a bugbear." [29] Two days after that, on February 22nd, 1892, Verhoeff turned twenty-six, and Jo prepared a dinner to celebrate his birthday — along with George Washington's. It was an excellent dinner, Verhoeff thought, but he was still in a petulant mood: ". . . I did not enjoy it as much as I would have if Peary had overlooked my error of the 20th," he wrote in his diary.

Furthermore, he did not like "the woman" Peary had brought along, and Jo did not waste any affection on him. When Verhoeff had the fire watch she braced herself for a few chilled hours in her quarters, which depended on heat from the stove in the big room. Verhoeff seemed to have a mania for saving fuel; one day he kept the fire going on six tomato cans of coal, and water spilled near the stove froze almost instantly.[30] "It is useless to remonstrate with him," Jo wrote. "He is determined to do just the opposite of what a person wants him to do." [31]

Verhoeff was indeed a puzzle. Not only did he not get along well with the Pearys; he engaged in frequent arguments with the other members of the expedition and with the Eskimos. He quarreled with Gibson; referred in his diary to Matt Henson as "the nigger"; shoved away from his proximity a nose-blowing Eskimo with such force that he "unfortunately tore his birdskin shirt." [32]

Later, Peary was to be known for his stern assessment of a man like Verhoeff, and to have no sympathy for a subordinate who was tried and found wanting. Now, however, he became solicitous of Verhoeff: he gave Verhoeff a pair of bearskin breeches and, another time, a pair of gloves, and on one occasion remarked to him that his meteorological observations would be "one of the principal features of the expedition," as Verhoeff stated in his diary.[33] Then Peary informed Verhoeff he would be leaving him at Red Cliff House to make these observations, instead of taking him on the long inland ice journey, and this probably represented something of a diplomatic triumph for Peary: the unreliable, unpredictable Verhoeff had been dumped from a role in the expedition, but without his realizing or resenting it. Still, Verhoeff remained a problem. "I hated to [take the gloves], not liking him," Verhoeff wrote of Peary and his gift, "[but] I could hardly refuse, and took them." [34]

Along with the men, Peary tested his equipment. Later he was to be recognized as one of the most ingenious of the Arctic explorers, but even now his cleverness was evident. He drew plans for lighter yet stronger sledges and devised loads down to the last ounce, for compact boats to probe the coastline, for light but warm sleeping bags, for many other items. One of the sleeping bags was being occasionally tested in March by the men, who slept in a snowhouse away from the warmth of Red Cliff. Only one person found the bag uncomfortable; that was the unnamed man with the "voracious appetite" with whom Peary had already become disillusioned.

> [He] . . . got his bag and went out with me, but when I came into the house at 7 A.M. this morning he was, much to my surprise, in his bunk, having come in in about an hour, after I had gone to sleep, with some lame excuse about his mitten falling off. He seems to be a coward as to the cold.
>
> I wore a Jaros undershirt and a pair of short reindeer fur stockings inside my bag and was comfortable and slept well,

though not all the time, owing to the novelty and my desire to watch myself carefully.

. . . I think it is a very good indication of the superiority of my sleeping gear over that of [Sir Clements] Markham . . . or [George] Kennan. Markham's men slept in misery or not at all in temperatures of minus fifteen to minus twenty-five degrees in the tent . . . and Kennan speaks of minus thirty-five degrees as his limit of comfort with a sleeping rig weighing, I should judge from his description, more than twice as much as mine.[35]

The rest of the winter working time Peary devoted to a study of the Eskimos, a few of whom lived around his headquarters. He listened to their speech, observed their habits and mannerisms, and photographed them. Peary had a knack of inspiring confidence in Eskimos — of winning their friendship — and he honestly liked these Arctic people. This winter work laid the groundwork for his future dealings with these natives, who were to prove essential to his success. From the Eskimos Peary learned how to build snowhouses, how to drive a team of dogs with only a whip to guide them, how to fashion fur clothing loose enough to allow for the circulation of air but still be windproof and snowproof.

Jo was less enthusiastic about the association. She was shocked by some of the customs: Eskimo women would strip to the waist, along with the men, when a snowhouse interior became too hot; and an Eskimo man visiting from another settlement without his *koonah*, or wife, had at his disposal the *koonah* of the owner of the igloo where he was visiting. "If he brings his own," Jo wrote with obvious disgust, "they trade for the time being."[36]

The ethnological studies and his planning kept Peary busy — kept everyone busy, in fact, and deliberately so; for Peary believed that an expedition with too much idle time would deteriorate rapidly. As soon as Peary observed the first hint of returning light, however, he hastened plans for taking to the inland ice; and, happily, he could walk now. In mid-February he, Astrup, and Dr.

Cook departed on a trial journey that almost ended disastrously and taught Peary a lesson: never try sleeping unclad in his new, light, efficient bag, leaving the clothes outside, no matter how comfortable it might be. Thereafter none of Peary's men went to sleep in the field with their clothing outside the sleeping bag.

The first night out on the icecap they found shelter in a snow-house still standing from the fall work. Instead of a dome this igloo had a flat roof made of skis with snow blocks arranged on top of them; and the amateurism nearly proved fatal. After supper they undressed and crawled into their bags. They were asleep when a raw spring blizzard struck.

. . . [I was] awakened by the roar of the storm and the snow driving in my face. Looking over the foot of my bag, I could just see, in the faint light of day, that the cutting drift had eaten off the angle of the igloo where roof and end wall met, had completely filled that end, and was rapidly covering us. As I watched it, roof and wall melted away as fine sand before a water jet; and by the time I could arouse Dr. Cook, adjust my hood, and tighten my bag, it required a good deal of effort to force myself up through the superincumbent weight of snow. The doctor also succeeded in liberating himself, but Astrup, who was lying on the other side of the igloo, could not get free.

Telling Dr. Cook to keep a breathing hole open for Astrup, I rose up in my bag, forced the ski apart, rolled out over the wall, bag and all, and reached the shovel at the entrance, then rolled back to the end of the igloo, and crouched against the wall on the outside to get my breath. Then I crept around to the side where Astrup was, and crouching before the howling wind, tore a hole through the side wall and freed his head and body, and with the doctor's assistance, pulled him out.

Here we were in our sleeping bags, clad only in our under-clothing and with our fur garments and footgear buried deep under the snow. We could not have stood up before such a gale if we had tried. All we could do was to crouch, half sitting, with our backs to the storm, in the breach I had made in that part of the igloo wall which was still standing. We sat there hour after hour until nearly night, when the doctor and Astrup were again both fast, and needed assistance to release them from the drift. While performing this work of necessity, we managed to dig from under the snow a little pemmican and a few biscuits, and ate them. Astrup then wriggled alongside me, and the doctor rolled a few feet to leeward of where the house had been, and thus night settled down upon us.

We were lying out on the icecap over two thousand feet above sea level, wholly without shelter, on the top of the drift, beneath which our snow hut was buried. The snow flew past us with such a roar that I had to shout at the top of my voice to be heard by Astrup, who was lying partly upon me. After an hour or so, his weight and that of the snow became oppressive, and I worked myself loose and crawled a little to one side and to windward, into the wind ditch alongside the big drift over the house. Here, in a sitting posture, with back to the wind and side against the drift, I sat out the night. By lowering my chin upon my breast, I could keep most of the drift out of my face, and by raising my head I could feel rather than see the two dark prostrate objects close to me to leeward, and at intervals shout to them to inquire if they were warm enough.

Occasionally I dozed a little, but most of the time I was studying how we should extricate ourselves from our predicament if the storm continued for several days. My greatest source of anxiety was the fact that the suddenness with which we were compelled to free ourselves from the drift had left our outer clothing and footgear deep under the drift, my dogskin trousers being the only thing that was brought out. I knew that we were good for at least twenty-four hours longer in the bags, but if the storm continued longer than that, I should have to try and dig out a *kooletah* and a pair of *kamiks*, and get to the house for clothing.

Dozing again, I suddenly awoke to hear a rattling as of hail against my hood, and putting my hand out through the sleeve of the bag, [felt] great drops of rain [drive] against it, freezing as they struck. Moving in my bag, I felt that it had stiffened greatly, but fortunately was not yet frozen down. Calling to the boys, I told them to roll their bags gently from side to side every few minutes to prevent their freezing down, and then anxiously waited developments. The continuation of the rain would, I knew, make the digging out of our clothing impossible, and if I had to go down to the house, I should have to wear the upper part of my bag cut off for a *kooletah*, my dogskin trousers, and a pair of reindeer-skin sleeping socks which I had in my bag cover. I was worse off than either of the others, for they had on complete suits of underwear, including stockings, while I wore only an undershirt.

To my infinite relief the rain did not last much more than an hour, and then the snow resumed its sway. Very soon, too, the wind ceased its steady, monotonous roar, and began to come in intermittent squalls. This, I hailed with delight, as a sign of the near breaking of the storm. I fell asleep again. When I next awoke, I found the opening of my hood closed with balls of ice, but the wind was much less violent, and the intervals between the gusts were longer. Putting out a hand and tearing away the ice, I looked out, and to my delight found moonlight flooding the inland ice, the moon having just broken through a rift in the black clouds over Herbert Island. It had stopped snowing, but the wind was still whirling the fine snow along the surface.

I immediately conveyed the pleasing intelligence to the boys, and learning from the doctor that he was cold, I got over to him as well as I could in my sleeping bag and curled myself around and against the head of his bag, to windward. This expedient did not succeed in making him more comfortable, and as the temperature was rapidly lowering I rolled back, got the shovel, and succeeded in digging a hole, down into the snow. I then got the doctor's bag loose, pulled the sleeves out of the frozen crust, adjusted his hood, and helped him to wriggle to the hole, into which he tumbled and curled himself up. I . . . placed my trousers over his head to keep the drift off, and curled myself round the windward edge of the hole above him. I was very glad to find that the complete protection from the wind thus afforded him, together with the exercise of moving, restored his temperature and rendered him entirely comfortable.

In this way we lay for several hours, the wind gradually dying away, and the light of day increasing. Then as Astrup was more completely dressed than any of us, I requested him to make the attempt to dig out our clothing. I was obliged, however, to go to his assistance, and break his bag free, clear the ice from the opening of his hood, adjust it, and help him to a sitting posture. In doing this, one of the sleeves of his bag was unfortunately torn off, and when he began to shovel, his arm was so cold that he could do no effective work, so I told him to lie down, and I took the shovel. It was now 8:45 A.M., Tuesday, and after a long time, and with much trouble, owing to the hard snow, the coldness of my hands, and the difficulty of working hampered by my sleeping bag, I dug out a *kooletah,* a pair of trousers, and a pair of *kamiks.* Astrup then got out of his bag into these, and after a brisk run to limber himself up, took the shovel and continued the work of excavation. The temperature at this time was plus 3 degrees Fahrenheit, with a light breeze blowing.

As soon as Astrup had dug out another *kooletah,* a pair of trousers, and a pair of *kamiks,* I sent him to help Dr. Cook put them on. The doctor was now thoroughly chilled again, and anxious to get out of his bag, so that he could warm himself with exercise.

While he did this, I excavated my corner of the igloo and got out the stove, tea, sugar, and milk, and lit the lamp for a pot of hot tea. It was now 11:45 A.M., and the southern sky was a mass of crimson, rose, purple, and green clouds. There was one dazzling yellow spot where the sun was about to burst into view. I pulled the Dahlgren and Academy ensigns and the sledge banners from my bag cover, shook them out, fastened them to the ski and alpenstock as flagstaffs, and then drove these into the firm snow. At that moment the wind freshened and the bright folds of our banners, the fairest in the world, flew out into the sparkling air.

Then the yellow sunlight fell upon the highest bluff of Northumberland Island west of us. A minute later Cape Robertson, to the northwest, blazed with a crown of glory — and then the great yellow orb, for whose coming we had so longed, peered over the icecap south of Whale Sound.

In an instant the snow waves of the inland ice about us danced, a sea of sparkling, molten gold. Neither gold, nor fame, nor aught can purchase from me the supreme memory of that moment when on the icecap, far above the earth, with the rustling of the Stars and Stripes in my ears, I laughed with the laughing waves of the great white sea, in greeting to the returning sun.[37]

Peary returned to Red Cliff, and on the third of May he departed on the big journey. His plans had been refined long ago. For the trip he would have a small party — four men would start out, but two would turn back after providing some early support. He would use Eskimo dogs, twenty in all, to haul the light, strong sledges — the dogs not only were hardy beasts; they could be fed to each other if the pemmican supply should become dangerously low, and, in the direst of situations, they could provide food for man too. The loads were thoroughly checked and weighed; only the barest essentials of pemmican, condensed milk, biscuit, compressed pea soup, medical supplies, and navigation equipment were loaded. Space was allowed for one Winchester carbine with a full magazine and one box of cartridges. Not even a tent was included; the men would sleep in snowhouses built as needed.

Peary, Astrup, Cook, and Gibson comprised the traveling party.

Henson went along too, to help during the first few days, but he was to return after that.

Peary encountered typical luck: three dogs died of *piblockto*, a madness brought on by extended exposure to the terrible Arctic weather, and a fourth broke his traces and escaped; Peary ordered Gibson back for more alcohol and extra snowshoes, and was approached by a complaining Henson who spoke of a painful heel — so he had to send Henson back too; storms of wind and snow delayed them, once for forty-eight hours.

On May 24th Cook and Gibson turned back. They took with them two dogs, further depleting Peary's force, a sledge, and food for twelve days. Peary and the young Norwegian Astrup continued on toward the unknown area ahead over marble-hard *sastrugi* — wind carvings on the snow — that battered sledges and eventually smashed the largest of them. Peary was on the verge of discarding it, then used it, secured to the side of another one, as an ingenious three-runnered catamaran.

Progress became agonizingly slow. Four days after Cook and Gibson had turned back, Peary and Astrup came upon soft snow on a rising grade that made travel so difficult the dogs refused to pull until conditions improved. Then they relented and went to work, but in another bit of hard going later on the men actually pulled the reluctant dogs. They encountered crevasses, necessitating a long detour; ran into a windstorm that stopped them for another forty-eight hours; hit a steep, slippery surface that gave both men and dogs numerous bad falls.

A series of undated notes, all in Peary's handwriting and all in his 1892 diary, described the hardships:

> The hard surfaces, the hummock slopes, and the strong cross wind have made the "ski" worry and tire me very much. Frequent falls. Yet they are superior to snowshoes.

> Dogs would not pull sledge this morning in the deep soft snow, so Astrup and I got in the traces with them. The pace

then seemed very slow and the forenoon seemed rather a blue one for me.

Eyes troubling me very much in afternoon and at last decided to try a pair of the dark glasses. Relief instant and complete — though much darker I can see much clearer than before.

Note [the] alternating stroke of ski in good going, like motions of connecting rods of locomotive, also crisp swish, swish on the snow like steam escape from cylinders. God grant these ski may keep up their stroke to Greenland's *ultima Thule* [northernmost point].

Feel less like writing than for last three or four days even. It seems almost sure my dream of years is ended. This cursed land is forcing more and more to the east and south. I have not yet been to the 82nd meridian. But I will do all that man may do.

It is now twenty-seven hours since I turned out and during twenty-three of them have been traveling over the roughest kind of ice and ground, all the time with a troubled mind, part of it in bitterness of spirit. The combination has nearly done me up. I defer the writing up my trip down into the valley till tomorrow.

Peary was obviously in a spiritual valley himself at this time, but the valley he referred to was a literal one. He and Astrup had stumbled across a descent from the icecap leading to a moraine and had made camp there. Without halting Peary had gone on to climb a mountain that he estimated lay five miles away; there, he hoped, he would get a view to the eastward. The mountain proved to be almost three times as far as he had estimated, however; sharp rocks cut his *kamiks* — or footgear — to pieces; and the mountain failed to provide any enlightenment as to what lay to the eastward anyway. Bitterly, Peary returned to the moraine camp, but he had one consolation: he had noticed signs of musk oxen. After a five-hour sleep he returned to the area with Astrup and the dogs — but without sledges — and shot two of the animals. Men and dogs gorged on this fresh meat, rested, and continued on eastward, hoping to get a view. Twenty-six miles from their moraine camp they finally stumbled upon it unexpectedly: a high plateau dropping off in an awesome wall almost four thousand feet high. Before them they had an unbroken panorama. Peary named this height Navy Cliff.

Before us stretched new lands and waters, to which, with the explorer's prerogative, I gave names, as follows: The bay at our feet, opening into the Arctic Ocean halfway between the 81st and 82nd parallels of latitude, was named Independence Bay in honor of the day, July 4th; the red-brown land beyond the fjord which had stopped our forward northward progress was called Heilprin Land; and a still more distant land beyond the entrance of a second fjord, Melville Land. The enormous glacier at our right, flowing due north into Independence Bay, received the name of Academy Glacier, and the bold rugged land beyond it, Daly Land.[38]

From where he stood, Independence Bay far below him seemed to extend northwestward, no doubt on to the west coast, as a channel: a great cleft separated the nearer plateau summits from those beyond. This, then, proved the insularity of Greenland, Peary thought. He was, however, wrong; the cleft was not a channel, and land's end in Greenland lay another hundred miles away. Later Peary's enemies were to use the mistake in an effort to embarrass him, and they labeled the cleft "Peary Channel," but certain explorers who followed Peary to Navy Cliff voiced an understanding of how the mistake had been possible. Among them

were Peter Freuchen, second in command to the Danish explorer
Knud Rasmussen on the First Thule Expedition of 1912, and
Lauge Koch, another distinguished Danish explorer.

In any event, Peary was unable to probe farther northward.
The surface was much too rough for his sledges; his dog team was
dwindling; and his supplies were running low. He and Astrup
built a cairn on Navy Cliff, left a record of discovery dated July
5th, then retreated to the moraine camp, got the sledges, and
dashed southward for Red Cliff House — or at least they tried to
dash. The first few marches were easy, but then they met with
the same problems as before: storms, crevasses, tired and dying
dogs, rough ice surface. Again the diary entries testify to the
trials:

> July 14. Today has been a dismal one for me and I have had
> a severe attack of blues, so I had to send Astrup ahead and
> drive the dogs myself in order to divert my thoughts.
> July 17. . . . Eyes almost useless. Odom[eter] breaks. Ta-
> manoh [one of the dogs] on sledge, I driving afternoon. Ski
> and snowshoes. Musk ox tongue, stew, extra pea soup. Self out
> of condition, pain in bowels due to bit of musty pemmican.

On July 21st Peary figured he had only ninety pounds of pemmican to feed two men and the six remaining dogs for the estimated twenty more days of the return trip, but they succeeded.
On August 4th a party from Red Cliff under Professor Heilprin, who had returned on the *Kite*, met them near the edge of the
inland ice. Peary's trip not only proved his stamina but also his
navigational ability: although he had been able to get only three
observations on the return journey, his dead reckoning position
was only five miles removed from his true location.

One last trial remained for Peary before the *Kite* sailed.

Gibson and Verhoeff were in a "boat camp" several miles from
Red Cliff, Gibson chasing birds for his ornithological collection

and Verhoeff scouring for mineral specimens. One morning
Verhoeff came into camp long overdue and explained he had
walked six miles past the camp before realizing his mistake. Gibson laughed and joshed Verhoeff for the error, then heard Verhoeff tell of being compelled to climb a glacier during his wanderings, cutting more than a hundred steps with his axe. "I suppose
Mr. Peary would have considered it dangerous," Verhoeff remarked.[39]

Gibson prepared to leave, in the boat, for Red Cliff, but Verhoeff wanted to poke around the vicinity a while longer. He asked
to have the boat sent for him in three days, but he was never seen
after that. For four days after Verhoeff's disappearance Peary
sent out search parties that climbed over rocks, peered into crevasses, trudged across the ice, fired rifle volleys, left food caches;
and he offered the natives rewards for finding Verhoeff. The only
probable trace anyone ever found was a small collection of rocks
evidently placed on a large, flat boulder by Verhoeff to lighten his
knapsack prior to crossing a glacier. His footprints were visible in
the vicinity.[40]

Peary left for Verhoeff four hundred pounds of provisions,
marked by a cairn, and the *Kite* left for home August 24th. Four
days later Peary wrote in his diary, "Last night after we turned in
Jo was actually homesick for Red Cliff House." [41] Peary himself
soon yearned again for the sights and sounds of Greenland, and
for another crack at his big opportunity. Shortly after his return
to the United States he startled his friends and relatives by announcing his intention of lecturing during the winter to raise
money for another expedition, which would return to Whale
Sound by late June of 1893.

Chapter 8

ROBERT PEARY returned from the expedition of 1891–1892 on a growing tide of the fame he sought. That expedition had been deceptively easy, despite all the momentary troubles that had beset it, and the results had been widely publicized and enthusiastically received by geographers and scientific societies. Among the many letters of congratulation came one from Fridtjof Nansen, the man who had beaten Peary across the inland ice. Nansen signed the letter, "Your admirer."

> As I am one of those who have seen a little of the inland ice and who have followed your expedition with the keenest interest and sympathy I hope you will not think it impudent when I now send you my most heartfelt congratulations with your wonderful achievements and grand results. Certainly not many will better understand what a piece of work you have performed, and not many have awaited with more impatience to hear what you would find in the unknown North of the inland ice.[1]

Peary's recent success inspired him to plan to return to Greenland as soon as he could make the necessary arrangements: obtain more leave, raise the money, select personnel, get a ship and supplies.

Most urgent of his immediate problems was obtaining leave of absence from the Navy. Many of Peary's colleagues had begun to

look with disfavor on his explorations. Some resented his growing fame, particularly since he was little more, in their judgment,
than a civilian allowed to wear a naval officer's uniform. Others
disapproved of his apparent neglect of naval duties — this despite
the fact that, in certain other countries, military services encouraged exploration by their qualified personnel — as would, in fact,
the United States, in later years.

For help in persuading the Navy to grant him another leave,
Peary turned to the Philadelphia Academy of Natural Sciences,
which had sponsored his 1891–1892 work. The Academy president, General I. J. Wistar, was taken by Peary's enthusiasm for
further exploration of Greenland, and for a possibility of reaching
the North Pole, and he presented Peary's case to the secretary of
the Navy so effectively that Peary was given a three-year leave.

Now money became the foremost problem, but Peary's growing
fame was sufficient for the lecture platform to promise a quick and
sure way of raising a good deal of the necessary funds. In the
autumn of 1892 Peary approached a well-known lecture agent, J.
B. Pond, but Pond tried to delay him. It was too late, Pond said,
to arrange any lecture tour of 1893.

Again Peary's enthusiasm prevailed, and Pond set about sched-
uling lectures. After it was over, Pond remarked that Peary's tour
was one of the most successful he had ever arranged.

Peary took his always-professional attitude to the platform. If
he had to learn showmanship, which he despised, he would do
that — to further his work where it mattered: in the Arctic. For
Peary's lectures Matt Henson dressed, and perspired, in the furs
he had used for Arctic travel, and Peary used as stage ornaments
his sledges, snowshoes, harpoons, cooking utensils, and other
equipment.

He even exhibited the half-dozen dogs that had survived the
1892 traversal of northeast Greenland. The animals, managed
during the tour by Henson, added not only color but occasional

humor to the lectures: when Peary talked too long the dogs became restless and, as if they had been taught, joined in a howling protest that ended the lecture soon thereafter.

In January of 1893 Peary had only four days without lectures. For most talks he received from one hundred fifty to two hundred dollars, but for one — in Philadelphia — he was paid six hundred dollars.

". . . The sole purpose of my lectures," Peary explained to the editor of the Washington *Post*,[2] "is the raising of the necessary funds for the coming Arctic expedition. I have preferred, if possible, to defray the entire expense of the next expedition myself, and the lectures seem to offer the means of doing this." Peary wanted no more trouble with expedition members like John Verhoeff, whose two-thousand-dollar contribution in 1891 scarcely made up for the disturbances he created.

Peary hoped to sail in June, and he drove himself nearly to exhaustion in keeping the lecture schedule while still handling overall planning. He spoke 165 times in 103 days, earning from these lectures twenty thousand dollars. After deducting expenses, he was able to put thirteen thousand dollars toward financing the expedition. Between appearances he kept two secretaries busy with his detailed planning.

An important job was selecting personnel for the expedition. From among hundreds of letters that poured in from hopeful persons of all ages and both sexes Peary carefully picked out the few intelligent or otherwise interesting queries: he realized that an expedition such as his would attract a good many crackbrains and malcontents, and he knew such persons must be weeded out. Just one flawed character might cause disaster for an entire expedition.

He chose his people slowly, after studying their biographical résumés and trying to read between the lines, and after careful observation of the individuals during personal interviews. He demanded self-reliant men with the mental makeup to withstand the dreary Arctic winters without depending on the society of others. He also, however, sought jovial men, who could contribute to mutual pleasure when thrown into the society of others during the winters. Eivind Astrup, the youthful Norwegian from the previous expedition, was selected this time without such scrutiny, however, as was Dr. Cook, the amiable 1891–1892 surgeon who had efficiently cared for Peary's broken leg. Another automatic selection was Matt Henson, Peary's manservant. Astrup, Cook, and Henson all had Peary's confidence. Later Cook decided not to go, and Peary was forced to look for another surgeon.

Occasionally Peary based a decision purely on intuition instead of on methodical analysis, and he chose one member of the forthcoming expedition in this manner. Hugh J. Lee, a young Easterner, mailed his application, waited awhile for an answer, then sent Peary a postal card requesting an answer and demanding that he not be "kept like Mohammed's coffin, suspended between Heaven and earth." [3] The card convinced Peary that Lee was a strong-minded youth who could probably help take some slack out of sagging spirits during the dreary Arctic night, and he sent him a letter of acceptance. It proved to be a fortunate choice.

Eventually Peary's Second Greenland Expedition — which would actually represent his third visit there — was composed of Samuel J. Entrikin, first assistant; Astrup, second assistant; Evelyn Briggs Baldwin, meteorologist; Dr. Edwin E. Vincent, surgeon; Lee, George F. Clark, George H. Carr, James Davidson, and Walter F. Swain, assistants; Henson; and an independent member, Frederick Stokes, an artist who paid his own way.

Each of these men received the same contract, one that was to be used by Peary in all his later expeditions. It stated that Peary was to be the sole commander of the expedition, that each "signee" would faithfully obey all directions and carry out instructions of Peary and ". . . will loyally aid and support the said Peary by all means in his power, to accomplish each and every object and purpose of the expedition aforesaid, in such manner as the said Peary shall deem best and require." Finally, each man agreed not to write or lecture or otherwise to give out information on the expedition, and agreed to turn over to Peary all diaries and journals kept during the expedition. The latter clause was an important one to Peary: he knew that writing and lecturing would provide his chief means of raising money for future work, and he did not want to have these profits divided.

In return, Peary promised to provide transportation from a specified departing place and return, and to furnish equipment like snowshoes, a rifle and ammunition, hunting knife and belt, sleeping bag. The salaries, invariably small, were to be paid upon return.

To the general dismay of the public, Peary announced that his wife would again make the trip too, and this time she was expecting a baby in September. Accompanying Jo, then, would be a nurse, Mrs. Susan J. Cross. The inclusion of an assistant-and-companion for Jo still failed to placate most people, who were insistent that Peary ought to leave his wife at home.

Jo herself had, however, been left at home much too often. When Peary was devoting all of his time to traveling, lecturing, and expedition planning she had stayed at home — and, unlike her husband, she had little to occupy her time, and she had despaired of herself and of their marriage. Once she wrote him an unusually railing letter, when he asked her to join him for part of a tour:

> I shall not attempt to tell you how wretched I feel, both mentally and physically, because in your good heartedness you would make yourself miserable.
> . . . Try to think kindly of me when you give me a thought. My greatest fault is my love for you to the exclusion of everyone else and it is too late to remedy it now. Had I known how matters stood when we were first married things might be very

different now. But I do not feel equal to the separation from you all over again and shall therefore remain at home.

She added a postscript, however, with old feeling:

Do take care of yourself. Remember without health your money will do you very little good. If you conveniently can let me hear from you often. Your letters are all I have left me now. . . .[4]

Why should a man leave a charming, devoted wife, one now expecting a child of his, and leave a comfortable naval billet, all in preparation for another trip to the northern wilderness? The old desire for fame and money provided part of the answer, but Peary, after one serious expedition to the Arctic, was veteran enough to realize that fame could surely be earned more easily elsewhere. The fact is that demands, hardships, and disappointments — although they were nothing compared to what they would be — had burned into Peary a greater degree of maturity. Now he felt:

Noble daring has made the Arctic ice and waters classic ground. It is no feverish excitement or vain ambition that leads man there. It is a higher feeling, a holier motive — a desire to look into the works of Creation, to comprehend the economy of our planet, and to grow wiser and better by the knowledge.[5]

This time, Peary announced, he would take more men on the icecap, begin the journey earlier, and hope to accomplish more. Three parties totaling eight men would travel from the west coast northeastward across the ice to Independence Bay, which Peary had viewed in 1892 from Navy Cliff and near where he had killed musk oxen. There one party of three men would continue northward along the coast in the hope, perhaps, even of reaching the North Pole. Another group of three would follow the coast southward to Cape Bismarck, a point on the east coast located about 77 degrees north latitude, and map the previously unknown area, then return across the ice to the main base on the west coast. The third party of two men, both of them accomplished hunters, would remain in the Independence Bay region, to lay in a meat supply from the musk oxen there — for the return trip of the northern party, and of themselves, across the ice to the main base.[6]

He would also take, for experimental use, eight burros from Sante Fe, New Mexico, although he planned to rely on dogs as sledge animals, and some carrier pigeons for rapid communication with his main base. The proposed use of burros was based on their success as transportation in the Rocky Mountains and in other cold areas of the Western states.

These plans were formulated by an overly optimistic Peary, a man who had, for once, been deceived by the ease with which he had conducted his earlier expedition. He later regretted his indiscretion, particularly his failure to recognize the limits of endurance of his Eskimo dogs and his befogged judgment that led him to try to take a large party into the field. He was to admit he had been carried away by enthusiasm. Rarely afterward was he to be found so brimming with advance optimism about the smoothness of Arctic work.

Moreover, he had been too optimistic about the financing. As he prepared to sail, in "a trim, black-hulled, yellow-masted bark" named the *Falcon,* he became aware that his lecture profits had fallen considerably short of expedition requirements; and to aggravate matters, a growing silver panic had wiped out some promised contributions. Nevertheless, Peary had a last-hope plan he reluctantly resorted to for raising the rest of the money. Somewhat inured to showmanship after his lecture tour, he decided on exhibiting the ship and its people to curious throngs at East Coast ports for an admission price of twenty-five cents. After its inaugural display at Philadelphia, the *Falcon* sailed down the Delaware River on June 26th, 1893. Further exhibitions at Brooklyn, Boston, and Portland erased the deficit as the quarters poured in, and on July 8th the *Falcon*, whose master was a Newfoundlander, Captain Harry Bartlett, swung away from her pier in Portland Harbor and headed north.

> I had hoped to visit for an hour or so my little Eagle Island, but our direct course was too far from it, and I did not care to delay the ship solely for that, so I was content to see its green dome standing out against the misty background of beautiful Casco Bay. As the sun went down, the wind freshened, raising a little sea, which thumped against the weather bow, and occasionally came splashing up on the quarterdeck.[7]

The next day was a rough one, especially for a nonveteran like young Hugh Lee, whose seasickness kept him in his bunk. Peary sent down oranges for him, and the steward brought some crackers. This combination he was able to eat, but he remained below for the next few days.

The *Falcon* coaled at Saint John's, Newfoundland, and stopped at ports in Labrador and Greenland to procure dogs. The last part of the voyage north, across dreaded Melville Bay, usually jammed with ice, went by with amazing speed — in twenty-four hours fifty minutes — and on August 3rd the *Falcon* moored quietly in Bowdoin Bay, in Inglefield Gulf. One of Peary's first tasks was to look for John Verhoeff, who had vanished on the last expedition, but no trace was found. He questioned the Eskimos, who hesitated to answer because they never speak of the dead. Finally they said they had seen no trace of him.

Peary now selected the site for his headquarters, which he was to call Anniversary Lodge. Construction and unloading commenced; Peary sent out walrus- and reindeer-hunting parties for meat supplies; Astrup led a group onto the icecap to cache supplies for the crossing later, but miserable weather rendered this work a disappointment. On August 20th the *Falcon* nosed southward on its homeward voyage.

Now disappointments came — in the ineffectiveness of the burros and the homing pigeons. Moreover, the poor burros were having trouble from another quarter: Peary's savage sledge dogs suspected that burros were good to eat, a notion that later events proved for them to be true — when several of the animals died and were fed to the dogs. After that Peary was forced to maintain a close security around the remaining burros to keep them alive.

Some homing pigeons, too, fell victim to the dogs, and others were killed by falcons. Only one message was to be carried successfully by a pigeon —and that, from a point only twelve miles out on the icecap. Most of the pigeons were dead before the winter arrived; those that remained then became stupid with the cold and the dark. One day the last remaining pigeon put his head through the bars of his cage and had it instantly snapped off by a dog.

Peary was disappointed, but he was nudged back into his old concept of Arctic life: that a stranger would have to reconcile himself to the region instead of trying to fit the region to him. Peary wrote:

> I am led to believe that this region is adapted only for those species of life which are found here and that any other species either of bird or animal can at best have a precarious and short-lived existence here.[8]

One new life, however, succeeded in thriving. In the early evening of September 12th, 1893, Jo Peary gave birth to an 8.7-pound baby girl, who was given the name Marie Ahnighito. The baby had deep-set blue eyes and quickly impressed her nurse, Mrs. Cross, as being unusually bright and strong. Never before had a white child been born in such an extreme northern latitude.

The first six months of her life were spent in continuous lamp-light [Peary wrote]. When the earliest ray of the returning sun pierced through the window of our tiny room, she reached for the golden bar as other children reach for a beautiful toy. . . . Throughout the winter she was the source of the liveliest interest to the natives. Entire families journeyed from far-away Cape York to the south, and from distant Etah to the north, to satisfy themselves by actual touch that she was really a creature of warm flesh and blood, and not of snow, as they at first believed.[9]

Even after the Eskimos had satisfied their curiosity, however, Marie Ahnighito's nickname remained: she was the Snow Baby. Jo Peary was a proud mother; she commented that Marie "is just as good as a baby can be . . . sleeps nicely at night and only wakes to drink and be changed." [10] The awesomeness of new fatherhood, however, at first overwhelmed Peary, who shrank from even touching his newborn for the first eighteen days of her life, an omission that led his wife to conclude, ". . . He don't like my baby." She doubled her attentions, and — as a precaution against her own death — she fed the baby a bit of condensed milk regularly to get Marie used to a bottle.

Disaster did not enter Anniversary Lodge, however; it occurred outside. First, the services of two key men engaged in the vital work of laying down caches on the inland ice were lost, Astrup with a severe stomach disturbance and Carr with a back injury after a fall on the ice. Then, on October 31st, while Peary was absent from the lodge, a giant iceberg broke off from nearby Bowdoin Glacier, thundered into the sea, and created a huge wave that bellied up the ice-covered bay and broke, on the shore, in a roaring cataract of foam and water. A steam launch and two other boats were smashed and, worse, every barrel of oil except the one in use at the lodge was engulfed in swirling water which tossed the precious fuel about and slammed it against the rocky shore. When the wave receded it carried the barrels of oil with it.

An appalled Hugh Lee had witnessed the calamity from beginning to end from just outside the lodge door. He hurried with the bad news to Peary, who was some five miles distant preparing to move onto the icecap for a brief journey. Lee later recalled that when he informed Peary that all of his fuel had been swept into the bay Peary paused in dismay, then said with unconscious histrionics, "The fates and all hell are against me, but I'll conquer yet." [12] They both hurried back to Anniversary Lodge, where all available hands spent a full day retrieving bobbing oil barrels from the ice water. They found three or four had been completely smashed and many others damaged. Much of the oil had been lost, and Peary canceled his plans to install an electric-light plant for the lodge.

On March 6th, 1894, the Second Greenland Expedition commenced the long journey across the inland ice. In the party were Peary and seven other of his men (who were to turn back after four or five days), five Eskimos, twelve sledges, and more than ninety dogs. This represented an earlier start by nearly two months over his 1892 trip — and an initial traveling party of three times the size. Furthermore, this time his men were hauling on their sledges tents and deerskin sleeping bags. Despite all this relative luxury, the traveling party was doomed to a wretched existence on the ice, and eventually to utter failure.

The debacle began on March 10th, when one of the dogs developed the dreaded *piblockto*. Two days later Lee and Astrup became infirm, Lee with a frozen toe and Astrup with his old stomach trouble. Both had to be returned on March 14th to Anniversary Lodge by the two strongest men of the party, Peary and Clark, who delivered their charges and dashed back to the main party.

On March 22nd they met bad weather: furious headwinds that hurled a stinging drift into them, all in a temperature of from 35 to 40 degrees below zero. After three miles the dogs refused to pull the sledges farther, and Peary had no choice but to camp. He, Entrikin, and Baldwin put up one tent and lighted an alcohol cooker; the three other men occupied another.

The dogs were fastened as usual, each team was divided into groups, and, dinner over, we turned in. About five o'clock next morning I was awakened by a sudden increase in the force of the wind, which now blew with such violence that, had not our tent been all in one piece, connected with the floor cloth on which we were lying, I should have expected to have had it blown away at any moment.

The drift which accompanied this storm was almost indescribable, and had the members of the party been any less perfectly clothed than they were, it would have been impossible to have gone out of our shelter. As it was, however, Baldwin made his regular observations at the observatory sledge, about one hundred feet from the tent, and he and I took turns in carrying hot tea and pea soup to the three men in the [other] tent, about fifty feet distant. Throughout the day and the following night, the wind steadily increased in violence, until it became impossible to shout so as to be heard from one tent to the other, even with the utmost effort of our lungs.

On Thursday afternoon, the drift forced an entrance into the [other] tent, and in order to escape being smothered, its occupants were obliged to get out as best they could and retreat to [our] tent. In doing this, Davidson had his heel, and Clark a toe, two fingers, and a thumb, frost-bitten. As soon as they were safely in our tent, Entrikin turned out of his bag and gave his place to Clark. I turned my deerskin sleeping trousers over to Davidson, and the doctor curled himself up on the foot of the big bag. This left a small space between the pole and the tent opening, in which Entrikin and I could stand. This space was constantly decreasing in size from the drift, which, in spite of our best efforts, continued to force itself through the fly, after the entrance of the boys. After a time, there was room for only one of us, and we alternated in standing up, steadying ourselves by the pole, now and then curling up on the snowdrift for a few winks of sleep, and making tea several times during the night to warm up the boys and keep up their spirits. The straining and flapping of the tent, the deafening roar of the wind, the devilish hissing of the drift, the howling and screaming of the poor dogs, made a pandemonium never to be forgotten.

One consoling feature was the fact that, owing to the quality and construction of our fur clothing, no one of the party suffered severely from the cold while in the tent. Personally, though without sleeping bag or any other covering beyond my deerskin traveling garments, I was entirely warm and comfortable throughout the storm.

Early on Friday morning, March 23rd, the wind began to subside, and at seven . . . I was out looking upon a scene that made me sick at heart. Half my dogs were frozen fast in the snow, some by the legs, and all were in a most pitiable condition, their fur a mass of ice and snow driven into it by the pitiless wind. Several had freed themselves and had destroyed the double sleeping bag and many of the harnesses which had blown off the tripods. Baldwin's anemometer, barograph, and thermograph, which, as the result of his ingenuity and perseverance, had kept on recording throughout the storm, showed that for thirty-four hours the average wind velocity had been over forty-eight miles per hour, and the average temperature about minus 50 degrees Fahrenheit, with a minimum of over minus 60. . . . When these figures are considered in connection with our elevation of some five thousand feet, the unobstructed sweep of the wind, and the well-known fact that icecap temperatures accompanied by wind are much more trying to animal life than the same temperatures at sea level, it is believed that the judgment will be that this storm beats the record as the most severe ever experienced by any Arctic party.[13]

Davidson now became the latest invalid requiring hospitalization at the lodge. Because of the growing list of wounded there, Peary sent Dr. Vincent back with him. Clark, who had also suffered frostbite, chose to go with Peary, although he was aware that should he have to return later he would be forced to travel alone and on ski: Peary could spare no more men, sledges, or dogs for ambulance work.

Already his intended three-way split at Independence Bay was an obvious impossibility, and he would, in fact, have to choose just one alternative there: get musk oxen, then go on northward toward the Pole or turn southward and follow the coastline to Cape Bismarck.

He was destined to do neither. Traveling became more difficult: sledges smashed on the marblelike *sastrugi;* dogs weakened and died or were killed and fed to the others; Entrikin froze the bottoms of his feet, then strained his back; one night Clark froze his nose to his sleeping bag; dogs refused to pull; another dog developed *piblockto* and bit nearly all the animals in the two other teams before he was shot. Two marches later the fury of another storm confined them to their tent for three days and nearly finished their dogs. "When the storm ceased," Peary wrote, "many of them were buried completely in the snow, several frozen down, and two were dead from exposure." [14]

Still Peary went on, but after another march *piblockto* struck two more dogs.

One of these dogs, . . . Agitator, a powerful, big, wolfish brute, the last survivor of the dogs purchased on the Labrador coast, presented just before he was killed as savage and gory a spectacle as I have ever seen. He had run amuck through the team, and, half blind as he was with froth and blood, had been mercilessly torn and shaken by the dogs that he had attacked. As the rifle was leveled at him, he stood exhausted and panting, with head and neck swollen to twice their natural size, ears torn in shreds, eyes bloodshot, bloody foam dripping from his jaws, and his entire body flecked with foam and blood and clotted tufts of fur. Though so weak that he could scarcely stand, he was just gathering himself for another spring at the dog nearest him, when the bullet passed through his brain, and he collapsed in a quivering heap on the blood-bespattered snow.[15]

On April 10th, at a point 128 miles from Anniversary Lodge, Peary wearily gave up this attempt to return to Navy Cliff and Independence Bay. In support of a future effort, he cached most of his pemmican and other supplies at his last camp, marked the site with a sturdily braced pole that could be seen from a distance of two or three miles, and, with the other three men — Entrikin, Baldwin, and Clark — retreated toward the lodge. They arrived on April 20th in pitiful condition: Entrikin's and Clark's feet had been badly frozen; Peary and Clark had suffered snowblindness; Baldwin's physical condition was generally poor. Compounding their discomfort, all four were covered with body lice, a vocational hazard of Arctic exploration in those years. For two weeks after their return none of the four had energy for any activity.

After his period of recuperation, however, inactivity began to be grating to Peary — especially after such a great failure. He felt he must be up and around to salvage something in the months ahead. He and Jo sledged around fifty-mile-long Olriks Bay on Whale Sound, an area never accurately charted, but the work of exploring it was soon completed.

His next project was an intriguing one. For seven or eight decades Arctic explorers had been hearing reports of a mysterious "iron mountain" somewhere near Cape York; John Ross, on an 1818 expedition, had seen knives made by the natives from the metal. No outsider, however, had been able to persuade the natives to point out the location.

On his 1891–1892 expedition Peary had obtained some information from the natives with the intention of locating the site, but time would not allow him to pursue this course. He realized that the description "iron mountain" was an exaggeration, and he suspected it was actually a meteorite. Furthermore, he knew most of the young Eskimo men had visited the location, whether or not they talked about it, and he sought one to take him there. The offer of a gun brought an acceptance from an Eskimo named Panikpah, and on May 16th Peary, Lee, and the native guide left Anniversary Lodge with a sledge and ten dogs. They followed the rugged coastline southward toward Cape York, but after two days, with the weather worsening, Panikpah chose a course of discretion. He quit.

Peary and Lee continued on, and at Netiulumi, a small Eskimo village, they found another Eskimo, Tallakoteah, who said he was familiar with the "iron mountain" and would lead them there. He spoke of three *saviksue* — great irons — of varying sizes. The smallest, he said, was the size of a dog, the name the Eskimos had given it. Another, called "the woman" because of its shape, was larger. Largest of all was "the tent," located on an island in Melville Bay. Encouraged by the man's confident talk Peary hurried his party on southward, followed by several curious Eskimos, but the journey was one of the most difficult of his experience. Thick blowing snow cut their visibility, and deep snow and slush made travel heavy. Peary's Eskimo guide began singing an impromptu song describing the deep snow, telling of numerous cracks in the ice southward toward Cape York, warning of the ice breaking up behind them to prevent their return, detailing the pain in his legs, and predicting a deep covering of snow that would hide the iron stones. Finally Peary silenced him temporarily by reiterating his intention at least to visit the site of the stones, but the native was not finished with his annoyances.

At 3 P.M., after getting into several cracks and getting wet to my waist, we find open water reaching in against the land. Go ashore over a shaky bridge of floating cakes and follow along the land to the north point of Wolstenholm Sound and Granville Bay. . . . Stopping here my driver takes me a long wild goose chase to the front of the big glacier and after various wanderings points to a big snowdrift as the site of the stone. I tell him he is a fraud and return to the sledge. Numerous other sledges have come up now and my driver says he is going *back* . . . afoot and I can take one of these men to go on with me. I tell him go and good riddance and he makes up his pack and starts back. Lee begins melting water in an open fireplace and I make arrangements to sleep in Ahngodohlaho's tupic and let him use my dogs tomorrow in return for driving them.

Hardly have these arrangements been completed when my driver returns and says he will go on. His little game of bluff has failed to work.[16]

Before arriving at their destination they were beset by more snowstorms, by broken ice in a bay that they crossed by stepping from one cake to another, by open water that necessitated a detour over a thousand-foot-high plateau. Finally, on May 27th, Tallakoteah indicated they had arrived, but no "iron mountain" was visible. The Eskimo eyed the snow-covered terrain closely, noticed a bit of blue traprock poking out above the snow, and began digging. This, he said, was a pile of stones used in pounding and shaping fragments from the "iron mountain." Five feet away, he declared, was the iron mass known as "the woman," and he hurried to the sledge for a sawknife to excavate the snow. He had dug a pit three feet deep and five feet in diameter before "the brown mass, rudely awakened from its winter's sleep, found for the first time in its cycles of existence the eyes of a white man gazing upon it." [17]

Fascinated, Peary listened to a discourse by Tallakoteah on "the woman." The iron stone had resembled a woman in a sitting position, Tallakoteah said, but it used to be much larger and higher:

the Eskimos had worn it down, and many years ago some natives had broken off the head and carried it away. Tallakoteah also showed Peary how the ancient knives seen by John Ross had been made.

Before striking out northward for Anniversary Lodge Peary scratched a rough "P" on the meteorite and left a record of his discovery in a cairn 112 yards away. He did not look for the two other stones, but he intended to return later in a ship to pick them up.

After a two-hour nap and supper Peary and Lee commenced the trip back to Anniversary Lodge.

> This return journey [Peary wrote] was one of the invaluable experiences in spring sledging in the Arctic. Part of the time we were storm-bound, buried in drifts at the base of the wild shore cliffs. Then we were struggling at a snail's pace through deep slush, intersected by hidden cracks and wide leads of open water. The disintegration of the sea ice had proceeded so rapidly since our downward trip that we were repeatedly compelled to take to the shore, climb the shore bluffs, sometimes carrying sledges and outfit on our backs, and make long detours overland.
>
> In one place we were obliged to scale a nearly vertical curtainlike drift, the crest of which rose 1,050 feet above sea level.
>
> Up this we carried the sledge loads on our backs, along zigzag steps cut in its face, then pushed and pulled the sledges and dogs after.[18]

Their food gave out, but when they arrived at an Eskimo settlement, Nachsarsami, on Wolstenholm Sound, they expected to find something to eat. There, unfortunately, the Eskimos could supply only some rotten walrus meat, which Lee could not stomach despite his hunger, and which made Peary sick for the rest of the trip. The climax of the journey came with a wild sixty-mile-an-hour toboggan slide down the icy northern slope of Tyndall Glacier,

which overlooked the village of Netiulumi, where Tallakoteah
had joined them. Peary and the Eskimo, on the first sledge,
"dashed down [the] cyclopean toboggan chute, the great red-
brown rock buttresses enclosing it, rich and warm with the glow-
ing sunlight, whirling past us with dizzying rapidity."

> The bay ice below rose rapidly to meet us; two or three bergs
> imprisoned in it grew as grows the locomotive of the lightning
> express when thundering straight at one at a speed of sixty
> miles per hour. . . . At last, veering sharply to the left into the
> snow-filled gorge beside the glacier to avoid the crevasses in its
> lower portion, we reached the level of the bay, breathless, with
> clothing snow-filled, and our dogs animated snowballs.[19]

Behind, Lee, in another sledge, closed his eyes, which were
smarting from recent exposure to the sun, pushed off, and followed. From time to time he opened his eyes, painfully, and once
saw tracks of the first sledge veering sharply left. Using his body
as a brake by dragging it in the snow he was able to stop at the
edge of a steep ice bluff, to change course, and to continue his
tumultuous ride to the bottom of the glacier. Peary and Lee
dropped a relieved Tallakoteah at his home and went on to Anniversary Lodge, where they arrived June 6th, ten days after leaving
the meteorite. Their return march had been phenomenal; Lee
said that three marches, those of June 2nd-3rd, 3rd-4th, and 5th-
6th, covered about sixty-five miles each, were made with little
sleep and no food, and only by dragging sledges through deep
snow and over giant glaciers.[20]

Peary and Lee arrived at the lodge too exhausted to contemplate any further activity for a while. They looked forward to the
probable arrival of the *Falcon:* although a return voyage in 1894
had not been planned definitely, Peary anticipated that his friends
in the United States would send the ship because of a concern for
his supplies and for his wife. Such an event, however, portended a

not entirely happy occasion. Because of Peary's failure to recross the icecap, he had determined to try again in 1895, but he felt a growing anxiety, and with good reason, about the willingness of other members of his expedition to stay another year. On June 29th, he observed, in his diary, ". . . there is discontent in the party." This discontent had been evident for some time; and on numerous occasions the surgeon, Dr. Vincent, had been deliberately rude to Peary.

On July 31st Eskimos brought news from the south of the arrival of a ship, and Peary dispatched Entrikin to investigate. Two days later he returned, accompanied by two persons from the *Falcon:* Henry G. Bryant, president of the Philadelphia Geographical Society and commander of this auxiliary expedition, and Emil Diebitsch, Jo's brother. Ice had stopped the *Falcon* farther south, but they brought the mail, including a letter from Peary's mother urging him to return and to confine his future explorations to the United States, and musing, "I am trying hard to feel that all is well — that you, Jo and baby will [have] health and strength as well as the gratification of feeling that your efforts have been crowned with success." [21]

This letter only served to heighten Peary's determination to remain another year; he was psychologically unable to cope with the thought of returning to the United States an admitted failure.

By August 20th the ship had been able to force a passage to Bowdoin Bay, where it moored off Anniversary Lodge. Meanwhile, Peary's wife and child, for the sake of their safety, prepared to return to the United States; and now also was the moment when Peary was to learn how many of his men would volunteer to remain.

One person besides Matt Henson, Peary's manservant, volunteered: Hugh Lee, the young man who had prodded Peary for a decision about his acceptance to avoid being "suspended between Heaven and earth." Peary's hunch about the strongmindedness of young Lee had been right. Although Lee was later to write in his diary of a growing fear of the inland ice journey coming in 1895, his ethics dictated that he stay with Peary. "Mr. Peary is having some quite hard luck," he wrote his mother in a letter dated July 8th. "Sometimes it seems as if I could almost cry, but that would do no good of course. The boys have all gone back on him and I am about the only one who is faithful to him — poor little weak me. Oh, what can I do for him, what can I do for him! Almost nothing. If anything is the matter at home that you need me I shall be in a sad state for he needs me and I shall hate to leave him. It will be hard, hard indeed. You do not know how I feel towards that man. The more the boys talk against him, the more I like him. . . . All the boys are so down on him and if there is any fault on either side, and I believe there is, it is all on their side as nearly as I can make out. . . . All the boys know that I am true to my contract; that I am loyal to Mr. Peary. . . ." [22]

Lee also said:

[Peary] told me he had asked each of the others if he would stay another year, and that each had refused. Then he told me that Matt would stay, and asked: "How about you?"

I replied: I'll stay with you.

With a look of joy he said: "Do you mean it?" and I said: "Sure." "Do you really mean it?" he asked, and when I assured him I did, he said: "Well, shake on it." [23]

On August 26th the *Falcon* left Bowdoin Bay for home, taking Mrs. Peary and her Snow Baby and all of Peary's men with the exception of Lee and Henson. It also transported Peary and Matt Henson and five Eskimos two hundred miles down the coast to the vicinity of glistening Petowik Glacier, where these seven would leave the ship in a whaleboat, the *General Wistar,* and work their way up the coast, on a minor exploration, back to Anniversary

Lodge. The last night aboard the *Falcon*, which was to be his final contact with civilization for a year, Peary was up, writing, until four o'clock in the morning; but when he did turn in sleep eluded him. At 9:30 A.M. he rose, and an hour later, on August 28th, he and Henson and the five Eskimos took to the whaleboat for their journey northward.

Peary's thoughts were gloomy. He was depressed by the return of most of his assistants, and dispirited by the coming year-long separation from his wife and child. In this fragile mental condition, temporary though it was, he could not refrain from glances backward, all of which he recorded in his diary:

> . . . It must have been an impressive sight to those on board to see the little boat tossing away from the ship's side and heading northward into the coming Arctic night. . . . I have eyes only for the white handkerchief fluttering from the port of Jo's cabin. — So ends with the vanishing ship the ill-omened first half of my expedition and begins the second. I wonder did Jo think of Tennyson's lines as she watched my little vanishing sail.[24]

Elsewhere Peary quoted Tennyson's lines to which he referred: "Sad as the last beam glittering on a sail / That sinks with me, that sinks with all we love below the verge." [25]

After the boat journey had been completed Peary wrote:

> . . . I reach the lodge at 10 P.M. [September 6th] and find Lee writing by the light of a bit of candle. He looks badly and tells me he has not been feeling well since the ship left, and that last Saturday he was confined to his bed. He thinks it is malaria, but after talking with him a while I find it to be a pronounced case of nostalgia. Poor boy, he has been very homesick and lonesome, has eaten but little and that irregularly, and is all out of sorts. . . .

. . . I cannot sleep in her room tonight, so after a refreshing bath I put on clean clothes left by her hands and roll myself in a couple of deerskins on the seat in the dining room. . . .[26]

I find myself trying to see [my baby] in coming years. First, will she know her father when she sees him again, and will she still be glad to come to him? Will she always be as bright and quick and strong and healthy as she is now, and last, what will be her fate in life, happy or unhappy? [27]

"By brute force" [28] Peary turned his thoughts elsewhere. The need for a winter supply of meat for himself and his men necessitated his leading a group of Eskimos to nearby deer pastures on a hunting expedition; then, to lay in food for the dogs, he and the natives obtained walrus at their feeding grounds in Omenah Sound.

This activity sparked a renewed enthusiasm, and Peary foresaw only two catastrophes that might defeat him in 1895: an outbreak of *piblockto* among the dogs, or the death of one of the three remaining members of the expedition:

I place[d] the latter possibility second intentionally because without dogs it would be folly to think of attempting the conquest of the "great ice," while the reduction of our members to two would not necessarily mean the same. The journey to Independence Bay had once before been made by two, and there seemed no reason why it should not be made by two again.[29]

Apparently Peary was unworried about his ability to locate the invaluable caches left on the inland ice during his retreat the year before — a surprising lack of concern for a Greenland explorer of his experience, but a fault of which he was never again guilty. The caches had been deposited at distances of from twenty-six to one hundred twenty-eight miles from Anniversary Lodge, and they contained all but a few of the supplies needed for the journey across the icecap. Peary planned to visit the caches immediately after the hunting expeditions — which he could not postpone because of the lateness of the season — and, if necessary, to re-erect the markers pointing out the location of his precious piles of supplies.

In October, with this activity in mind, he sent Lee, Henson, and one Eskimo, all with a sledge and twelve dogs, onto the icecap to dig out the caches nearest Anniversary Lodge and to re-erect the signals. After they returned he planned to pass the winter "leisurely," readying equipment for the long sledge journey, maintaining good physical condition, conserving "every energy, physical and mental." [30]

They returned after only four days, however, and without having found any caches. They had, in fact, traveled no farther than the vicinity of the first cache, one containing alcohol, located twenty-six miles out on the icecap. There, before returning, Lee had left a cache of his own supplies, for use later. An extraordinary depth of new snow had hindered them during the journey, making travel exceedingly heavy, and, they reported, had almost obliterated two bamboo-pole signals — not over caches — erected during the preceding spring. At that time the poles had stood nine feet above the snow; now only a foot was visible.

With great dismay Peary listened to this news. Then, impatient to see for himself, he wanted to start for the icecap at once, but he realized his returned dogs needed food and rest. Three days later, on Monday, October 8th, he, Henson, and one Eskimo — Maksingwah, popularly known as "Flaherty" — sped toward the alcohol cache, leaving at daybreak of a calm, clear, bright morning — a rapturous beginning that signified nothing.

Toward evening of the second day, in the vicinity of the alcohol cache, Peary peered around the white wilderness and saw in the distance westward, sharp and clear against a yellow horizon, a pole poking out of the snow to a height of perhaps a foot. It appeared to be a few hundred yards away, but when Peary left his companions and struck out for it the distance lengthened to a mile and the one pole became four, standing nine feet high. They marked the cache Lee had made only a few days earlier.

Dejected, Peary returned to the sledge. "The cold blue shadow of night, sweeping down the northeast, had taken full possession of the field surrendered by the light," and Peary gave the word to stake out dogs and to pitch the tent. Hot tea, a small ration of biscuit, and frozen seal meat provided some refreshment after the disappointing day.

At midnight Matt rose and went outside for a look at the weather. The sky was cloudless; stars shone brightly, and a brilliant aurora sparkled on the northern horizon. By six o'clock, however, fog and clouds had obliterated the scene.

. . . The wind had veered to the southeast, and that dead gray emptiness of minute snow particles, which I knew so well, shrouded the universe. I had the tent turned to bring its back to the wind, the sledge brought alongside, the dogs refastened in front of the tent, and everything carried inside — preparations which more than one disagreeable experience had taught me to make. These completed, I re-entered the tent and Matt followed me.

Absorbed in my thoughts, I did not notice for some time that Maksingwah had not entered with us, and that I had heard no sounds from him outside. The suspicion at once came to me that he had decamped, rather than take the chances of an October storm on the dreaded *sermiksoak* — icecap. Looking out and seeing nothing of him, I tied on my snowshoes, and, picking up our sledge tracks, found his footprints overlying them, and pointing down the back track. I did not follow him for any distance, as, if we were booked for a long storm, he would be of no earthly use to us, while his absence would very materially economize our food supply, and enable us to stand a longer siege.

Poor fellow, I learned afterwards that it took him four days to reach the lodge, arriving at the end of that time so weak with hunger and cold that he could barely crawl.

The wind increased to a steady whistling gale, the air became saturated with horizontally flying snow, and those Arctic barometers, the dogs, were every one curled in a ball, backs to the wind, and noses and feet buried in their bushy tails. Reluctantly I resigned myself to the prospect of another of those dreary storm-bound episodes upon the "great ice," only hoping that I might be as fortunate as hitherto in sleeping away the majority of the long hours. All day and night the monotonous music of the storm continued. Late in the afternoon of the next day, the wind slackened a little and enabled us to get out, feed and untangle the dogs, and muzzle several suspicious members of the team that might be expected, under the influence of that archdevil of mischief and destruction which in storms on the "great ice" possesses the Eskimo dog, to eat their harnesses and traces. Then the fury began again and continued till six weary gnawing days and nights, the most accursed I ever spent upon the icecap, had crawled their slow lengths into the past.

My little tent, pitched at an elevation of five thousand feet above the sea level, stood upon the absolutely unbroken, unobstructed surface of the "great ice." The fury of the wind drove the snow through the walls of the tent in a constant shower of impalpable white dust, which settled upon us and everything in it. The clouds and the driving snow combined to almost completely obliterate the little daylight remaining at this season of the year, and kept us in continual gloom. About twice in each twenty-four hours we lit the little oil stove, and made a cup of tea, ate a biscuit and some of the seal meat, then put out the stove, pulled our hands and arms inside our fur sleeves, and, rolling on our faces to avoid the snowdust, tried to sleep again.

But after the first three days I could not sleep and could only lie and listen to the infernal driving of the snow against the tent, knowing that the demoniac white downpour was destroy-

ing the last chance of finding my caches, destroying all the
work of the previous year on which I had counted so largely to
assist me the next spring, reducing my resources to the very
minimum, and perhaps even destroying every chance of success
next year. Plans for the future failed me. Interest in anything
refused to be aroused; thoughts of wife and blue-eyed baby, of
mother, pictures of boyhood, happy scenes and memories before this devil of Arctic exploration took possession of me, rose
and ranged themselves opposite to the precious hours of my life
being wasted, the sacrifices of me and mine, all perhaps to end
in naught, till it seemed as if with this, and the unceasing hissing of the wind and snow, I should lose my reason. . . .[31]

Peary eventually returned to the warmth of Anniversary Lodge,
but he found little comfort there. He began his endurance of the
monotonous Arctic night, always the dreariest time for any explorer, with doubled gloom: virtually all of his provisions and
every ounce of his alcohol and pemmican were now buried under
the monstrous blanket of the inland ice. He saw himself as a man
shipwrecked upon an uninhabited shore, with nothing left him but
the clothes upon his back.

Not once, however, did he decide to give up the spring work. If
his pemmican was gone he would take frozen deer meat for men,
and walrus for dogs, although this meat supply would weigh four
times as much as pemmican. If his alcohol had disappeared he
would rely on kerosene, heavier and much less efficient. Even so,
he could take provisions sufficient only for the trip to and from
Independence Bay; food for any extension would have to come
from the land there. Such planning, precarious though it seemed,
helped him through the long night. Throughout it, he remembered later, he was haunted by a fear that some new catastrophe
would prevent him from even beginning the journey; and in a
frequent nightmare he was transported home without having
made any attempt to cross the icecap again. He would waken

with infinite relief, he said, to find himself in bed at the lodge, to hear the familiar howl of the winter wind tearing at the house, and to realize the work still lay ahead.[32] Once, when Henson and Lee were both ailing and Peary himself was suffering from an injured back, Peary wrote that he would like to be able to put his companions in a sealed vault and spoon feed them, to be sure they would remain healthy for the coming struggle.

The night before that struggle began Peary mulled over his chances for success, then wrote his wife:

> Anniversary Lodge
> March 31, 1895

My Darling;

It is the eve of our departure for the great ice, and I sit down to write you what I know I shall later hand you myself. I do not know why, but I cannot collect my thoughts to write as I wish. The winter has been a nightmare to me. I have been to the shrine regularly ["the shrine" was an isolated recess along the rugged coastline where he and Jo used to go for a few quiet moments], but the cold, damp, frost-lined room has made me think of the tomb. The only bright moments have been when I was thinking of you and old times. My wife, my darling, I have kissed the place where your head rested, have kissed my blue-eyed baby's socks, and I carry with me next [to] my heart your last letter and your little guidon. These will go with me to the end, where and how it may be.

I start with provisions and equipment evolved almost from nothing. As you will see from my journal which is in the larger of the tin lockboxes under the floor of our room, the enormous snowfall of last summer lost me everything on the icecap — biscuit, milk, pea soup, cranberry jam, pemmican, and worst of all, alcohol. I am obliged to use kerosene for fuel and this the Saint John's article of such poor quality that it becomes like condensed milk at temperatures not far below zero. I have been obliged to devise a cooker in which I can keep a small flame

going constantly during the upward trip. For meat I have venison, some cooked and some raw, and for dog food walrus meat.
I can carry full rations only for the outward and return trips to
Independence Bay and tea, milk, and biscuit for three months
there and beyond. For meat for ourselves and dogs during that
time I must depend entirely upon the game of the country.

I have named my sledge made on the Greenland pattern the
Josephine after the woman I love and a little trailer sledge
Chopsie after my baby. I start with thirty-five dogs of my own
and thirty hired ones. I have with me four natives, Nuktah,
Soker, Annowkah, and Kardahsoo, who will form a supporting
party and have promised to accompany us for ten days, which
ought to carry us past our farthest of last spring. [Two other
Eskimos, Nupsah and Akpalisoaho, were to help the expedition
to the icecap.] I have had a great deal of trouble in getting
dogs, thanks to the loyalty of the Norwegian member of the
expedition [Astrup], who has told the natives that he was coming here in a year or two and if they kept their dogs for him he
would give a gun for every two. I owe Ingerapadoo and Akpa-
lisuahlio, members of the boat crew that went to Cape York,
each a gun. The others I have settled with. I have a sledge
contracted for with Poodloanah for Chopsie and I have a standing offer of a flask of powder for a young bearskin for her. Of
the three narwhal heads and tusks on the roof, one for Emil
[Diebitsch], whose kindness I shall always remember, one for
[Herbert L.] Bridgman [Brooklyn newspaper editor], who is
more than thoughtful, and . . . the other for you.

The papers and records are in the steamer trunk and the two
lock . . . boxes. These with the ammunition are cached under
the floor of our room and the remaining provisions piled over
them. There has been no chance to put them anywhere else
owing to the constant presence of the Eskimo. After thinking
the matter over carefully I felt they would be safer from theft
and fire here than anywhere else. Two of the guns are also under the floor, three behind the books and your shotgun in one of

the closets. One shotgun and one carbine I have loaned to Nuktah, who will remain here till the ship comes. I have promised him [Frederick] Stokes' house. The other three men who accompany us will summer at Kanrah, and I have promised them that portion of the house east of the partition between what was formerly dining room and kitchen and the men's room. Should I not return the rest of the house should go back on the ship. Put on exhibition it will make you independent. All the keys I have put back of the books on the very top shelf.

Good-by my darling.

Bert.

That night Peary, Henson, and Lee enjoyed a last warm bath, soaping themselves lavishly. They shaved leisurely and carefully, and clipped each other's hair in a "prizefighter's" cut — partly with the intention of eliminating the happy hunting grounds of the body lice that had plagued them on earlier journeys. For this reason, also, they had hung their traveling furs outdoors for three weeks, hoping that the subfreezing March temperatures would route out any unwelcome inhabitants that might have found lodging there while the Eskimo seamstresses had been at work.

Early Monday morning, April 1st — after a few hours' sleep — they rose, dressed, left their various last letters with natives for later delivery to the ship in the event of their deaths, and began their journey: up to the moraine, the "shore" of the inland ice — up to the awesome, dazzling, bewitching, perilous icecap that was to Peary both friend and foe.

On the outward trip Peary searched for his lost caches but found only one of them, a minor supply depot of ten cases of biscuit and a case and a half of milk. He conducted an exhaustive search for the giant cache, put down the year before 128 miles from Anniversary Lodge when he had admitted defeat and turned back, but the stores — including, of course, all his pemmican and alcohol — could not be located.

Heartsick, he was on the verge of admitting defeat again, primarily because of his responsibility now for two other lives — Henson's and Lee's. Although he had steeled himself for this eventuality, he had hoped for better luck; Peary was a congenital optimist, and of course had to be, regarding his Arctic work.

Now, near the site of the lost giant cache, with the four Eskimos ready to turn back toward the coast, he consulted his two companions. Lee reported the exchange later:[33] Peary said he had no right to gamble all their lives by going ahead. Should they go on and fail to find game at Independence Bay, all three knew, they probably would be unable to return to Anniversary Lodge. Lee and Henson voted to continue, as Peary certainly would have chosen to do anyway had he been responsible only for his own life, and they took leave of the returning natives. One of the Eskimos carried a letter from Peary for eventual delivery to Jo: ". . . In the event of mishap," it concluded, "no human help can find or reach us."

Despite his own peril, his thoughts were with the four Eskimos as they vanished southward over the raw horizon. "For six sleeps and six long rapid marches," he said, "they had followed me unquestioningly into the awful heart of the [icecap], where none of their tribe had ever . . . dared to go before. Never before, even in their longest pursuit of the polar bear across the frozen surface of Smith Sound, had they been out of sight of the cliffs and mountains of their savage coast. . . . And now they must hasten back *alone* with feverish speed, before a storm could obliterate our sledge tracks, and leave them lost, bewildered, and bewitched, at the mercy of the dread demons of the [icecap]."[34]

Peary now was left with two companions and forty-two dogs. Bound northward again, he pioneered with the sledge *Josephine,* pulled by twelve dogs. His experience made him a master of steering a straight course, a difficult task on the Arctic Sahara, where there were no landmarks to guide on. Henson and Lee followed, in that order, with the rest of the sledges and dog teams.

The trip continued to be harrowing: Lee, whose health had been flagging for months, became ill and rode the tent sledge for three days. While he was sick all the dogs, normally his responsibility, broke loose at feeding time; swept through camp, overturning equipment; and fell upon the walrus meat about to be doled out by Peary and Henson. Those two men, caught in the pack of the ravenous, yelping animals, leaped for safety as the savage dogs snapped at their footgear and clothing, at the walrus meat, and at each other. On the following day a blizzard roared down upon them, forcing them to camp, under the usual miserable conditions, for forty-eight hours. Dogs weakened and died or were killed for food for the others; Lee's sledge was smashed beyond repair on rough ice — and his toe was frozen, requiring morphine doses to ease the grueling pain; equipment not essential to survival was discarded, to lighten the sledge load. By May 5th they had consumed all food allowed for the outward journey, and still the land near Independence Bay eluded them.

On the following day they sighted it, or thought they did: an irregular blue blob ahead and to their left. Peary realized it might be a mirage — and they could be fooled easily: their eyes had been strained severely by the trip across the glaring ice. Further observations left no doubt, however, that it was land.

Later they camped on the crest of the icecap more than five hundred miles from Anniversary Lodge, and Peary calculated his situation. He now had eleven dogs, all of them exhausted and three nearly dead, and three men operating at about 50-per-cent efficiency after the dreadful trip. Should he not find game, he guessed, none of the dogs would survive more than a third of the return journey, and the weakened men would be reduced to hauling the sledges themselves.

In desperation, Peary and Henson packed a few supplies and their rifles on the small sledge *Chopsie*, left Lee in camp to rest, and sped toward the land. Peary also left all of his dogs at the camp — they pulled the sledge themselves — for he knew that if he failed to get meat his animals would never consent to climb back on the icecap. If he found game, he reasoned, he could lead the dogs to the carcasses, where they could feast.

He and Henson traveled in a straight line toward the land, and soon they were able to look directly down on it: the peaks and valleys of a new region lying far below, in the yellow light of a Greenland midnight. Peary imagined himself descending from the sky upon his prize, which proved to be an area west of Independence Bay.

His daydreams of earlier years, when he had imagined himself the first human being to look upon a new land, again became reality; and despite his situation the reality did not bring total disappointment. Peary wrote:

> Cortez . . . looked down from the mountains which circle the great plain of Mexico, upon the glistening lakes, and the wonderful city; and Balboa, upon that "peak in Darien," looked down upon the smiling Pacific, but what an unimaginable contrast here!
>
> For them trees rustled in the warm, perfumed breeze, and the panorama spread before them glowed with fullest tropical opulence.
>
> For us hissed the driving snow, borne on the freezing breath of the heart of the "great ice," and the new land far below was but a barren heap of fragments of earth's skeleton.
>
> Yet, by contrast with the frozen desolation immediately around us, even those bare primeval bones seemed warm and inviting.[35]

Only when he descended to the land was he thoroughly disappointed. After a long search he and Henson failed to find game, although they did see tracks of small animals and old droppings of musk oxen. Dejected, they returned to the camp on the ice. There, after he and Henson had enjoyed a long sleep, Peary proposed a last gamble: he should return to land with Henson and stay until they found meat. The only alternative was to commence the exhausting return journey immediately in their weakened condition.

Peary's two companions agreed that they should stake their lives on the land. "I felt . . . that . . . in that cool, deliberate moment we took the golden bowl of life in our hands," Peary wrote, "and that the bowl had suddenly grown very fragile." [36]

Typically, however, he later disavowed the drama of this moment. ". . . I feel now, as I felt then, that we were neither rash nor foolhardy . . . but simply . . . could not act otherwise. . . ." [37]

The entire party proceeded to the site of the 1892 moraine camp, and there Peary dropped off Lee. Emphasizing the finality of the decision, he and Henson this time took all the dogs with them to the land, where the men were nevertheless forced to drag the sledge from snowdrift to snowdrift over loose stones. An all-day reconnaissance turned up no sign of living musk oxen, and Peary began to despair. Perhaps, he reflected, the musk oxen he had seen here three years earlier were migratory; or perhaps his hunting success of three years ago had frightened them away. As day waned, however, they spotted a hare and killed, cooked, and devoured it. This was the first substantial meal they had enjoyed since leaving the site of the big cache thirty-five days earlier, and though it satisfied them momentarily, it later aroused hunger pangs previously dulled by near-starvation. It also taught Peary a valuable lesson on the advantages of using a small exploring expedition: the hare had provided all the food he and Henson could eat at one meal. Had there been more men, Peary could only have rationed the meat.

The next morning they stumbled across a rapturous sight: fresh tracks of musk oxen, in a valley that lay between Navy Cliff and the site of the successful 1892 hunt. Eagerly they fastened the dogs, all still in traces, to a boulder, then muzzled them, to prevent their chewing their way to freedom. They followed the musk oxen to a nearby plain, where they caught the animals — a herd of twenty-two — in a midday rest two hundred yards away. From behind a giant rock both Peary and Henson trembled with excitement and both realized they must not risk shooting from such a distance. Furthermore, their eyes had been weakened by ice glare. Quickly they decided to rush the herd, for better position, and to trust, hope — pray — that the animals would stand their ground.

Breathing heavily with excitement, they paused a final few moments in their hiding place. Matt whispered a question: Did Peary think the beasts would charge? Peary said he hoped so; for then they would be certain to make a kill.

Peary leaped from behind one side of the boulder and Matt from behind the other, and both men ran straight for the herd. The noise aroused the curiosity of a giant bull, who turned, faced his attackers, and expressed his defiance in snorts and stomps. Every animal in the herd also turned toward them, and Peary was sure of a kill. He and Henson had raced to within fifty yards of the herd when the bull charged, Peary raised his rifle and fired on the run, and the bull sank on his haunches. The herd wavered and began to scatter; Peary and Henson fired a literal barrage and killed four more musk oxen before the animals disappeared.

Savagely, they turned to skinning the animals. As they worked they cut off and swallowed strips of the tender, warm, raw meat. Then Matt went for the dogs, and they gorged on hunks of the rich, steaming food until their stomachs were full. The rest of the meat was cut up for immediate needs and for the return journey; some of it went to the famished Lee, delivered to him by Henson.

A later attack on the same herd felled more animals, so that eventually Peary had obtained six grown animals and four calves. With this additional meat supply Peary could have safely extended his explorations around Navy Cliff and Independence Bay but for the still-weakened condition of his party. Again he acted with discretion; he limited his field work to a fresh visit to Navy Cliff, where the view along the southern coast of Independence Bay was much clearer than during his earlier visit. This time he saw "several miles of the south shore of the bay, a land of precipitous black cliffs trending eastward from the cape which confined Academy Glacier on the east," and was able to correct the map made earlier, when clouds had obscured that coast.

This trip also resulted in the discovery, from a vantage point on the icecap, of a towering mountain some seventy-five miles due north. Peary named the height Mount Wistar. Five years later he was to sight the mountain again, this time from another point — east — and through the intervening observations establish beyond any doubt the insularity of Greenland.

Finally, the trip reinforced some earlier meteorological observations made by Peary, observations that only he, of all men, was able to make, firsthand, at this time:

One thing very much in favor of the navigator across the northern inland ice of Greenland is the fact that he will encounter practically no head winds. The regularity of the winds of the "great ice" of Greenland, as I have found them during an actual sojourn of over seven months upon the icecap, and visits to it of greater or less duration in every month of the year, is phenomenal. Except during atmospheric disturbances of exceptional magnitude, which cause storms to sweep across the country against all ordinary rules, the direction of the wind of the "great ice" of Greenland is invariably radial from the center outward, perpendicular to the nearest part of the coast land ribbon. So steady [in direction] is the wind, and so closely does it adhere to this perpendicularity, that I can liken it only to the flow of a sheet of water descending the slopes from the central interior dome to the coast. The direction of the nearest land is

always easily determinable in this way; the neighborhood of
great fjords is always indicated by a change in the wind's direction; and the crossing of a divide, by an area of calm or variable
winds, followed by winds in another direction, independent of
any indications of the barometer.[38]

Another result of the journey, although a negative one, was
finally to explore for Peary his idea of reaching the North Pole
over the inland ice. His two journeys to Independence Bay had
shown conclusively that the smooth icy highway northward he
had hoped to find was not there.

The return to Anniversary Lodge was a race with death, despite
the life-saving musk oxen obtained in the Independence Bay region. The trip began early on June 1st; for it Peary had nine dogs
and meat rations for them for fourteen days; half-rations of tea,
biscuit, and oil for thirty days; and rations of frozen venison for
seventeen days. For a time he considered allowing the men to eat
the venison, but this would have meant that after the dogs gave
out — as they surely would — the men would have been compelled to drag their sledges the rest of the way home. He decided,
then, that the men would try to live on the biscuit ration, scant
though it was, and the dogs would have the meat.

They raced homeward with amazing speed. In one twenty-two-
day period they averaged twenty and a half miles each day across
the ice, and that included a short march of only four miles one
day, June 9th, when Lee became so ill and weak he dropped on
the inland ice to die.

Peary and Henson were a mile or so ahead when Peary turned
to look for Lee and saw him lying in the snow far behind them.
Peary rushed back to help his man, but Lee suggested that he go
on. "We will have no more of that kind of talk," Peary answered.
"We will all get home or none of us will."[39] Peary made camp
and nursed Lee for the rest of that day, giving him hourly cups of

warm milk containing beef peptonoids and brandy. By the following morning he was well enough to continue, and, a few days later, Peary joshed him about his postal card request, following his application for expedition membership, not to be left dangling between Heaven and earth. "Well, Lee, have you made up your mind yet whether it is Heaven or earth?" Peary asked, and Lee answered, "I certainly have. It's neither. It's hell." This was the only reference Peary ever made to the postal card.[40]

After the first hundred and fifty miles of the return Peary's dogs began to give out. A few, weakened beyond hope, were shot and fed to the others; some simply died. The men, after giving up their venison, were later forced to eat dog meat. The last mile or two of each march became sheer torture, "dragging the life and vital force" out of men and dogs. Finally, as the mountain summits of Whale Sound came into view, one dog — Panikpah — was left, and three starving men. Descending from the icecap, the dog found the rocks too much for him, and he lay down some distance from the lodge. Peary left him there, knowing that after a rest the dog would continue. "When he did come in," Peary wrote, "I fed him with my own hands, and before I had eaten anything myself."[41] A week passed before Peary "felt like doing anything but lie down" — and eat.

It was with difficulty that the appetites of any of us were restrained within bounds, though I knew and endeavored to impress upon the boys the probably disastrous effects of eating heartily in our exhausted condition, and with our stomachs accustomed for so long to meagre rations of the simplest and most digestible kind. Matt had a serious attack of indigestion almost immediately after he had finished [one] meal, and I was up most of the night trying to make him comfortable; succeeding at last with the assistance of hot water bags and medicines. Since then all have been troubled with almost constant diarrhea, the greater portion of what we eat passing us unchanged. This has made us, if such a thing were possible, even weaker than before.[42]

He had failed again, and this fact clouded a homecoming for Peary. Lee remarked in his diary that during the last marches on the icecap, made in the area of giant crevasses, Peary had barged ahead carelessly, as if hoping to avoid the necessity of going home again a failure.[43]

Whether or not Lee was correct, certainly Peary was not himself, nor were the other two men, for days after their return. On the morning of July 4th, Peary wrote in his diary, he wakened to hear Lee and Henson chatting in an adjoining room. He stirred just as one of them uttered the word "poison," and they fell quiet. Probably they were talking of food poisoning — this was during the time of their acute sickness — but the word stayed with Peary's subconscious, and three days later, after he had eaten a pastry prepared for him by Henson, he wrote, on July 7th, "I wonder if I am really going mad. I tried another piece of my cake last night but it tasted bitter and I did not eat any of it. Last night I dreamed that Matt was trying to poison me and the dream seemed so real I have not been able to shake off the impression it made upon me."

Eventually he was able to rid himself of this melancholy, but the feeling of failure remained. Later, when the relief ship *Kite* arrived to evacuate Peary, Henson, and Lee, Peary was to receive this letter from his mother, whose entreaty had an effect opposite to that intended: it spurred Peary to greater effort in the future.

Bertie Mine,
     . . . I need not tell you of my great disappointment last September. Nor of my great anxiety to have you at home. I was sorry for you, my child. I can imagine how much you suffered

before you decided to stay another year in that dreary place. I would have borne it for you if I could. I have a mental photograph of you as you turned your face northward away from Jo and baby. I do not often look at it. To have you home again is first in importance with me. . . . If you have not accomplished all you had hoped to do not be disheartened; take a cheerful view of your failure. *Many* have failed. . . .[44]

One last disappointment remained, and it came with the arrival of the *Kite*, a ship Peary was not even sure he wanted to see in the first place. ". . . I felt the sharpest extremes of feeling," he wrote. "At times it seemed as if I could not wait another moment for the ship to bring my brown eyes and my blue eyes to me; then I felt that even were the ship here I could not go on board and say I had failed. . . . At times I even hoped that the ship would not come, so that I might make another attempt the next spring."[45] Now, suddenly, the vessel was here; cries of "*oomiaksoah!*" — the ship! — awakened Peary from a sleep early in the morning of August 3rd. Soon afterward Jo's brother Emil Diebitsch, from the *Kite*, strode into the lodge.

"My first question may be imagined," Peary said, "and learning that they were not on board, my interest flagged. . . ."[46]

Then he learned of his wife's heroism back home. Through her efforts, and the efforts of Emil, money had been raised for this very relief expedition. After Jo had unsuccessfully petitioned the Navy Department to send a ship for her husband, she had reluctantly taken the only other course open to her: raising the money herself, work that she despised. She solicited contributions; she lectured on life in the Arctic, for her a most distasteful chore; she cut her spending to austerity. Through her efforts money was obtained to charter the *Kite*, and here it was.

While it was here Peary decided to make the most of it. On the return trip he went by Cape York and picked up two of the meteorites there. With great difficulty they were loaded aboard the ship: "the woman," found to weigh 5500 pounds, and "the dog," 1000 pounds. Peary also visited the site of the largest meteorite, "the tent," but he realized that transporting it home could be accomplished only after careful planning; "the tent" weighed from ninety to one hundred tons. In the summer of the following year, 1896, he was to return for it in the *Hope,* a ship of only 307 tons, but a threat posed by pack ice was to force the vessel to flee before accomplishing the mission. Then, in the summer of 1897, he was to return again in the *Hope,* this time successfully loading the huge meteorite by a feat of engineering. Years afterward the three meteorites were to be sold by Jo Peary to the American Museum of Natural History for forty thousand dollars,[47] leaving Peary the target of barbs cast by his critics, who were to accuse him of stealing the Eskimos' metal supply. Since explorers and whalers had begun venturing north, however, the Eskimos had not needed the "great irons," because their knives and other necessary metalware had been provided by these adventures.

Acquiring the two meteorites was, for Peary, the brightest accomplishment of his otherwise dismal 1893–1895 expedition. The greatest accomplishment for one of its members, however, was simply staying the full two years. For the rest of his life Hugh Lee was to remember with pride his service with Peary.

Lee was the type of young man Peary tried to find for his expeditions, but with lackluster success: Lee was intelligent, steadfast, energetic, and subordinate. Men with other qualities frequently clashed with Peary, but not Lee. Although every other male member of the 1893–1895 expedition, save Henson, had left Peary at the midpoint, Lee had this to say years later of his leader:

> Peary was a very determined man; he was absolutely ruthless, so far as punishing his own flesh was concerned. It was not his way to say: "Do this or do that," but rather, "Please help me do this." He was gentle and kind and . . . understanding, which is true greatness. . . .[48]

Part IV

NEARING THE GOAL

Four-year expedition

(1898–1902)

Seventh trip (1905–1906)

Polar attainment (1908–1909)

Chapter 9

THE AMERICAN GEOGRAPHICAL SOCIETY held in much higher
regard Peary's accomplishments of 1893–1895 than did Peary himself. In 1897 it awarded him its Cullom Gold Medal, for establishing the insularity of Greenland by determining the conver-
gence of its northernmost coastlines, and for explorations in the
area of Inglefield Gulf. The following year the Royal Geographical Society of London gave Peary its Patron's Gold Medal, and the
presentation speech by the Society president, Sir Clements Markham, glowed with tributes to the American explorer.

Such recognition lent inspiration to Peary for future efforts.
Now he began considering the possibility of forcing passage by
ship through the ice-jammed strait linking Baffin Bay and the
Arctic Ocean and lying between Greenland on the east and Ellesmere Island on the west. He would ram his way through this passage — Smith Sound, Kane Basin, and Kennedy and Robeson
channels — into the Arctic Ocean, where he would establish a
base at the northern tip of Greenland or of Ellesmere Island for an
"assault" on the North Pole. Such a feat of navigation, assuming it
was possible of accomplishment, would allow Peary to commence
his grueling journey two or three hundred miles farther north
than he could otherwise have expected. Furthermore, he would
devote several years to reaching the Pole. Should he fail one year,
he would try again the next, and so on. Meanwhile, he would live
largely off the land, obtaining vital meat supplies by hunting.

While he dreamed, he realized that three main wants blocked his way: another leave of absence from the Navy, money, and a vessel powerful enough to crash through the ice barriers of those northern seas.

By now the naval establishment had closed its ranks tightly against Peary. From the secretary of the Navy on down, it was opposed, by a great majority, to any more leave — during which an officer was on half pay — for this presumptuous naval officer, even though his explorations were helping to fill in blanks on the Hydrographic Office charts — and though his later probes of the Arctic Ocean would prove to be a breakthrough that would eventually result in atomic submarines, half a century later, operating with assurance of adequate depth in what was to be an area of strategic importance. In the Navy Department, jealousy — combined with sincere conviction that Peary ought to devote himself to naval duties — had increased with each newspaper headline devoted to Peary; furthermore, the threat of a war with Spain was increasing daily, and the Navy would most certainly be deeply involved. Under these conditions a routine request of leave of absence was out of the question, even in the mind of the man who was usually able to muster a feeling of optimism in the face of discouraging odds, but Peary astounded his Navy colleagues by talking of still another expedition north, and this time of four or five years' duration.

On April 12th, 1897, he opened an official envelope and was dismayed to read that the Navy Department had ordered him to report for duty at Mare Island on the West Coast, possibly to get him away from the Eastern United States and certain influential supporters there. He countered by submitting a request for a five-year leave, then turned for help to his newest acquaintance of prominence — Morris Jesup, a wealthy New Yorker who was president of the American Geographical Society and a man who had been most favorably impressed by Peary's determination.

Jesup agreed to round up from prominent friends letters endorsing Peary's request.

The Navy Department now was far above being impressed by such wire-pulling, however, and reacted quickly, sending Peary a blunt negative reply. With that exchange he seemed to have used up his resources.

A few days before his departure for the West Coast, however, he enjoyed unusual good fortune. By chance he met a prominent New York Republican, Charles A. Moore, who had just helped to elect President McKinley. Moore cared nothing about Arctic exploration, but Peary's unyielding character appealed to him. When Peary told of his difficulty in getting a leave of absence Moore inquired, "How much leave would you like?"

"Five years," shot back Peary.

"Very well. I'll get it for you!" came the startling reply.

Mr. Moore went in person to the secretary of the Navy. "You'll do me a favor?" he asked. The secretary jumped at such a chance to reward a man who had done so much to put the Republicans in power. But when he heard that Peary was the object of the other's philanthropy his color flamed up and he shouted: "*Anything* but that, Moore!"

"Oh, very well," retorted the politician coolly. "Then I'll get the President to order you to do what I want. . . ."

Mr. Moore crossed the street and was closeted with Mr. McKinley within an hour. His immense power in the great metropolis gave him entrée where another would have cooled heels or failed. "You remember, Mr. McKinley, that you said to come to you if I ever wanted anything?"

"I do," said the President courageously. He knew the danger of recalling campaign promises. But Moore was a man who had never once claimed his reward, so he braced himself for something stupendous.

"I want Lieutenant Peary of the Navy granted five years' leave in order to continue his great work in the North."

The President leaned back in his chair. A smile of relief played over his kindly features. "Oh, is that all, Moore!" he chuckled. "Of course I'll do it." He sent for his secretary and dictated a memorandum to the Navy Department.

"May I take it over myself?" asked his visitor. . . .

Notice of five years' leave granted reached Lieutenant Peary forty-eight hours later.[1]

Money and a ship also appeared to be forthcoming. Morris Jesup persuaded a group of businessmen, the nucleus of an organization later to be known as the Peary Arctic Club, to underwrite the expedition with a guarantee of four thousand dollars each for the planned four-year period; and another admirer, Lord Northcliffe, the London newspaper publisher, donated a steam yacht, the *Windward,* which had been used for an earlier expedition to Franz Josef Land. The *Windward* had only auxiliary steam power, certainly not sufficient for Peary's ice-smashing purposes, but Northcliffe offered to install new engines in the vessel.

Before those promises had been fulfilled, however, Peary's luck began to ebb again. He had planned to go north in the summer of 1898 and stay four years if necessary, but on February 15th of that year he saw his prospects clouded again — by the explosion and sinking of the battleship *Maine* in Havana Harbor. Although responsibility for the tragedy was never affixed by a United States Navy court of inquiry, the event hastened a declaration of war on Spain, on April 21st.

Again Peary found himself in a bind. Although the Navy did not revoke his leave — and Peary concluded not to give it up, assuming that civil engineers would not be vital to his service, war or no war — the conflict wiped out a good many of the promised contributions. Furthermore, a machinists' strike in England prevented the installation of engines in the *Windward.*

Delay was out of the question; leave of absence was too precious to waste waiting in the United States. Worse, Peary learned that a Norwegian explorer, Otto Sverdrup, was planning to lead an expedition, in the polar ship *Fram*, into the same area Peary expected to visit, and with objectives similar to his. This development infuriated Peary, who felt that Sverdrup was thus guilty of poaching.

Peary cabled to England instructions to dispatch the *Windward* on to the United States, at her normal three and a half knots, and he hurried his plans for departure. He mulled over the delays that the *Windward* — a ship "with as much power as a year-old baby" — would no doubt cause, and he chartered another ship, the *Hope*, for his northward journey.

On July 3rd Peary and his wife parted — with emotion that can only be imagined, since no mention of it was made in diary entries of that date. Four days later, just after the news had arrived of the United States naval victory over Spain at Santiago, in Cuba, the *Hope* left Sydney, on Cape Breton Island in Canada. With Peary, destined for Arctic duty, were Henson and a doctor, T. S. Dedrick, Jr. This time Peary had determined he would use small sledging parties; for any further help he would engage Eskimos.

The *Hope* reached Peary's immediate destination in Greenland, Etah, only a short time before the lumbering *Windward*. Peary then sent both vessels on walrus hunts — routine work for every Peary expedition upon arrival at and before departure from Greenland: to provide the Eskimos with a winter meat supply. On the 13th the *Hope* left for home and the *Windward*, with Peary, Henson, and Dedrick on board, commenced a crossing of the Kane Basin. Five days later Peary's feeble ship was beset by ice and held fast — for the long winter — near Cape D'Urville, far south of Peary's intended destination. This was a serious blow to him; now, he concluded, his best chance was to find Fort Conger, Greely's headquarters of fifteen years earlier, and use it as an advance base; he could unload his supplies at Cape D'Urville and sledge them to Conger, two hundred fifty miles distant, using the autumn moons. Since the day Greely and his men had left Conger on their disastrous retreat southward down Ellesmere Island to find a ship no one had visited the place.

Peary would not, however, be able to begin sledging his supplies northward for weeks; ice would be in no condition to allow such travel. In the meantime the restless Peary, a man for whom time now was ever critical, began devoting himself to explorations west of Kane Basin, an area generally unknown: the islands, bays, capes, and inlets of the east coast of Ellesmere Island.

Once during this autumn he walked into the camp of his rival, Otto Sverdrup, quite by accident. "I had a short and not effusive meeting with Sverdrup," Peary wrote,[2] with a brevity that implied his coolness. Peary was relieved to learn from Sverdrup that the *Fram*, too, had been unable to push through the Kane Basin ice and had been halted far south of Sverdrup's goal. This had forced the Norwegian to modify his plans — and to withdraw from the competition, to the north, with Peary.

Still, Peary was not mollified by this development. Invited to stay for coffee, Peary refused, left Sverdrup's camp, and continued on his way.

By October, ice conditions allowed Peary to begin transporting his supplies from Cape D'Urville, where they had been landed from the *Windward,* toward Fort Conger. He followed the ice foot of the Ellesmere shore — the belt of ice formed between high- and low-water marks — and he used the frequent headlands jutting out along the cheerless coastline for depots. He limited these operations to the time of brightest moonlight — and in this part of the Arctic the moon, like the sun later, travels in a helix above the horizon without setting, as long as its declination keeps it above the equator — about two weeks every month.

December arrived, with 50-below temperatures, before Peary was ready to complete the journey to Fort Conger, although he had been eager to learn whether the supplies abandoned there might still be usable and to investigate the condition of the building. On December 20th four Eskimo volunteers, Peary, Henson, and Dedrick sped northward, knowing they must complete the trip during the period of lunar light.

Traveling along the ice foot, however, was torturous. Strong headwinds and heavy drift slowed their progress so that by the ninth day they had covered only half the distance. Two more days and the moonlight would begin to give way to impenetrable blackness; yet progress became even more difficult. Food was low; a freezing wind blinded them; the ice grew steadily worse — an "efflorescence made the sledges drag as if on sand" — and finally became impassable. At Cape Cracroft, near the northern end of Kennedy Channel, one Eskimo became so numbed by the biting wind that, to save him, Peary ordered a halt, dug a burrow in a snowdrift, and left him there, with another Eskimo and nine of the weaker dogs. Later the other two Eskimos were to return for them; when they did, they would discover that their countrymen had eaten some of the dogs and had struck out for the ship, rather than venture any farther into this frozen wilderness where only wild animals, and only the hardiest of those, lived.

The last part of the trip was made in total darkness. Men and dogs groped and stumbled, blindly, through a chaos of broken, heaved-up sea ice; two dogs died in their traces; one camp, made under an ice cake, was so cold that sleep was impossible for the men — no matter how muscles and eyes ached — and they pushed on after brewing hot tea; Henson and an Eskimo lagged behind, forcing Peary to retrace painful steps to assure himself of their safety; Peary injured his right arm and lost the use of it. Finally Peary reached an area he believed — by the "feel" of the shore, which he had never seen before, except on maps, and could not see now — to be the entrance of Discovery Harbor, near where had been built Fort Conger. Several more hours of groping showed Peary that it was the eastern entrance.

Sometime around midnight, January 6th, 1899, they came, in blackness, upon a low, snow-covered frame building. Somehow Peary had been able to lead his starving group across the riprap of ice, through the appalling night without dawn, to a house that he had never seen before — that no man, surely, had seen in fifteen years. Had he not found it, of course, he and all the others would have died.

They forced an entrance into the building and got out their oil stove. Using it for illumination they looked around the eerie room. If ever a house seemed haunted, this one did — certainly with memories. Peary knew the whole story:

A. W. Greely had been a lieutenant in the Signal Corps of the United States Army when, in 1881, he had commanded an expedition organized to carry out a plan of establishing circumpolar stations in accordance with an 1879 recommendation by the International Geographical Congress. He and twenty-five men went north in the S. S. *Proteus,* which left them with enough food for three years. Greely had established this very base — Fort Conger.

The *Proteus* was to return in two years for the men, but if it failed to appear Greely had orders to break camp and journey southward, subsisting on rations that were to be cached along the route by supply ships. A series of misfortunes, some due to the ice and others due to bungling, resulted in landing only a few supplies.

In the summer of 1883 the *Proteus* returned. Near Cape Sabine, however, ice crushed the vessel and it sank. The crew was able to escape and to return to the United States on a smaller vessel, but Greely and his men were left marooned farther north. Now, according to the plan, Greely was to head south, using the caches he would find along his route.

Unfortunately, he would find virtually nothing. Washington officials, realizing this, frantically organized a relief expedition. It departed early in May, 1884, under the command of Winfield S. Schley, later to be known for his role in the Spanish-American War.

Schley eventually found Greely and seven others, all of them nearly dead, camped at Cape Sabine. Greely's tent had blown down over him, but he had been helpless to do anything about it. He had not eaten anything for two days, and the others had swallowed only a few chunks of soaked sealskin.

The rescuers built a fire, heated milk, and fed the men. Then they carried them to the ships offshore. Some of the survivors, delirious, begged the sailors not to shoot them, for Greely had been forced to order the execution of a man who had stolen rations.

Schley's sailors discovered this man's body on the beach; it was said most of his flesh had been eaten. Bodies of the other dead men were found in a similar condition. Schley prohibited the discussion of cannibalism among his sailors, hoping to spare the feelings of next-of-kin, and he suggested to the Navy Department that the remains of the dead be sealed in metal coffins.

Now, fifteen years late, Peary studied the headquarters of this tragic expedition:

[We] found the interior presenting the utmost confusion. Floor of both officers' and men's quarters and kitchen blocked and littered with boxes, packed and empty, pieces of fur, cast-off clothing, rubbish of all descriptions. In the kitchen partially consumed tins of provisions, tea, coffee, etc., were scattered about, their contents spilled on table and floor. In the men's quarters dishes remained on the table just as left after lunch or dinner of the day when the fort was deserted. Biscuits were scattered in every direction, overturned cups, etc., seemed to give indications of a hasty departure. To my surprise, the biscuits on the table, though somewhat tough, were not mouldy or spoiled. These things were meted out while a fire was being started in the range. Coffee in the bottom of one of the tins opened for sixteen years was found to have sufficient strength that by using a double amount, drinkable coffee could be made. After some considerable delay, owing to difficulty in making the range draw, we were all enjoying an ad lib supply of coffee and biscuits.[3]

Even as Peary sipped his coffee and reflected on the perils of Arctic travel as endured by the Greely expedition he became aware of a danger closer to home: he had noticed, with dismay, "a suspicious wooden feeling" in his right leg. An Eskimo helped him remove his *kamiks*, and Peary "was deeply annoyed" to find that the toes on both of his feet were seriously frostbitten. Dr. Dedrick removed the frost, bathing Peary's feet in bowls of ice water, but both men knew the toes had been badly frozen and would no doubt have to be amputated.

The Eskimos built a fire in the adjoining officers' quarters, and Peary and his two assistants slept there that night in their chilled, damp clothes, under whatever blankets they could find from the Greely supplies. The next morning, ironically, they all had colds, after having avoided them during the trip — in temperatures that had ranged to 63 degrees below zero.

Peary's toes obviously required attention, and Dr. Dedrick prepared to take them off. Using primitive methods and old medicines he performed the operation, removing parts of seven toes.[4] Now began the darkest period of Peary's life. For six weeks he was to lie on his back at Fort Conger, in doubt about whether he would ever walk again, whether he would keep the rest of his lower limbs. He and his men were snowbound, stormbound, and nightbound, more than two hundred miles from the *Windward*. Under such hopeless conditions Peary wrote, in heavy pencil on the wooden wall beside his bunk, a favorite quotation from Seneca: "*Inveniam viam aut faciam*" ("I shall find a way or make one").[5] Many years later Peary was to recall his ordeal at Fort

Conger, in a speech before the student body of Rensselaer Poly-
technic Institute at Troy, New York:

> . . . Here I lay helpless on my back for six weeks, . . . listen-
> ing to the howling of the winter winds and the cries of my starv-
> ing dogs, until in the latter part of February there was sufficient
> daylight to enable us to attempt to return to the ship. Through-
> out these interminable black days, though I could not at times
> repress a groan at the thought that my God-given frame was
> mutilated forever, still I never lost faith, in spite of the encour-
> aging statements of my physician that a man who had lost even
> a big toe, could never again walk effectively. I *knew* that I
> should yet do the work which I had set before myself.[6]

Six weeks after his arrival at Fort Conger Peary remained a
helpless cripple, unable even to stand. The forced inaction was
even more unbearable to him than his physical condition, however, and he decided to return to the ship, where, also, a more
sophisticated operation could be performed to get his feet in better shape. The only possible way for him to make the trip would
be lashed to a sledge, which would have to be carefully tended
over the awful ice foot by his men. Returning light, though dim,
provided some consolation; the landscape was "distinctly visible."

> . . . I remember few more grim and desolate scenes than the
> environs of Fort Conger as I took them in while being lashed
> onto my sledge, a helpless cripple, the bitterly cold February
> morning that I left the fort to return to the *Windward*.
> The dead white slopes of the hills lifting to the blue-black
> sky, the dead white expanse of [Discovery] harbor and [Lady
> Franklin] bay reaching away to the ribbon of pale steely light
> past the black dot of Cape Lieber where, in ten days, if the
> weather held clear, the sun would appear. . . .[7]

Peary refrained from mentioning in his letters and diaries his
own pain in returning to the *Windward*. It can only be imagined:

the torture as his sledge slipped across the ice and slammed into a variety of frozen barriers, jarring his tender stumps. In diary entries of February 18th-February 28th, dictated to Dr. Dedrick, who wrote them down, he gives only an indication of the hardships endured:

Saturday, February 18. Left Fort Conger at early daylight on the return to the ship, myself on the little Conger sledge drawn by five dogs and driven by Ahngoodloo, our provisions and camp gear on Sipsu's sledge drawn by eight dogs. . . . A few miles of rough ice outside and below Cape Baird gave the sledges a severe shaking up. . . .

Sunday, February 19. . . . Was dragged up the inner slope of ice foot, lowered down the seaward slope, and . . . practically carried across the rough belt of ice to the smooth ice outside. Keeping well out from shore and with the doctor and Matt in advance [we] were able to keep on good ice most of the day though encountering several very disagreeable stretches of rubble. . . .

Sunday, February 26. Either it is getting colder or else I am feeling the cold more, for today I have had the second musk-ox skin wrapped around my back and shoulders. . . .

Monday, February 27. . . . At the big snow slope near Cape Frazer I and my sledge are unceremoniously thrown over on one side, and sliding and dragging make the bottom. . . . This has been a long march for the doctor and Matt although a comparatively easy one for me. . . .

Tuesday, February 28. . . . The ship [was] reached the middle of the afternoon. No one being aware of our approach until we were close aboard, then almost instantly every face was at the gangway. The journey of some two hundred fifty miles, half of it before the return of the sun and with the burden of a crippled man, has been completed in eleven days without mishap or danger [an average of 22¾ miles each day]. The doctor and Matt, as well as the Eskimos, have completed a by no means slight feat in walking this distance in eleven days. They have had a harder time of it than I, and there could be no more faithful fellows than my two Eskimos, who, walking all day long at the upstanders and driving the dogs, have then turned to at night without a word of complaint to erect or excavate our snow shelters. After having my wraps and lashing removed and transferred to the deckhouse, where I could pull off my clothes that I had worn continuously for eleven days, I personally feel little the worse for wear. Temperature at the time of our arrival was minus 64 degrees. The average for the day has been over minus 60 degrees. As I expected, we have been practically given up by those on board the ship, and plans had been laid to bring up a detachment of Eskimos with which to form a relief party. . . .[8]

Two weeks later, on March 13th, Peary underwent another operation; all but the little toe on each foot was removed. A month later, without waiting for the stumps to heal, he began another series of sledging journeys, although he was forced to ride, at least for the following few weeks, and to use crutches when walking. He returned to Fort Conger and retrieved the Greely expedition records there; he resumed his explorations to the west of Kane Basin and completed his map of that unknown region. Before summer he was walking; frequent diary references mentioned an annoying pain, particularly in his right foot, after a jarring, bruising walk across the ice or after occasional soakings in chilly water. Sometimes, despite all his loathing to do so, he was forced to call a halt for rest.

In early August of 1899 the thick-ribbed ice finally loosened its grip on the *Windward*, and the ship proceeded to Etah. There a relief ship, the *Diana*, arrived on August 12th, with some encouraging news for Peary. Even as he had lain on his back, helpless, at

wind-swept Fort Conger, scribbling notations about finding a way
or making one, a group of wealthy businessmen, under the persuasion of Morris Jesup, had formally organized themselves into the
Peary Arctic Club with the primary aim of giving Peary financial
support for his Arctic work. The voyage of the *Diana* was, in fact,
one of their first official contributions. In charge of the ship was
the club secretary, Herbert L. Bridgman, publisher of the Brooklyn newspaper *Standard Union.*

The *Diana* also brought other news from home: Peary had become the father of a second daughter, Francine, born in January.
In a long letter Jo told him of this event, and many others; and
Peary spent most of a day reading and rereading the letter. As
was typical, she had tried to avoid writing anything that might
depress him, but she had not been able to repress an observation
that life was slipping away from both of them.

When he answered the letter, Peary wrote:

> You are right, dear, life is slipping away. That cannot come
> to you more forcibly than it has repeatedly to me in times of
> darkness and inaction the past year. More than once I have
> taken myself to task for my folly in leaving such a wife and
> baby (babies now) for this work. But there is something be-
> yond me, something outside of me, which impels me irresistibly
> to the work. . . .[9]

Bridgman listened with horror to the story of Peary's frostbite
and amputations, and urged him to come home, but without success. The *Windward* and the *Diana,* after the usual walrus-
hunting trips to obtain food for the Eskimos, sailed for home, leaving Peary, Henson, and Dedrick at Etah, the Greenland Eskimo
village Peary had chosen for his headquarters. His advance base
remained at Fort Conger, however, and despite his unfortunate
experience of the previous year with winter moons, he used the
moonlight to transfer his fresh supplies from Etah, where they

had been unloaded, to Payer Harbor, across Smith Sound near Cape Sabine. Later, from Payer, he transported the supplies, by stages as before, to Conger. When he arrived there on March 28th, 1900, he learned to his satisfaction that his Eskimos had shot twenty-one musk oxen near the place. His food supply thus benefited, and his morale was given a lift. The availability of game near Fort Conger gave him a feeling of security — but it also had a side effect that was to involve him in an unfortunate, bitter dispute later on: Peary became contemptuous of the leadership of the Greely expedition, which had abandoned Fort Conger in such haste, in such obvious fear of starvation, yet with a meat supply nearby for the looking. Peary's blunt observations regarding this later got to General Greely, who became infuriated.

For the spring work, which was to commence in April, Peary was at first undecided whether to strike out for the North Pole by way of Cape Hecla, about one degree of latitude north of Conger in Grinnell Land — on Ellesmere Island — or to cross frozen Robeson Channel and to try from the northern tip of Greenland. Eventually he decided on the latter alternative, reasoning that if he should fail to reach his primary objective, the Pole, he could complete the mapping of the northern coast of Greenland, linking the "farthest north" points reached on the west and east coasts — Lieutenant J. B. Lockwood's, near Cape Washington on the northwest coast, and Koldewey's, at Cape Bismarck on the east coast. On April 11th he and Henson and five Eskimos, with seven sledges, departed from Conger, leaving Dedrick and the other Eskimos behind for hunting forays to be conducted from the fort. Almost immediately Peary's usual luck showed itself: one of the Eskimos — Ahngoodloo, who had helped to return Peary from Conger to the *Windward,* became ill, and Peary himself saw the native back to Conger. Then Peary crossed the ice of Robeson Channel and rejoined his party.

That sledge expedition was to be one of the most remarkable

Arctic journeys made. After leaving Fort Conger and crossing Robeson Channel, Peary hugged the North Greenland coast, soon venturing again into a region no man had mapped. He came near to closing his traverses in that part of the world by rounding the northernmost portion of Greenland, a point named by him Cape Morris Jesup, then pressing on southeastward toward his Independence Bay.

Although Peary was not to be able to progress a great distance across the sea ice to the North Pole, the trip provided him invaluable experience for later efforts. It became the first instance of his use of supporting parties to assist a main party in areas where the country could not be counted on for game; the supporting parties each brought a sledge or group of loaded sledges that provisioned the entire traveling group, and when those provisions were almost exhausted that supporting party turned back. This trip, moreover, gave Peary his first real experience with travel over Arctic Ocean ice; until now he had been more of a glacial specialist, in Greenland.

The major part of the journey, however, was along the forbidding Greenland coast: groping over the same vicious ice foot that ripped footgear and capsized sledges, climbing the cliffs for passage inland when open water blocked their path, fighting the maddening raw wind that hit them insistently, squinting to see through blinding snowstorms and seeing nothing, pounding feet against ice that occasionally blinded Peary with pain. Depressing their spirits, and frightening the Eskimos, was the continued groaning of the icepack, always in motion near them, which sometimes sounded like the moans of dying souls, while, all around them, the black gloom cast by surrounding cliffs lent an appropriate atmosphere to the ghostly recital.

Shortly before midnight on May 8th Peary came upon the site of the "farthest north" of Lieutenant J. B. Lockwood and Sergeant D. L. Brainard, both from Greely's expedition. He found Lockwood's record in a cairn, and, following custom, removed it for return to civilization, leaving a copy in place of the original.

Peary knew that before Lockwood and Brainard had turned back from this point they had sighted in the distance ahead a cape given the name Washington; possibly this was the *ultima Thule* of Greenland. With considerable anxiety Peary sledged on toward that cape; then, reaching the blue ice foot, hurried on for a view of the coastline ahead.

> Great was my relief to see on rounding this point another great headland, with two magnificent glaciers debauching near it, rising across an inlet beyond. Cape Washington is not the northern point of Greenland, as I had feared. It would have been a disappointment to me after coming so far to find that another's eyes had forestalled mine in looking on the coveted northern point.[10]

Four days later, Peary came upon a cape lying in the distant gloom, and the feel of the country made him confident that *this* was indeed *ultima Thule*. One more march brought him to the place, and an eager observation beyond showed him that his guess was correct. He named the cape Morris K. Jesup, for his benefactor, then began considering his next move. From the northernmost point of Greenland he had declared he would set out over the sea ice for the Pole, and he surveyed conditions in that direction.

Conditions, however, were not promising. The scene was one of broken, jumbled ice and giant ridges, often shrouded by fog, and — beyond — a smokelike "water sky" that, he knew, hovered above open leads of water. Still, he began, and he made three marches northward.

> Have given my feet repeated blows today upon hidden blocks of ice that made me sick to my stomach and half blind

for a few moments. Two especially severe knocks on the illy cushioned end of my right foot made me almost fear that the bones may be injured.[11]

From an ice pinnacle fifty feet high he looked northward and saw "a chaos of broken and heaped-up ice," dim prospects indeed for a man who had just traveled over heavy ice broken and thrown up to heights of twenty-five and fifty feet. Moreover, he saw ahead, marked by an ominous "water sky" that Peary came to dread with the same intensity as failure, a wide lead of open water, no doubt blocking further progress northward. Peary realized the water might freeze over, but he also realized the futility of waiting. This spring he was not equipped for a serious attempt to reach the Pole; he turned back toward land, intending to carry out the alternate plan of exploring southeastward along the Greenland coast. An observation at his northernmost point on the sea ice, made March 16th, showed him to be at a latitude of 83 degrees 50 minutes north.

"A high latitude will keep till next spring," he wrote. "As it is, I am unquestionably second on the list." [12]

On May 22nd, with rations for the outward march running low, Peary finally turned back toward Fort Conger, more than four hundred tortuous miles away. He had reached a point later known as Cape Wyckoff, about the 83rd degree of latitude, and had seen for himself, beyond all doubt, the insularity of Greenland. Some hundred and fifty miles down the coast lay Independence Bay. Representing further success, during this part of the journey Peary had caught a glimpse of "a magnificent mountain" far to the west, and he recognized the peculiar contour of Mount Wistar, which he had seen in 1895 lying far to the northward, from the vicinity of Independence Bay. Little of North Greenland now remained an absolute blank.

On the return trip Peary deposited records in cairns at Cape Morris Jesup and at three other locations; his record at Cape

Jesup was to be recovered nine years later by Donald B. MacMillan, a member of his 1908–1909 expedition. On June 10th, 1900, an hour and a half after midnight, Peary arrived at Fort Conger.

Hunting occupied Peary and his men during summer and autumn. Once, soon after his return from the sledge journey, Peary, Henson, and four Eskimos visited the Lake Hazen region west of Conger and killed more than one hundred musk oxen, a boon to the food supply for both men and dogs. Still more animals were obtained elsewhere.

Unknown to Peary, the *Windward* had returned to Greenland some two months after his own return from the long sledge journey. Little more than two hundred miles to the south were his family, mail, and a host of friends, but he was totally unaware of this — and the people aboard the *Windward* were unable to communicate with him. The ship reached Etah August 19th after great difficulty in forcing a passage through the ice, but Peary was not there. The Eskimos said he had gone to Payer Harbor, on Cape Sabine, and the *Windward* made an arduous, eight-day voyage across narrow — but ice-clogged — Smith Sound to find Peary, but he was not at Payer Harbor either.

Safety for the *Windward* was waning; ice would soon block its return home. While its officers were pondering a course of action, an onshore wind suddenly sprang up one night and drove the ship on the rocks. With the vessel in immediate danger of being lost, everyone aboard but the crew was sent ashore — over the ice — and supplies were hurriedly unloaded. Despite the fears of everyone, the *Windward* escaped undamaged, but ice now imprisoned the ship, and it was held in the Arctic for another winter.

The time was a particularly trying one for Jo Peary. Her husband, after writing out his ideas for successful Arctic exploration fifteen years earlier — even before he had launched his career — had found few of them not worthy of being followed now, including the sentence that stated: "The presence of women an abso-

lutely necessity to render the men contented. . . ." [13] On board
the *Windward* was an Eskimo woman, Allakasingwah — or "Ally,"
as Jo called her — and her baby. The woman innocently boasted
of her relationship with *Pearyarksuah*, not realizing the enormous
difference in mores.

Jo Peary was stunned by the revelation, but without losing her
composure; she was a woman who invariably masked deep feeling. She began a long letter to her husband, for delivery whenever communication with him could be established: "Today I feel
as though I should not see you this year and I must put on paper
what I had hoped to talk over with you. . . . You will have been
surprised, perhaps annoyed, when you hear that I came up on a
ship . . . but believe me had I known how things were with you
here I should not have come." [14]

Nevertheless, when "Ally" became seriously ill later Jo was solicitous of the woman's welfare, and she elicited a promise from
the natives that the baby would not be strangled in event of his
mother's death, as was Eskimo custom. "Ally" recovered, however, and the persuasion became unnecessary.

In later letters Jo displayed her stanchness of character. Peary
was not destined to receive any of these letters, however, until the
following spring: even after the *Windward* personnel had guessed
he was at Fort Conger, no autumn or winter party from the ship
was to reach him, because of difficult ice conditions, trepidation
of would-be messengers, and refusal of the Eskimos to venture
that far north, even for a promised reward. In her letters Jo
wrote:

. . . Should this reach you you must *not think of coming down.*
You must save yourself for your northern work. [Ally] has
told me how very tender your feet are and you must do nothing
that would in any way interfere with your work; besides,
stormy weather might detain you as it did last year. . . .

You wrote me that *failure* would not affect you seriously. I want you to know that whenever you return your friends, who are many, will think you the bravest, pluckiest explorer that ever went into the field. . . . Whatever you do you must take care of yourself. . . . Sometimes I think you are a physical wreck. If this is so, come home and let Marie and I [*sic*] love you and nurse you. Don't let your pride keep you back. Who will *even* remember it ten years from now? . . .

Don't forget to let me know about your coming down and if I am to meet you anywhere. Etah, the lodge, or Fort Conger will make no difference. Oh, Bert, Bert. I want you so much. Life is slipping away so fast — pretty soon all will be over.[15]

Two hundred fifty miles north, Peary settled down into a winter routine. Despite his restless nature, he usually enjoyed the quiet moments that preceded a major effort; these times of privacy seemed to renew his energy. With his singular self-sufficiency he did not need a close, continuing companionship in the North; such a relationship would have been, in fact, disagreeable to him. Once his wife wrote to his mother, "Marie is like her father — she needs no one . . . [although] she prefers some persons to others. . . ."[16] Now Peary added unknowing corroboration: "Wonderful this cabin, this mellow light, this warmth, this freedom from care or annoyance, this freedom to do as I please; it will unfit me for [later] life I fear, and yet it is needed. . . ."[17]

. . . There has never been a time for me in the Arctic before so free from annoyance, worry, or irritation. I have no interruptions, have my place entirely to myself, and can work as I please.

No previous winter either has my house been so comfortable as is this.

I turn out between 5:30 and 6:30 A.M., make my own coffee (one quart) which I can do in fifteen minutes; have my coffee and biscuit, call doctor at eight — devote forenoon to writing or arranging material in most compact form. Doctor gets dinner at twelve, and I go in his place to eat it.

Then I get in my twenty-four hours' supply of wood, ice, biscuit, etc. Then I do whatever is on hand outdoors. Afterwards work on equipment.

At 6 P.M. supper, sometimes in doctor's place, sometimes self. Then the evening for writing, reading, or planning. About ten to eleven I turn in after preparing my kindling for morning and my coffee kettle.[18]

Although Peary made no mention of it in that particular entry, relations between him and Dr. Dedrick were becoming more and more strained. The doctor had resented Matt Henson for months, feeling that Matt was usurping his own position — an imagined one — as Peary's chief assistant.[19] Dedrick had been particularly incensed to hear the Eskimos laughingly refer to Peary as the middle finger, Henson as the ring finger, and Dedrick as the little finger.[20]

After only a few months in the Far North Dedrick began to brood, but at first his dissatisfaction was limited to his diaries;[21] for Dedrick's personality prohibited his speaking up in a strong voice, although he occasionally wrote down resolutions to do so. Peary's only initial unhappiness with Dedrick came from the doctor's inherent slowness; the man seem incapable of hurrying, even when speed was vital.

Now, however, Dedrick was becoming an annoyance, and certain of his erratic actions were made more striking by the man's wild look: he had let his hair grow down to his shoulders, and he had stopped shaving so that he had a long, pointed beard. Dedrick dropped into Peary's quarters for long chats; spoke with increasing authority on a variety of medical topics, yet became inconsistent and forgetful in words and actions; voiced inability to carry out certain assignments because of ignorance of procedures; asked for greater authority and more work, yet when given it sometimes begged off because of illness or other indisposition. In his diaries he scribbled painful recollections of striving for virtue and for manhood; of longing for the companionship of his wife, whom he had married in 1896; of disgust with the purely sexual relationship available from Eskimo women.

Mainly, however, Dedrick indicated a jealousy of the relationship between Henson and Peary, and he demanded that Peary write out for Henson a set of instructions detailing responsibilities of all. These instructions, Dedrick suggested, should emphasize his own position as second in command.

Peary made an effort to placate the doctor. Henson had, in fact, become something of a problem to Peary too, and Peary determined to speak to him. Beforehand, Peary made notes on the topics to be covered:

Intend start in this winter with every possible source of annoyance, irritation, or misunderstanding removed.

Have cleared up some matters with doctor. Now it's your turn, then the Eskimos. . . .

Not only reality but even appearance or suspicion of unfairness to be avoided. . . .

Must come to me about everything, no matter how small, for use or consumption.

Am old enough now and you have been in my service long enough to show me respect in small things.

Have a right to expect you will say sir to me always.

That you will pay attention when I am talking to you and show that you hear directions I give you by saying yes sir, or all right sir.

Have no fault to find when we are alone together, but when doctor or number of Eskimos present or we are on board ship you are very different. . . .

Now is there anything which, if different, would make things pleasanter for you? [22]

The situation failed to improve. As Peary completed preparations for his spring attempt to reach the North Pole, Dedrick pronounced Henson unfit for the journey — indeed he was ailing — and observed that Peary's condition left something to be desired, too. When Peary spoke of delaying his spring work until he was better fit for it, Dedrick asked why he could not go himself — this despite his lack of proficiency with a sledge and his unpopularity among the Eskimos.

Eventually Peary set a date for commencing the attempt — April 5th, 1901 — and decided that Henson and one Eskimo would accompany him. They would head directly north from Ellesmere Island. Dedrick and another group of Eskimos would proceed north only a march or so, acting as sort of a support party, then turn back. Dedrick pondered the nuances of this, fretted, pouted, and days afterward submitted his resignation, then later backed down from quitting.[23]

Before Peary departed he wrote numerous letters, mostly in regard to disposition of his affairs in the event of his "nonreturn." Despite his increasing difficulties in dealing with Dedrick, he left the doctor in charge of the advance base, with authority to use his own discretion should Peary not return[24] — but at that time Dedrick had not turned in his resignation.

To his mother Peary wrote a letter she would never read:

. . . Hardly an hour, certainly not a day, has passed, that I have not longed for you, and Jo, and my babies. I have been *very* foolish. I can see it now when it is too late, and *very very* selfish, and yet I know that you have forgiven me, for you have been with me so many times, and averted trouble [for] me. In my journey of last spring, things happened in which I know you took a part, and yet they seem so strange that were another person telling me of them, I should be incredulous.

Among others the following. In three instances bears passed close to caches of food which I had made for our return, caches which were very important if not vital to our return, without disturbing them. Another time a bear walked over a cache, yet let it alone. Once, open water which barred my passage froze over to let me pass, and twelve hours later was open water again.

Repeatedly I had the most vivid dreams of you. I know you are watching over me.

I am not sick, mother, not worried nor discouraged. But I am older and I see many things more clearly.

God bless and keep you till I come. . . .[25]

After only eight days Peary turned back, upon reaching Lincoln Bay. There he realized that the sea ice would prohibit a significant advance. Probably, however, he had resigned himself to only a token spring effort, anyway, because his expedition obviously was not planned for an extended effort. He returned to Fort Conger; then, on a late-April trip south, he encountered a party from the ship, bound northward to try to locate him. They brought him his mail, and he learned of Jo's arrival, and of the death of his second child, Francine.

From Jo:

Our little darling, whom you never knew, was taken from me on August 7th, '99, just seven months after she came. She was only sick a few days, but the disease took right hold of her little head and nothing could be done for her. . . . I shall never feel quite the same again — part of me is in the little grave.[26]

Then, from Jo's brother, Emil:

. . . Jo has had more than her share of sorrow and trouble, but has borne everything with fortitude. Her share of the North Pole burden is the nerve-destroying worry, which no watching world applauds, but which can hope to find recognition only in the hearts of those who see her always ready to do anything, to suffer anything for the good of the cause.

I hope for both your sakes that your task will soon be finished and that you will attain the summit of the earth and hear for all the rest of your days the praise of the applauding world. If, however, it should be denied you to reach the Pole — as it has been denied to all others — you can rest on the laurels you have already won in the North and feel assured of the admiration and respect of all who appreciate perseverance, pluck, and courage. . . .[27]

Peary read his mail; and, after a rest, struck out for the *Windward*, where he was reunited with his wife and daughter on his forty-fifth birthday, May 6th, 1901.

Three months later the relief ship *Erik* arrived, on August 4th, and brought Peary more sad news. A letter from his cousin Janette Wiley told of the death of his mother:

I know that the absence of a dear familiar handwriting has already told you what my heart shrinks from writing, and you will be somewhat prepared for the contents of this letter. . . . In one of her bright moments [before the end] I asked her if she knew she was very ill. She answered, "No." I then told her she was, and that we wanted her, for our sakes, to try hard to get well, and she replied, "I am not anxious to." I said, "Had you rather go than stay?" and her answer was, "Yes." . . . I am sure that for some weeks before she went away, she felt you were no longer living, and I think a part of her life went out at that time. . . .[28]

Peary's grief was almost overwhelming, as his diaries show, but still he stayed in the Arctic, for one last attempt to reach the North Pole, in 1902. The *Windward*, freed from the ice at last, returned to the United States on August 24th. The *Erik* was to follow five days later, but before its departure Peary's surgeon, Dedrick, submitted a second resignation,[29] which Peary accepted readily, "to take effect on [Dedrick's] arrival in New York," where Dedrick was ordered to proceed by the returning *Erik*.[30]

Instead of returning on the *Erik*, however, Dedrick confounded everyone by insisting that he remain in Greenland. He would establish his quarters at Annoatok, he declared, and would be available to Peary in case of need. Peary's blunt answer that he wanted to see no more of the doctor failed to change his mind; neither did the persuasion of the people on board the *Erik*. When it appeared to Dedrick that he was about to be returned to the United States against his will he slipped ashore.

The *Erik* landed one other person, this one formally: Peary's steward Charles Percy. On August 29th that ship, too, sailed for home, and once more Peary was isolated in the Arctic. This time he planned to use Payer Harbor for his winter quarters, although he would continue the system of sledging supplies northward toward Fort Conger — for he would leave for the Pole from the northern tip of Ellesmere.

The recently renewed contact with his family and the grievous news from home made him doubly susceptible to a feeling of nostalgia that, at times, became melancholic when he could not keep busy:

. . . The loss of mother keeps coming to me. Night, day, morning, evening, recollections of scenes and times and places in which she was associated, come rushing over me followed by the thought, "Never again. . . ."[31]

A strange dream last night of the *Windward* swept by the ice against the rocks, broken in two and sinking instantly, with Jo and Marie in the cabin and I standing on the ice.[32]

I can hardly realize that there is a world . . . different from this "black hole." Ah, Jo and Marie, was I criminally foolish in staying? Shall I really never see you again?[33]

At Payer Harbor that autumn an epidemic described as dysentery struck the Eskimos. Peary cared for the natives himself, giving no thought to summoning the man he was to refer to as his "crazy doctor," but by November 19th six Eskimos had died. Finally, the disease spent itself, and Peary polished his plans for the polar journey.

On April 6th, 1902, Peary, Henson, and four Eskimos left the land near Cape Hecla, a distant, far-northern point of remote Ellesmere Island, and began their struggle across the perilous ice of the Arctic Ocean. "As the sledges plunged down from the ice foot," Peary wrote, "their noses were buried out of sight, [and] the dogs wallowed belly deep in the snow." [34]

Thus began Peary's major effort of the 1898–1902 expedition — but, before commencing it, he had been in the field for a month and had covered four hundred miles "of the most arduous traveling" in temperatures ranging from 35 degrees below zero to almost 60 below.

For the next fifteen days Peary and his men found themselves in a frozen purgatory where they were forced to zigzag and double on their track to avoid areas of impassable rough ice, then open water; to lift sledges bodily over numerous ice barriers; to clear a roadway with pickaxes.

By April 20th the expedition was gasping, and Peary was aware that the end of its attempt was near. A zone of old rubble ice blanketed by deep snow exhausted both men and dogs. Next they encountered a lead of young ice; Peary's sledge crashed through and was almost lost to the depths before it was retrieved. Then a biting wind lashed them, blinded them with snow and ice particles, and cut visibility to only a few yards, even when they could attempt to look.

Going on was hopeless. On the following day Peary, heartsick, wrote in his diary:

The game is off. My dream of sixteen years is ended. . . . I have made a good fight, but I cannot accomplish the impossible.[35]

Observations placed him at 84 degrees 16 minutes 27 seconds north — a new farthest north for the Western Hemisphere. He gave the dogs a double ration of pemmican, then broke out the flag Jo had made for him and took several photographs. Before he set out on the return journey he heard from the distance beyond a sound resembling a heavy surf: a lead crushing together before the northerly wind, he speculated. Ordinarily this would have been an occasion for exultation; he would find no open water ahead. Now, however, he began his retreat, and the return marches seemed exceedingly long and trying. Despite this, Peary found himself unable to sleep for more than an hour at a time. ". . . I feel very tired," he wrote. "My appetite has not been good since we turned back, and I have had but one good sleep . . . and I experience an annoying feeling of extreme lassitude and heaviness." [36]

On May 3rd he reached Fort Conger, where he remained three days, resting, before going on to Payer Harbor. He was at Conger on his birthday, May 6th, which he noted in his diary: ". . . Forty-six. Too old for this kind of work." Later:

My dream of sixteen years is ended. I close the book and turn to others less interesting, but better suited for my years.

Were I younger I might feel bitter that my training, experience, love for the work, and strenuous efforts should be first handicapped by a compulsory start from a low latitude, and then rendered futile by insuperable conditions. As it is, I accept the result calmly. I have put the best there was in me into it. The goal still remains for a better man than I, or more favorable conditions, or both.

As I look back I see nothing to regret — equipment was all right, the plan of campaign was right and carried out to the letter as long as obstacles were superable. Neither were we hampered or impeded by the rigors of the climate, or accidents, long experience having eliminated these.[37]

Adding to his discomfiture, Dr. Dedrick began to plague him with an occasional uninvited, unannounced visit, using a variety of excuses for making the calls. At first Peary was patient, without being cordial, but eventually he was forced to reiterate his ultimatum to the doctor: stay away. Eventually the doctor took passage, apparently on a whaler, for the United States.

Peary's spirits continued to sag:

. . . My feelings are not of the brightest. I think of four years ago when in spite of the setback of not getting my ship farther north, I looked full of life and hope and anticipation at this . . . shore mellow in the August sunlight, and dreamed of what I should accomplish. Now a maimed old man, unsuccessful after the most arduous work, away from wife and child, mother dead, one baby dead. Has the game been worth the candle? And yet I could not have done otherwise than stick to it. I have made my fight as I said I would and I believe a good one, and have missed my goal only because of insuperable obstacles — not because of supineness, or weariness, or carelessness, or mismanagement. I shall be glad to get away from everything here, and yet as I look at the cliffs a feeling akin to homesickness comes over me, but it is for the youthful foolish hopes and dreams with which they have been associated (youthful if one can regard forty-two years youthful as against forty-six). But I am more than four years older now than I was then.[38]

. . . As I look about on the scenery that a few years ago would have filled me with enthusiasm, as I think of my high hopes then, and contrast them with my present lack of energy,

of interest, of elation; as I think of the last four years and what I
have been through; as I think of all the little petty details with
which I have been and am still occupying myself, it all seems so
small, so little worth the while that I could cry out in anguish of
spirit.[39]

On August 5th the *Windward* hove into view, preceded by excited shouts from the Eskimos. Peary strained for a sight of his
wife and daughter, but could not see them at first and disappoint-
edly concluded they had not come with the ship. Then he recognized them, and as soon as the ship had moored he hurried aboard
for a reunion that allowed him to forget about his failure, momentarily.

After his return to the United States he was awarded gold
medals by the Royal Scottish Geographical Society and the
Société de Géographie of Paris. His recent anguish forgotten
now, he wrote Herbert Bridgman:

. . . I am as strong as ever in my belief that the Pole can be
secured by a determined effort via the Smith Sound gateway to
the Pole, and that it ought to be done and must be secured for
this country.

I am more than willing to throw such energies and experience and ability as I possess, into the work for two more years,
if sufficient funds can be obtained to insure a first-class equipment, it being understood that the first and foremost item of
such equipment is to be a powerful ship, the best of her class.[40]

Chapter 10

FOUR YEARS in the Arctic, and Peary came wandering back into naval duty feeling like "a lost cat."[1] His civil engineering proficiency enabled him to pass two examinations for promotion, however, and he rose from lieutenant to lieutenant commander, then to commander. The Navy even allowed him to accept the presidency of the American Geographical Society after his election in 1903.

Furthermore, he now had a friend in the White House: Theodore Roosevelt, inaugurated in 1901. Vigorous and bustling nearly to a fault, the inimitable "Teddy" liked men cut in his mold, and he had begun to follow Peary's exploits with enthusiasm long before becoming President. He warmed to Peary's pronouncements that the glory of reaching the North Pole first should fall to an American: United States prestige, already on an upswing after the defeat of Spain, would be further enhanced throughout the world, a broad endeavor with which Roosevelt was obsessed.

From the Far North Peary had once written Roosevelt, two years before Roosevelt had become President, and had voiced the hope that he would soon see his friend and supporter in the White House. Now that he was there, Peary's relations with the naval establishment became considerably smoother.

He was even given some choice assignments. One involved a

visit to England, to study plans of naval barracks. During this trip he also visited France.

He worked for a proposed reorganization of the Civil Engineer Corps that would increase the number of officers and provide an upward adjustment of rank of officers already commissioned. Characteristically, he went directly to the top with his lobbying, bypassing the sacrosanct chain of command: Peary wrote directly to President Roosevelt's secretary, William Loeb, Jr.[2]

Peary even entertained some hope of being named, sometime in the near future, chief of the Bureau of Yards and Docks. Because of his extended leaves or because of his talk of yet another Arctic expedition, however, the post went to another man.

This consideration of another voyage to the Far North provoked these letters from his wife and daughter even before he had arrived home from the expedition of 1898–1902:

. . . When Marie came home at noon [his wife wrote] I said to [her], "The *Herald* says the Peary Arctic Club wants your father to go north again."

She just flew to the paper: "Let me see it." Then after reading the paper she burst into a perfect torrent of words. Her eyes flashed and the tears rolled down her cheeks. I said, "Don't you have just as good time when your father is away?" "Yes, but I want my father. What's the use of having a father if you can only see him in spots?"

I said, well, the paper does not say that he is going. "Oh, you know very well if they give him the money he will only too gladly go to his beloved huskies." All this time I was nearly dying with laughter because she looked so comical. Her flushed tear-stained face, her eyes snapping, her head tossing, and all the time her tongue was going. Suddenly she stopped and looked at me in such a curious way, then said, "I do believe you are glad he is going — well, I am just going to write to him myself."

This she did while I was out this afternoon and I enclose her letter. . . .

November 14, 1902

My dear, dear Father-

Of course I know the papers are not always right, but I read that the Peary Arctic Club are trying to get your consent to go north again. I think it a dog's shame. . . . I know you will do what pleases mother and me, and that is to stay with us at home.

I have been looking at your pictures, it seems ten years, and I am sick of looking at them. I want to see my father. I don't want people to think me an orphan.

Please think this over.

Your loving
Marie[3]

The pleading was useless, however, for Peary had long ago become a man possessed by the demons of his ambition. He was not capable of giving up the pursuit of his dream that had been growing for two decades now, and he yearned for one more attempt at fulfillment. The arrival of a son, Robert, Jr., on August 29th, 1903, did not forestall his planning.

Foremost among his requirements for another voyage was a ship capable of reaching the Arctic Ocean, from where he could commence the polar journey rested and ready for the ordeal. The *Windward* had not been sufficient for his purpose, not even after new engines had been installed, in 1902. He proposed now building a ship to suit his needs, and he found support among members of the Peary Arctic Club, especially from Morris Jesup, who agreed to guarantee construction if Peary would raise half of the fifty thousand dollars needed.

Peary threw his seemingly boundless energy into the work. First he needed a leave of absence, but with President Roosevelt supporting him this no longer posed a problem. The Navy, in fact, expressed willingness to sponsor — though not to finance — the expedition this time, a development due entirely to the omnipresence of Roosevelt.

Orders for the leave came forthwith. In them Charles H. Darling, who was acting secretary of the Navy, stated:

> . . . *The attainment of the Pole should be your main object. Nothing short will suffice.* The discovery of the poles is all that remains to complete the map of the world. . . . *Our national pride is involved in the undertaking, and this department expects that you will accomplish your purpose and bring further distinction to a service of illustrious traditions.*
>
> *In conclusion, I am pleased to inform you that the President of the United States sympathizes with your cause and approves the enterprise.*[4]

Later, when delays required a modification of leave dates, the change was made without difficulty. Peary prepared for what he felt certain was to be his final, and successful, effort.

The condition of his feet had been greatly improved through an operation, in October of 1902, by Dr. W. W. Keen of Philadelphia. Dr. Keen amputated the outer joint of each of the remaining little toes, which projected beyond the stumps of the others. Then he slit the skin at the front of the feet and drew forward the tissue from underneath. This made a cushion for the stumps, and Peary was able to walk with less difficulty. He walked with a sort of glide, and he never limped, associates recalled in later years; but this was accomplished only through the same stern self-will that sent Peary back to the Artic time after time, even after heartbreaking disappointment.

By March, 1905, he had his ship, but getting it was not easy, even with the support of the Peary Arctic Club. Money proved to be a problem still, and supervision of the construction, which

Peary insisted on, left him with virtually no spare time for weeks.

Peary had designed the ship himself, and now he inspected every timber used, observed the bolts driven and the nuts set tight, watched over the calking and tarring. When completed, the ship was a taut, compact, efficient tool with which Peary could surely reach three or four hundred miles closer to his goal. He named it *Roosevelt*, in honor of the President.

The ship was only 184 feet long; breadth was 35½ feet. With this stubbiness the vessel could twist and turn rapidly and sharply through ice-jammed waterways. Draft load was only 16 feet, allowing the vessel to work close inshore around icebergs. The sides were egg-shaped, enabling the ship to rise when squeezed by ice and to avoid a fatal crush. Moreover, the sides were thick, reaching a maximum of 30 inches, and they were elastic and tough. The builders used wood instead of steel, which, of course, would have been vulnerable to slashes by the jagged ice and impossible to repair in the Arctic. Inside, the ship was heavily braced and trussed by steel beams as security against the tremendous pressures soon to be encountered in the icepack.

Three distinctive propulsion features went into the *Roosevelt*. First, the ship was built as a steam vessel with auxiliary sails, in direct contrast to all previous polar ships. Secondly, it had a valve-operated bypass that allowed steam from all the boilers at full pressure to be turned into a large low-pressure cylinder, thus doubling the power for a short time and giving the ship a reserve for extrication from dangerous situations. Thirdly, its shaft was of 12-inch diameter steel forging, a size used in steamers of a much larger size, and the propeller was an exceptionally heavy one. In the event the *Roosevelt* found itself helpless in the ice the ship carried powerful deck appliances — windlass, steam capstan, and winch — to warp the vessel out of precarious positions and to haul it off the bottom if it went aground. As a further safeguard, the raking counter was built to shield the propeller and the rudder; the propeller blades were detachable, and the rudder could be hoisted out of danger when required.

The ship was launched in March when Jo Peary smashed against the bow a bottle of champagne encased in ice, and, once again, the hectic last few months before sailing were upon Peary.

As always, hundreds of suggestions deluged him at this time, when the newspapers were filled with stories about his plans. Some were more helpful than others, but virtually all of them held up a mirror to the general ignorance of the Arctic regions. An Indiana man, Arthur DeLong, shared with Peary his idea of lining "coats, caps, and other garments, as well as the sleeping bags," with dried meats and other foodstuffs, to serve the obvious double purpose of keeping the men warm and, in an emergency, of providing nourishment — however unprotected this might leave them later.[5]

A man from Georgia, H. C. Barnard, was inspired to suggest a simple solution to the whole problem of Arctic exploration. Instead of striking out northward with dogs and sledges from the advance base, Barnard wondered, why not use electric automobiles? "If the sea up there freezes smooth and level I do not see why he could not use automobiles instead of dog trains and get right to the Pole in 'short order.' — The only trouble to be found with them would be to find a lubricant (for the working parts) that wouldn't freeze, I think, and isn't there some such lubricant in the world somewheres?"[6] The letter was forwarded to Peary with a solemn endorsement from the Bureau of Navigation, where it had been opened.

A resident of New Jersey, D. E. Parks, sent Peary a letter of introduction "to the president of Wieland, North Pole," a land described as circular, five hundred miles in diameter, with twenty million persons, and "a civilization greater than ours. . . . Kindly receive and care for [Peary]," Parks implored, "and when he wishes please allow and aid his return to his country."[7]

The work of launching this expedition was as exhausting and even more time-consuming than the work in the Arctic. Peary was able to see his family only rarely, and Jo was frankly concerned for his health.

> . . . You have been in a terribly unsettled condition, both mentally and physically, and I fear unless you do take a complete rest you will have a serious time.
>
> . . . I do feel for you, my dearest; I can't do much or indeed anything except keep quiet. In this affair, if you win I shall lose all love of life — if you lose, life will hold no happiness for you. . . .[8]

There was never any doubt where Peary's interest lay. In his lectures, delivered on a bustling schedule to raise more money, he made this clear:

> When I remember the hardships, the hunger, the cold, the weariness, the unceasing efforts, the years of time expended, part of myself sacrificed; and when I think of the splendid prize still waiting up there amid the eternal ice, needing only a little money to secure it, I have a feeling of contempt for the pretty pictures, and . . . I sometimes think [I] would almost sell my soul . . . for the opportunity to be at work *now*, with my loaded sledge and my faithful dogs before me, working across the polar pack towards that on which for sixteen years I have set my heart, instead of talking here to you, pleasant as it is.[9]

Again:

> . . . If I had the money myself, or could earn it even by such a bargain as used to be effected in the good old times when souls were a marketable commodity and always in demand by the devil, I would put the thing through single-handed.[10]

Peary even made a tentative inquiry at the Navy Department regarding the availability of money to help finance the expedition.

90° N. Lat. (North Pole
April 6° 1909

I have today hoisted
the National Ensign of
the United States of
America at this place
which my observa-
tions indicate to be
the North Polar axis
of the earth, & have
formally taken posses-
sion of the entire
region & adjacent
far, & in the name
of the President &
the United States of
America.
    I leave this record
& United States flag

in possession
[R] Robert E. Peary
United States Navy

On April 6, 1909, Peary reached the North Pole. He left this and one other record and the United States flag in possession.

Robert Edwin Peary, a boy usually full of mischief, nevertheless had his quiet moments.

As a Bowdoin junior, "Bert" Peary had established a reputation for working classroom problems his own way.

Josephine Diebitsch, daughter of a Smithsonian professor, and Peary were married on August 11, 1888. (Photograph from a later date.)

Until shortly before his death in 1920, Peary retained his tough, athletic appearance.

The discomforts of Arctic life were severe. Here, the deck of the *Roosevelt* is crowded with Eskimos, dogs, and supplies. (© National Geographic Society)

The *Roosevelt* contributed to Peary's 1908–1909 success by carrying his expedition to a Far North jumping-off point, Cape Sheridan, where it was then iced in. (© National Geographic Society)

Peary distributes gifts to a group of Eskimos who accompanied him on one of his expeditions. (Photo courtesy of the Library of Congress)

Peary and his wife, Josephine, share a quiet moment on the *Roosevelt*.

Egingwah, one of the four Eskimos who journeyed with Peary to the North Pole. (© National Geographic Society)

Besides Peary, Matthew Henson was the only non-Eskimo to successfully complete the dash to the North Pole. (© National Geographic Society)

Eskimos sound for the depth of the icy Arctic Ocean during one of Peary's expeditions. (© National Geographic Society)

The Cape Columbia monument, erected after Peary's return from the North Pole, commemorated his triumph. Mounted on the guidepost was a record of the expedition, framed under glass. (© National Geographic Society)

The journey across the frozen sea to the North Pole was frequently torturous and exhausting. (© National Geographic Society)

Peary in his furs during the successful 1908–1909 trip North. (Photo courtesy of the Library of Congress)

In January 1919, Peary made his last public appearance to bestow on Vilhjalmur Stefansson (center) a National Geographic Society medal for Arctic work. Pictured at right is Peary's critic, General Greely.

In the aftermath of the North Pole controversy between Peary and Dr. Frederick A. Cook, Peary became a leading advocate of aviation. (Photo courtesy of the Library of Congress)

Then, however, the funds were obtained from private sources, and a relieved Peary sailed for the bleak Arctic from New York during a blistering heat wave, on July 16th, 1905. "I did not realize until we were off, and the relaxation came, how utterly fagged out I was with the work, and heat, of the last weeks," he said.[11] The *Erik*, carrying coal and additional supplies, was to meet the *Roosevelt* in Greenland.

Members of the 1905–1906 expedition were Dr. Louis J. Wolf, surgeon, a thirty-year-old Oregonian; Ross G. Marvin, secretary and assistant, a young Cornell University graduate; Charles Percy, steward, who could not read a cookbook but whose meals were reputed to be unsurpassed; Matthew Henson, "personal attendant," now thirty-nine years old.

Master of the *Roosevelt* was a rugged, stocky Newfoundlander, Robert A. Bartlett, thirty, "blond, smooth-shaven, . . . and clear-eyed," as Peary described him.[12] Bartlett had first sailed, as mate, with Peary in the *Windward* in 1898–1899, and the two had struck up a mutual admiration. Later Bartlett, an inveterate pipe-smoker, was to win distinction as being the only man for whom Peary ever made an allowance for tobacco in his precisely figured sledge loads.

The *Roosevelt* handled admirably, Peary noted. "Captain remarks that she steers like a railroad train, meaning that she steers straight and easily. She is very quick with the helm."[13] Peary rarely was able to commence an expedition, however, without a major setback that beclouded the future, and this time the misfortune came from below deck: some boilers proved to be defective, and the ship was forced to proceed on half of her engine power. Nevertheless, the trip to Etah was pleasant enough otherwise, and by August 16th the *Roosevelt* had completed taking on supplies from the *Erik* and prepared to swing northward out of the harbor — and out of contact with civilization. "Below decks the ship was filled with coal until her plank sheer was nearly to the water; on deck were more than two hundred Eskimo dogs; and on the topgallant forecastle, and the tops of both forward and after deck houses, were over half a hundred Eskimos, men, women, and children, and their belongings." [14]

When the *Roosevelt* pushed into Smith Sound she began her first real battle with heavy pack ice, and the early results renewed Peary's optimism, which had wavered somewhat with the advent of boiler trouble. At first Bartlett was reluctant to slam the *Roosevelt* full speed at its formidable barrier, but Peary insisted on it, declaring he would assume responsibility for whatever happened. Then, even with little more than half power, the stubby vessel, ponderous with its overload, crashed into the opposing ice and was able to split it on impact or to wedge it aside.

"We are beyond the world's highways now," Peary wrote, "and shall see no sail or smoke except our own until our return." [15]

The ice became impregnable in areas, so that "a thousand *Roosevelts* merged into one" could not have negotiated a passage, and detours became necessary. Standing in Peary's favor now was his experience: he had observed ice conditions all along this narrow passageway between Greenland and Ellesmere Island at all times of the year, and the scenes had been stamped in his memory. The *Roosevelt* hammered, squeezed, and twisted her way northward, but her advance was distressingly slow and uncertain. For weeks Peary dared not undress for bed, and he slept only a few hours at a time.

North of the site of Fort Conger, which lay to port, the *Roosevelt* was pounding her way through a narrow strip of ice when a swirl of current swept the ice together like a "sudden scurry of fallen leaves before an autumn breeze," squeezing the ship between huge cakes, flinging her against the ice foot, and damaging the rudder. Temporary repairs were made, however, and the ship edged on toward Cape Sheridan.

. . . The *Roosevelt* has been fighting like a gladiator, turning, twisting, pushing with all her force, battering the heavy ice, and rearing upon [the cakes] like a steeplechaser taking a fence. . . .

It is slow and heartbreaking work. The *Roosevelt* is a splendid ice boat and if she had the power which she was designed to have she would be magnificent. The ice is very heavy, in large floes, some of them miles in diameter and the edges sheer walls of blue adamant.[16]

From time to time the ship was nipped by the floes, which visibly squeezed and forced her deck several inches upward, and left the ship vibrating "like a violin." Then her rounded hull came into play, and the vessel inched up out of the extreme pressure. On September 5th the *Roosevelt* made fast in a niche of the ice foot at Cape Sheridan, and Peary and Bartlett, worn out from the three-week battle since leaving Etah, retreated to their respective quarters, dropped into their bunks, and immediately fell asleep. "I do not believe there is another ship afloat that would have survived the ordeal," Peary wrote.[17]

An even greater test lay in store for the ship, however, eleven days later, when a huge ice floe, impelled by a flood tide, careened into smaller floes surrounding the *Roosevelt* and flung them at the ship. The *Roosevelt* reeled and vibrated, then seemed to shake off the effects of the blow. The broken smaller ice vanished harmlessly under the keel, but an edge of the giant floe pressed upon the ship, its awesome blue face tilting upward higher than the rail — and a few yards beyond soared a tall pressure ridge, towering even above the bridge deck, seemingly waiting to complete the *Roosevelt*'s destruction. The incalculable pressure of this ice mass squeezed the *Roosevelt* for a long minute; ship's ribs and bracing cracked like a rifle volley, the deck bulged upward, masts and rigging shook violently against the cheerless sky. It was a sailor's nightmare of The End of the World.

Then, suddenly, the egg-shaped sides of the ship, designed by Peary for just such an emergency, saved the *Roosevelt*. The vessel shook convulsively, and, with a mighty sigh that reminded Peary of an athlete sucking in his breath for a supreme effort, bounded upward until the propeller showed above water, free at last of the deadly vise. The floe shattered harmlessly underneath the ship; and with a roar the ice beyond crumbled into pieces. After that brush with eternity, Peary settled down into a mundane routine.

He began it by supervising the transfer of boxed supplies from ship to shore, where the boxes were arranged like house walls, covered with the ship's spanker sail, and protected from extreme cold by a buffer of snow blocks.

By October 1st hunting parties had obtained seventy-three musk oxen and twenty-seven caribou — or reindeer. Peary's jubilation was cut short, however, by a series of mysterious deaths among his dogs. Eighty of the invaluable animals had died before post-mortem examinations by Dr. Wolf and Peary showed the cause of death to be poisoned whale meat. Peary was forced to throw away the several tons remaining, and to depend entirely on the country, now, for feeding his dogs and most of his Eskimos. Fortunately, about this time four hunting parties returned to the ship from the Lake Hazen region and reported killing, and leaving in the field, a total of 144 head of musk oxen and caribou. With his ailing dogs continuing to die, Peary quickly decided to send all his Eskimos and dogs into the field, to subsist off this fresh meat and other supplies provided them, until their health was assured. Little daylight remained when they departed, toward the end of October: one hundred and two dogs, twenty adult Eskimo men and women, and six children. Thereafter, for the rest of the winter, Eskimo men returned to the ship, during the full moon of each month, bringing sledge loads of meat and picking up additional supplies as needed.

The ship, however, seemed almost deserted with the absence of all the Arctic guests, and as perpetual night engulfed it a distant, ghostly noise compounded for some a feeling of eeriness. It was the ominous sound of the ice, constantly in motion: first a loud murmur, next a hoarse roar, then an intermittent thunder, like a heavy surf breaking on some nearby shore.

With his knowledge of the causes, all this enchanted Peary rather than alarmed him. After dinner on the last day of October he left the ship, made his way across the ice to a "lookout hill" frequently used to observe the ice, and sat, on a rock, in quiet reflection, as he had done so many times in his life, even from his youngest days.

> The *Roosevelt* lies below me [he wrote], on one side the frozen shore of the Arctic *"ultima Thule,"* on the other the great white disk of the central Polar Sea with its mysteries and its terrors, its story of heroic effort, and its still unconquered secret. No other ship has been so far north in this region and but one other ship [the *Fram*] has reached so high a latitude anywhere in the entire circuit of the Polar Sea, and that one did not attain her vantage ground by stress of continued battle, as has the *Roosevelt*, but drifted to her position — helpless and inert in the grasp of the ice.
>
> Yet the *Roosevelt* lies there, sturdy but graceful, her slender masts piercing the fog and falling snow; a nimbus-circled glow of light at every port, and a broad bar of yellow luminance from the galley lamp shining forward over her and out through the mist, just as if she were a steamer anchored in the North River in a foggy night.[18]

Inside the ship, the men were housed snugly and kept busy — too busy, Peary planned it, for them to brood upon their winter situation. In his spare time Dr. Wolf read the works of an earlier

Arctic explorer, Isaac Hayes, and was impressed by the contrast of the two expeditions: the hardships Hayes described, and the smoothness of Peary's expedition.[19] By comparison, for instance, these meals were sumptuous, although served only twice a day. For breakfast there might be a dry cereal and ham and eggs, sausage, or brown bread and beans, with coffee; for dinner, liver and bacon; corned beef, musk ox steak, or trout, with vegetables, bread and butter, dessert, and tea. On evenings when the menu included musk ox steak Peary would look hungrily at the hot plate set before him and exclaim with relish, "Today we live!" [20]

Throughout the long night Peary not only kept his men busy, but also on occasion provided entertainment and other surprises: snowshoe and sledging races, for cash prizes; a special dinner for the Eskimos, with ship's officers acting as waiters; other dinners in honor of national holidays or in commemoration of family birthdays, which he invariably remembered and noted in his diaries.

On Christmas morning, 1905, Peary's men gathered around the breakfast table and discovered that he had left presents, sent north by Jo, at each man's place: a box of cigars, a box of Huyler's chocolates, bottles of grape juice and blackberry brandy, toilet soap, shaving soap, and a box of chewing gum. He opened his presents with them: two bottles of champagne from Jo and a pine-needle cushion inscribed with the words, "A breath from Maine," from Marie. The entire company enjoyed the fragrance of the pines.[21] That night, however, they were forced to forget about these amenities: the pack ice on the starboard side of the *Roosevelt*, perhaps loosened by a gale that had struck early that morning, broke away from the ice foot and left the ship entirely exposed on that side. Black water lapped against the planking and, in the distance, reflected the brilliance of stars that winked earthward on this puzzling night.

Hurriedly Peary evacuated the Eskimos who had returned aboard ship, and he ordered fires extinguished. The peril was not immediate, of course; it lay in what the ice might do to the ship when it returned. Peary set a full watch on deck, and others slept with clothes on, ready for work if called — or to abandon ship. The following day every available line was secured to the ice foot, on the port side, to hold the ship in its berth.

Peary waited, apprehensive of two possible disasters: when the ice returned it might push the *Roosevelt* onto the ice foot so far inland that refloating her would be an impossibility; or another violent gale might strike at any time, rip the ship from her berth, and carry her out into the moving pack — from where the chances of returning to the same locality would be exceedingly dim.

Neither happened, but for a month after the ice returned to starboard the *Roosevelt* was subjected to pressure of varying intensities. "It was a period of constant anxiety," Peary said, "with the ice pack surging back and forth along the shore on each tide and liable to crash in upon us at any time." [22]

On February 19th, 1905, the supporting parties for the North Pole journey began leaving the ship. Bartlett's left the first day, Marvin's the next, then Wolf's. Peary followed two days after Wolf. All four parties rendezvoused at Cape Hecla: seven men who had come up on the ship, twenty-one Eskimos, more than a hundred dogs.

Peary now planned to divide this force into five or six division parties, each one led by an expedition member who would have charge of two or three Eskimos and dog teams. The division parties were to move on to the sea ice from Cape Moss, about twenty miles beyond Cape Hecla, and take stations, fifty miles apart, along a direct route to the Pole. Supplies thus were to be transported eventually to an advanced base on the Arctic Ocean as distant as three hundred miles from Cape Moss, with each division party hauling loads over the assigned fifty-mile leg, then passing them onto the next group for further transportation, and going back for more. Peary's main party would save itself for a dash from the advance base to the Pole and back. Throughout the entire operation the trail would be kept well marked, and snowhouses would be erected at convenient locations for continuing use.

The plan was an ingenious one, but it was predestined to fail because of one vital shortcoming. For all of Peary's work in the Arctic, the veteran explorer still had not had sufficient experience on the sea ice. Although he realized the probability that floes would shift, he was not fully aware of the extent of the continuing drift, to eastward, of the Arctic ice. Keeping a long trail open across it proved to be impossible.

On February 28th Henson led a pioneer party off the solidity of Cape Moss onto the ragged ice foot, then onto heavily rafted ice and shifting floes. Five other divisions followed, on successive days; then Peary's departed on March 6th. As he left the ice foot he saw the sun briefly between crests of mountains to the south, and he felt it was a good omen. "An ideal day," he observed, "clear and calm and bitter cold, the southern sky vivid yellow, the northern rose-colored like my dreams." [23]

Peary's ingenious plan quickly broke down on the unpredictable ice. Parties stacked up at leads, where they were held up for days at a time waiting for the leads to close or for the water to freeze over; detours around other leads and around impassable ice became necessary, usually at the cost of losing the trail broken by the preceding party; storms forced the men to build quick snow shelters — and these same storms faulted the trail further.

On March 26th Peary's division caught up with three other divisions, all of them halted before a wide lead of murky water that Peary dubbed the "Hudson River." This proved to be the "Big Lead," a phenomenon that, he concluded, frequently appeared over the continental shelf, around the 84th parallel. For six frustrating days the lead held them there before young ice acquired sufficient strength to allow men, dogs, and sledges to cross, on

April 2nd. Three days later, however, they walked into the mouth of a wild, blinding blizzard that forced them to throw up a shelter, named Storm Camp, and to huddle there for another six days waiting for the fury to blow itself out.

By this time Peary had realized the futility of his plans for shuttling supplies across the ice to an advance base, and he determined to set out on a "dash" northward, with Henson's division, in a desperate effort to reach the Pole. Observations had shown him to be drifting steadily eastward; his longitude now was close to that of the *Roosevelt* at Cape Sheridan. Impatiently he waited for the infernal howling wind to abate, then he abandoned all equipment not absolutely essential for the trip, and started.

"The first march of ten hours," Peary wrote, "myself in the lead with the compass, sometimes on a dogtrot, the sledges following in Indian file with drivers running beside or behind, placed us thirty miles to the good; my Eskimos said forty." [24]

More leads, wind and drift, dying dogs, rafted ice continued to plague Peary, but the traveling improved somewhat on April 18th. Still, Peary became resigned to turning back without success. He realized that the rapidly deteriorating physical condition of his party, dwindling supplies, and weakening dogs would defeat him again. Three days later Peary found himself in a dangerous area of many leads and moving ice, and he surrendered again to the elements. An observation placed him at 87 degrees 6 minutes, farther north than any other man had ever traveled — but it was not far enough for Peary.

> . . . I thanked God with as good grace as possible, though I felt that the mere beating of the record was but an empty bauble compared with the splendid jewel on which I had set my heart for years, and for which, on this expedition, I had almost literally been straining my life out. . . .
>
> My flags were flung out from the summit of the highest pinnacle near us, and a hundred feet or so beyond this I left a bot-

tle containing a brief record and a piece of the silk flag which
six years before I had carried around the northern end of
Greenland.

Then we started to return to our last igloo, making no camp
here.[25]

On the back trail Peary was afire with anxiety. His eyes burned
and ached, and he feared that the effects of cutting snow and
wind, plus the painful exposure to sun during his sights, would
result in an acute attack of snow blindness. Furthermore, the excitement of the advance had vanished, and with it his enthusiasm;
now his feet dragged with weight. At the first return igloo Peary
flopped wearily on the sleeping platform, closed his seared eyes,
and rolled in agony, while one of the Eskimos made the tea.
Later, in an effort to relieve the pain, Peary chilled his eyes with
snow until the lids became numb, then he sank into a dreamless
sleep.

Still other worries dogged him later. Provisions were dangerously low; the Big Lead was ahead, with a possible delay — the
results of which were appalling to contemplate; the eastward
movement of the ice had now placed Peary north of the tip of
Greenland, and it might even carry his party farther eastward, so
that there would be no land at all at the southern end of the return
journey — only the East Greenland Sea.

In this precarious situation Peary's Eskimos became something
of a problem. Rarely did they dispute the explorer's decisions, but
now they had become obsessed with the idea that they had been
carried westward, not eastward, by the ice drift. Peary's observations showed him just the opposite was true, but he experienced
some difficulty in convincing the natives, who would surely have
lost themselves had their return route been left to their own judgment. Peary knew the only salvation for his party lay in a quick

return due southward toward the Greenland coast, where they would have to find and kill musk oxen to live.

With these concerns he and his men stumbled upon the Big Lead. Again it had become a broad band of black water, half a mile wide, and it stretched east and west across their path for a distance farther than Peary could see from the summit of a tall ice pinnacle. Lack of provisions made camping impractical, however, so Peary turned eastward, looking for a safe crossing.

On the following day he thought he had found it: a mixture of half-congealed rubble ice, barely strong enough to support them, spanned the lead. They had begun to cross, with the ice bending ominously under their weight — as salt-water ice will do — when the bridge failed them and began to go apart under their very feet. Quickly they scrambled back to the north bank, and there they camped on a floe that fronted on the deadly lead. With sinking hope they watched the lead widen inexorably; Peary changed his name for it from the "Hudson" to the "Styx."

He wrote:

Each day the number of my dogs dwindled and sledges were broken up to cook those of the animals that we ate ourselves. . . . One day leads formed entirely around the ice on which we were, making it an island of two or three miles' diameter.

Later, two Eskimos scouts whom I had sent east to reconnoiter the lead came hurrying back breathless, with the report that a few miles from camp there was a film of young ice extending clear across the lead — now something over two miles wide — which they thought might support us on snowshoes. No time was lost in hurrying to the place when it was evident to us all that now was our chance or never, and I gave the word to put on snowshoes and make the attempt. I tied mine on more carefully than I had ever done before. I think every other man did the same, for we felt that a slip or stumble would be fatal. We had already tested the ice and knew it would not support us an instant without snowshoes.

When we started it was with Panikpah, lightest of us all and most experienced, in the lead, the few remaining dogs attached to the long broad-runner sledge — the *Morris K. Jesup* — following him, and the rest of the party abreast in widely extended skirmish line, fifty to sixty feet between each two men, some distance behind the sledge. We crossed in silence, each man busy with his thoughts and intent upon his snowshoes. . . . Once started, we could not stop; we could not lift our snowshoes. It was a matter of constantly and smoothly gliding one past the other with utmost care and evenness of pressure, and from every man as he slid a snowshoe forward, undulations went out in every direction through the thin film incrusting the black water. The sledge was preceded and followed by a broad swell.

It was the first and only time in all my Arctic work that I felt doubtful as to the outcome, but when near the middle of the lead the toe of my rear kamik, as I slid [it] forward, . . . broke through twice in succession, I thought to myself, "This is the finish," and when a little later there was a cry from someone in the line, the words sprang from me of themselves: "God help him; which one is it?" But I dared not take my eyes from the steady, even gliding of my snowshoes, and the fascination of the glassy swell at the toes of them.

When we stepped upon the firm ice on the southern side of the lead, the sighs of relief from the two men nearest me in the line on either side were distinctly audible. . . . The cry I had heard had been from one of my men whose toe, like mine, had broken through the ice. . . .

When we stood up from unfastening our snowshoes and looked back for a moment before turning our faces southward [we saw that] a narrow black ribbon cut the frail bridge on which we had crossed. . . . The lead was widening again and we had just made it.[26]

Now, in contrast to the open water, a jumble of jagged, towering, slick sea ice barred their path —"such a hell of shattered ice," said Peary, "as I had never seen before . . . a conglomeration of fragments from the size of paving stones to literally and without exaggeration the dome of the Capitol, all rounded by the terrific grinding they had received between the jaws of the 'Big Lead' when its edges were together and shearing past each other. It did not seem as if anything not possessing wings could negotiate it, and I turned to my men to say a few encouraging words, but caught a glint in their eyes and a setting of the jaws . . . and I shut my mouth and said nothing, for I knew words were not necessary." [27]

During the next two marches they stumbled desperately southward, all of them taking frequent and painful falls. The ordeal was especially trying to Peary, whose poorly protected stumps received numerous raps, and at the end of the first march he discovered that his jaws ached from his continual teeth-grinding throughout the day. Soon, in the distance, the snowy mountains of Greenland came into view, and Peary recognized a promontory remembered from other days: Cape Neumeyer. That lifeless, wind-swept chunk of raw land seemed almost like an old friend to him now, and he set his course for it. Nearby, he felt certain, he could find hare and musk oxen.

While en route there, he came across another of his supporting divisions, one led by Charles Clark, a fireman from the *Roosevelt* crew who had received this supplementary assignment. With Clark were three Eskimos; all four men, Peary found, were nearly dead from starvation, having subsisted for the past few days on their spare skin boots. Like Peary's group, they had been cast eastward by the ice, and like Peary's Eskimos, they were certain the drift had been to the west. The distant mountains, they had guessed, represented the backside of Grant Land — which was the northern part of Ellesmere Island, from where they had embarked on the Arctic Ocean so long ago — and they had been struggling eastward, supposing that was the direction of the ship. Instead they had been traveling directly away from it.

Now the combined parties pushed on toward the coast. There, once more, Peary found musk oxen. So nervous was he that, before the first shot, he kicked off his snowshoes and sat on them for a few moments to compose himself. Then he rose, advanced toward the herd, fired, and brought down a bull. Another bullet dropped another bull, then he bagged five more animals. Again he devoured the warm, rich flesh, and again it saved his life and the lives of those with him.

In the waning days of May he and his men returned to the *Roosevelt*. There he reflected:

> What a delicious thing rest is. With Jo's picture on the wall above my head, with my face buried in Ahnighito's pillow of Eagle Island . . . needles, and its exquisitely delicious fragrance in my nostrils, I for the moment echo from the bottom of my heart Ootah's remarks, "I have got back again, thank God!" Yet I know that a little later I shall feel that I might have done more and yet got back, and yet again still deeper down I know that we went to the very limit and that had we not got across the "Big Lead," when we did, we should not have returned.
>
> Since reaching the ship I have had an aversion to pencil and paper, and have only cared to lie and think and plan. To think after all the preparation, the experience, the effort, the strain, the chances taken, and the wearing of myself and party to the last inch, what a little journey it is on the map and how far short of my hopes it fell. To think that I have failed once more; that I shall never have a chance to win again. Then to put this useless repining aside, and plan for my western trip, and when I have done my duty by this, to plan for mine and Eagle Island.[28]

The "western trip" Peary referred to was an exploration, with eight expedition members and Eskimos, of the unknown coast of

Grant Land, made while other members of the expedition were at work on soundings and other observations nearer the ship. The journey alone would have been sufficiently exciting to sate the appetites of many adventurers, but to Peary it was a weak second in importance to his big failure. He left the *Roosevelt* on June 2nd, 1906, only a week after his return, and he probed the rugged Grant Land coast westward to a distance of more than three hundred miles, and crossed Fridtjof Nansen Sound to the northern tip of Axel Heiberg Island before turning back. A headland at the tip of Heiberg he named Cape Thomas Hubbard, after a wealthy supporter in the Peary Arctic Club, and from its peak he gazed northward through his binoculars. It was to be a significant observation, for he thought he saw land far away.

> My heart leaped the intervening miles of ice as I looked longingly at this land, and in fancy I trod its shores and climbed its summits, even though I knew that the pleasure could be only for another in another season.[29]

A journey across the sea ice toward that distant land was out of the question: Peary knew he must return to the *Roosevelt*. He named his discovery Crocker Land, but it was never seen again. Probably the supposed sighting was the effect of a "superior mirage" peculiar to the polar regions, as William H. Hobbs has speculated, a phenomenon caused by an inversion in the atmosphere: a layer of warm air above one of cooler air toward the surface.[30] Eight years later the explorer Donald B. MacMillan, searching for Crocker Land, was to observe the same optical illusion from the same spot, and to attribute it to a mirage, or "loom" of the sea ice.[31] Whatever the reason for the sighting, the nonexistent "Crocker Land" was later flaunted against Peary by his critics as alleged proof of his unreliability, as was the nonexistent "Peary Channel" of northeast Greenland.

From Cape Thomas Hubbard, early in July, Peary commenced

his return trip to the *Roosevelt*, after leaving his record in a cairn on the cape. The summer season was so far advanced that thaw water and chilly rain pools spotted his path for the entire distance, three hundred miles, and he was forced to detour around lakes and rivers — or sometimes to ford them, wading waist deep and even chest deep in water. A typical day, July 10th, was described in his diary:

Yelverton Bay . . . — Out of my new domain, and back into the known world again.

It was calm while we slept at the last camp, and the sun was warm enough through the fog and clouds, to still further dry our clothing and gear.

Got an earlier start than usual and had good going, and decent weather (calm and overcast) until 9 A.M. when we struck the river from a glacier at the head of the bay, and after deflecting for two miles along its swampy banks, were obliged to ford it, one hundred yards wide, knee deep, and running with a current that threatened to sweep us and the dogs and sledges away. Then the thick fog [made] it impossible to pick a course through the lakes and rivers, [and] I camped.

Our tent here, as at the last camp, was in a slushy swamp, a small spot . . . made a little firmer by tamping the snow first with the snowshoes, and then with our feet. . . .[32]

On July 25th Peary accidentally intercepted a Grant Land sounding party led by Ross Marvin, who informed Peary that the *Roosevelt* had broken out from her winter quarters at Cape Sheridan on July 4th and thereafter had been able to squeeze southward twenty miles distant, where the ship had crashed against the ice foot, carrying away a propeller and ripping off the rudder and stern post. A jury rig for steering had been completed but was useless; ice continued to hold the ship.

Peary went on to Sheridan, rested two days, then set out for the ship, where he arrived at 3:30 A.M. July 30th, thoroughly exhausted, his feet almost useless, and now immensely concerned about the ship's capability, although he masked his worry. During the past five months — since his departure for the polar journey on February 23rd — he had been aboard the *Roosevelt* only eight days, and his feet now showed the effects of the wear: they were hot, aching, and throbbing; he felt the pain clear to his knees. For his journeys he had fashioned a pair of heavy tin inner soles, from pemmican cans, to give his stumps added protection, but when he reached the *Roosevelt* he found these soles broken in "dozens of pieces" [33] and his *kamiks* cut through. The next day, however, he remarked to Bartlett, "We have got to get her back, Captain. We are going to come again next year." [34]

The *Roosevelt*'s capability of fleeing from the Arctic, however, was in serious doubt. Imprisoned in the ice, her head continued to point northward, although the drifting ice carried her slowly southward. Her own steering apparatus was virtually destroyed, and, to make matters worse, the accident had opened a leak in the hull. Peary ordered provisions and equipment brought on deck, where they could be thrown onto the ice and the ship abandoned, should this become necessary. "I do not like the looks of things . . ." Peary wrote. "We are not well supplied for another year and I have been mapping out a program to put into effect in case we are caught here." [35]

The ice continued to hold them, and for days at a time it showed no movement to the south, where lay the only possibility of escape. "The prospects of getting out this season do not improve," Peary observed gloomily.[36] Another nip by the ice enlarged the leak, requiring continual use of the pump.

Am still unreconciled to the idea of another winter here [Peary wrote]. Charlie [Percy, the steward] came upon some Eagle Island pictures of Jo and Mugli [Robert Peary, Jr.] in a book today, and the sight of them nearly broke me up.[37]

Finally, more than three weeks after Peary returned to the ship, the ice began slowly releasing its grip. On August 24th the *Roosevelt* was able to turn southward and to begin creeping among the floes from crack to crack. It was mid-September, however, before escape was assured — and this came only after the crew "rolled" the ship through an area of tough young ice, by rushing back and forth across the deck. The coal supply was exhausted, and for a time spruce wood provided the fuel. Finally the ship broke free, was beached for repairs to the rudder, then continued on to the United States, where it arrived in New York at 6 P.M. on Christmas Eve.

News from home cheered Peary; his wife and children were well. "Marie has been at and near the head of her class all the year and is very proud of it. . . ." Jo informed him. "Robert grows too and looks more like his dad every day. His greatest ambition is to be big like daddy with a big mustache, not . . . chinny chin chin whiskers like uncle's. . . . Both children are imps, but life would not be worth living without them. . . .

"I pray you will return in safety . . . and come home. Think of it, *home* and to *stay*. . . . Just think, life is nearly over and we have missed most of it." [38]

For Peary, however, life still meant perhaps one more chance, after all, to reach his goal. Decades had gone by since he first voiced the youthful desire for fame. Now that craving had long since been satisfied, and had given way to the obsession with attaining a goal he had set, short of which he knew, and his wife knew, he would die considering himself a failure.

He explained his feeling before a banquet audience of the National Geographic Society late in 1906, when he was awarded the society's Hubbard Medal. President Roosevelt made the presentation; then Peary rose for his response.

The curious peered intently at the man who had endured so

many bitter years in such a remote place, wondering what he was really like.

They saw a hard, erect, slender man whose fifty years did not show from a distance. The broadest part of him was at his chest, and his hair and his drooping mustache were still auburn — from a distance the gray strands did not show. Only when an observer was within a few feet was it possible to see that the Arctic had left marks. Peary's ruddy face had been drawn by brutally cold weather, and the deep lines there were indicative of many bitter years.

His blue-gray eyes seemed to reflect the many disappointments they had seen. Perpetually narrowed, as if against the glare of sunlight on ice and snow, they made him appear to be squinting. This in turn gave them a veiled look, and he often seemed to be thinking about something far away.

Now, before the National Geographic Society audience, Peary once more bared these thoughts:

> The true explorer does his work not for any hopes of reward or honor, but because the thing he has set for himself to do is a part of his being, and must be accomplished for the sake of the accomplishment. And he counts lightly hardships, risks, obstacles, if only they do not bar him from his goal.
>
> To me the final and complete solution of the polar mystery which has engaged the best thought and interest of some of the best men of the most vigorous and enlightened nations of the world for more than three centuries, and today quickens the pulse of every man or woman whose veins hold red blood, is the thing which must be done for the honor and credit of this country, the thing which it is intended that I should do, and the thing that I must do.[39]

Chapter 11

"THE LURE of the North!" Peary once exclaimed. "It is a strange and a powerful thing. More than once I have come back from the great frozen spaces, battered and worn and baffled, sometimes maimed, telling myself that I had made my last journey thither, eager of the society of my kind, the comforts of civilization, and the peace and serenity of home. But somehow, it was never many months before the old restless feeling came over me. Civilization began to lose its zest for me. I began to long for the great white desolation, the battles with the ice and the gales, the long, long Arctic night, the long, long Arctic day, the handful of odd but faithful Eskimos who had been my friends for years, the silence and the vastness of the great, white lonely North. . . ." [1]

Always foremost, however, was the unfulfilled dream of final success, and Peary was desperately aware that his chances were waning with each vanished year. Thus he felt especially thwarted in the late spring of 1907, when delays in repairing and refitting the *Roosevelt* with new boilers caused postponement of still another expedition — this after President Theodore Roosevelt himself had been instrumental in arranging a three-year leave of absence for Peary from the Navy.

For a man who had been conscious virtually all his life of the pricelessness of time in regard to his work, half a century irrevocably used up was an appalling expenditure. The zenith of his physical strength was gone now, as were fragments of his élan and elasticity. More than compensating for this loss, however, was the accrual of experience and knowledge that can come only with age. These two assets, Peary knew, were his most valuable current holdings as an explorer, and he was fanatical in reserving their use for himself.

Peary was particularly intolerant of explorers who "intruded" on his own route to the North Pole: the American route, up the narrow waterway between Greenland and Ellesmere to Cape Sheridan, then from northernmost Grant Land directly across the Arctic Ocean. ". . . The knowledge [an explorer] has acquired of the particular route which he is . . . developing and by which he hopes, by repeated efforts, to reach the Pole, is as much a part of his capital as the gold and silver in the vault of a bank," Peary once declared, "and until he abandons that route, no one else, without his consent, has any more right to take and use it, than a stranger has to enter the vaults of the bank and take its treasure." [2]

Peary was fond of referring to the natives along the east coast of Greenland as "my Eskimos," and their dogs were available to him, alone, in bartering, he contended. Any other explorer venturing into the area was, to Peary, not only an intruder but, in fact, a poacher.

Nevertheless, his concern was not great when he first heard talk, in 1907, of an Arctic trip contemplated by his former surgeon, Dr. Frederick A. Cook, and a wealthy sportsman, John R. Bradley. In recent years Cook had earned something of a reputation as an explorer. He had served as surgeon with a Belgian Antarctic expedition in 1897–1899 and had earned an excellent reputation in assuring good health for his colleagues, who included an adventurous Norwegian, Roald Amundsen, later the first man to reach the South Pole. After this Cook had won national acclaim when he reported reaching the summit of previously unscaled Mount McKinley — on September 16th, 1906.

In the summer Cook sailed from Gloucester, Massachusetts, aboard the yacht *John R. Bradley,* named for its owner and commanded by Moses Bartlett, a second cousin of the master of the *Roosevelt.* The few persons who were at all aware of their departure had heard that Bradley invited Cook, an affable companion and one who knew the North, to accompany him on an Arctic hunting trip. Sometime between seven and eight o'clock in the evening of July 3rd, 1907, the *Bradley,* creamy white with new paint, stood out of Gloucester Harbor in a vanishing sunset.

Peary was among those who attached little significance to the voyage. A month after Cook had sailed he received an inquiry from a Canadian, W. A. Orser, an Ontario resident, regarding pending Antarctic expeditions. Peary answered the man: ". . . I am not aware of any American Antarctic expeditions being fitted out under anyone's command. Dr. F. A. Cook of Brooklyn, New York, is, however, interested in Antarctic matters and has been on one Antarctic expedition. I do not now recall his street number, but if you address a letter to him in care of the Brooklyn *Standard Union,* Fulton Street, Brooklyn, New York, he will undoubtedly receive it on his return from a yachting cruise, on which he started early in July." [3]

In the weeks that followed, however, several of Peary's friends began voicing an anxiety about Cook's intentions. Another explorer, Vilhjalmur Stefansson, returned from a trip to Alaska, where he had heard rumors that Cook's reported ascent of Mount McKinley was a hoax, and Stefansson hastened to inform Peary of this talk; the implications seemed obvious. Peary, however, brushed aside the admonition, declaring, "Cook is an honorable man." [4]

From Portland, Maine, came another word of caution, from

Peary's long-time acquaintance, Charles J. Nichols, who expressed doubt that Cook ever reached the top of Mount McKinley and predicted that Cook intended to fake an attainment of the North Pole. "Oh, no," Peary answered. "I do not believe Cook would do that."[5]

Still others informed Peary of their doubt about Cook's reliability, particularly in regard to his Mount McKinley claim. Among them were Belmore Browne, an artist and an expert mountain climber, and Herschel Parker, a Columbia University professor. Both men had been members of the expedition to scale Mount McKinley, but neither had been with Cook during his famous ascent. Both men had become sufficiently skeptical of Cook's statements to insist that the Explorers Club of New York ask Cook for proof of his feat. Cook left for the Arctic, however, without submitting his evidence.[6] Still, the only initial regret Peary seems to have had regarding Cook's sailing in 1907 was an entirely incidental one: Peary fretted over his own sailing delay; in another year he would be fifty-two years old. In virtually every wakeful moment he deplored his own inability to get away in 1907. The work contract for the *Roosevelt* called for completion of repairs by July 1st, but the job was not finished until September, much too late in the season for attempting a voyage to Cape Sheridan.

Other problems arose. Despite the continuing support of the Peary Arctic Club, its members contributed only a part of the seventy-five thousand dollars necessary to refit the ship and to get the next expedition underway. Raising the rest of the money was again Peary's responsibility, and he was faced with the usual punishing lecture schedule, further compressed, as always, by a variety of tasks squeezed into that program: handling correspondence, interviewing and selecting personnel, purchasing supplies. Then, just when he seemed to be out of the financial woods, his stanchest supporter, Morris Jesup, died; and Peary's grief was tinged by worry over the future of his expedition. Mrs. Jesup continued the backing, however, with a donation of five thousand dollars — to Peary's profound relief — and General Thomas H. Hubbard of New York offered his services as president of the Peary Arctic Club and a large donation.

For his next expedition Peary planned to rely on the same methods, equipment, and supplies that his overall experience, bolstered by the 1905–1906 expedition, had taught him were most sensible. He spoke of only a few modifications of his 1905–1906 plan. He would leave the north coast of Grant Land at Cape Columbia, instead of Cape Moss; would set his course over the Arctic Ocean west of north, to allow for the probably easterly ice drift; would keep his sledge divisions more rigidly massed, to prevent their being separated by movement of the ice; would locate his advance base, as before, as far out on the ice as possible, but would situate his major rear base north of the Big Lead, so that the supporting divisions would not again be held up by that frustrating lane of open water; would cache emergency supplies in Grant Land and in northern Greenland for the North Pole party, in case they were cast westward or, as before, eastward by ice movement.

On the ice itself Peary proposed to have a main party and four supporting divisions, each composed of an equal number of sledges, dogs, and Eskimos led by an expedition member who was capable of plotting navigational observations. The primary aim of these supporting divisions would be to place the main party, led by Peary, at a jump-off location within one hundred and fifty miles of the Pole with the pick of dogs, men, and supplies for the final dash. The most grueling work would be handled by a pioneering party, which would blaze a trail, and when the men of one pioneering party became exhausted another division could take over the work. The supporting units would turn back at five-day intervals, and during their return would keep the trail open and, if necessary, reknit it, so that the returning polar party, lightly provisioned after so long a journey, would not be delayed by the necessity of pioneering a trail.

Peary deliberated over these details, and all of his Arctic experience told him they were right. Even more impatient now for one more chance, he could scarcely wait for sailing. Away from home most of the time, he penned Jo brief, hurried notes in which he greeted her with an abbreviation, "M. D.," for "My Darling." [7]

In all this surge of activity Peary assumed an added responsibility: the presidency of the Explorers Club of New York. Indications were that he accepted the position reluctantly, for he certainly was not prepared to give the job much time. Moreover, by now Peary had been convinced that Cook was up to some devilment in the Arctic, and he disliked the thought of mingling with certain club supporters of the doctor. Possibly he was influenced toward acceptance by a letter from his wife, whose counsel he usually respected:

. . . I must say I hate the idea of your being associated with such men as Cook . . . and . . . [certain others in the Explorers Club]. They are all fakes. But in view of present conditions it might do you considerable harm to antagonize these people. Harm in this way — that they would assist Cook in every way just to annoy you.

Of course if you become their president it would increase your popularity in that direction (not that I should care for that very much).

These are all the points that occur to me now. Whatever you do, do it in a dignified manner as becomes the *greatest Arctic explorer of the age.*

Even if the sentiment of the club is against Cook now, if he returns during your absence they would be inclined to do more for him if you are not their president than if you are.[8]

*

In the spring of 1908, after several unpleasant episodes with the *Roosevelt* contractor and expedition purveyors over slow payments, Peary was convinced that nothing further would delay his sailing. His friendship with President Roosevelt resulted in a change of leave orders most convenient for Peary: his previous orders were revoked, and he was told to report for duty to the chief of the Coast and Geodetic Survey for instructions on making tidal observations along the Grant Land and northern Greenland coasts.[9] This meant that Peary would draw his full Navy pay during the expedition, thanks to his friend in the White House, who had written him: "I feel that you are doing most admirable work for science; but I feel even more that you are doing admirable work for America and are setting an example to the young men of our day which we need to have set amid the softening tendencies of our time." [10]

Accompanying Peary on his eighth expedition to the Arctic were the most able assistants he ever selected: Ross Marvin, the reserved Cornell University professor who had been a member of the 1905–1906 expedition; Matthew Henson, who had been with Peary, of course, since the tedious early days in Nicaragua; George Borup, a handsome, athletic young Yale graduate, a nonsmoker and a teetotaler, who had proved his endurance by finishing second in a collegiate 600-yard race at Madison Square Garden; and Donald B. MacMillan, an instructor at Worcester Academy in Massachusetts who had also excelled in college athletics — football and track — at Peary's alma mater, Bowdoin College. Surgeon was stout Dr. J. W. Goodsell of New Kensington, Pennsylvania. Master of the *Roosevelt* was, again, the vigorous Newfoundlander, "Captain Bob" Bartlett.

Fifteen other men comprised the entire expedition, all of them ship's officers or crewmen: chief engineer, second engineer, mate, boatswain, steward, cabin boy, five seamen, and four firemen.

When Peary sailed he was fully aware that Cook nursed an exalted aspiration for his Arctic venture. When the yacht *John R. Bradley* returned, after depositing Cook and his supplies in Greenland, owner Bradley bore remarkable tidings: Dr. Cook planned to try to reach the North Pole. This was a venture that Peary could not give full credence to, but it was upsetting all the same. Cook had no expedition, no experience on the treacherous sea ice. What really was his intention?

Whatever it was, before Peary sailed he wrote a letter to Herbert Bridgman, secretary of the Peary Arctic Club, decrying Cook's action in going North "for the admitted purpose of stealing a march on me."

. . . But . . . if the burden of bringing Cook back rests on Mrs. Cook's shoulders, I shall be willing to waive all personal feelings out of consideration for her difficult position, and recommend to the club that [he] be brought back for a nominal sum, on the auxiliary ship [*Erik*], which will go north this summer.[11]

Finally the *Roosevelt* was ready to sail. After a one-year delay, the ship sounded its whistle from a berth at the foot of East 24th Street in New York and backed into the East River. The time was one o'clock in the broiling afternoon of July 6th, 1908. Greeted by toots from the yacht fleet, tugboats, and ferryboats and by the shouts of a cheering throng, the *Roosevelt* steamed up the East River, past Blackwells Island, past the saluting presidential yacht *Mayflower*, and on to Oyster Bay, where President Roosevelt himself, Mrs. Roosevelt, and their three sons planned to visit the ship on the following day.

When he came aboard, the President appeared to be utterly oblivious of the peril to his white duck suit as he happily scrambled over the ship, poking into every space, even the engine room. He shook the hand of every one of the twenty-two expedition members, and he boomed a spirited Rooseveltian good-by to his host: "I believe in you, Peary, and I believe in your success — if it is within the possibility of man." [12]

From Oyster Bay the ship proceeded to Sydney, on Cape Breton, Nova Scotia. Peary and his wife went up by train to meet the vessel; their children made the trip on the *Roosevelt*, in the care of a family friend. Then, on July 17th, in brilliant sunshine, the *Roosevelt* got under way. Jo and the two children, waiting until the very last minute to go back, were on board.

Outside the harbor a tug came alongside for them. Robert, Jr., nearly five, saluted his father and said, "Come back soon, Dad." Then they were gone. "Another farewell," Peary reflected, "and there had been so many." [13]

Again the little *Roosevelt* steamed northward. The ship crossed the Arctic Circle into perpetual daylight on July 26th and six days later reached Cape York, a bold, snow-capped headland that marked the southernmost stretch of Arctic coast inhabited by Eskimos. The northern work of each of Peary's expeditions actually began here, with the initial negotiations to arrange for the services of men and their dogs.

Now those same Eskimos excitedly paddled their kayaks for the *Roosevelt*. "You are like the sun," they told Peary. "You always come back." [14]

Northward up the coast, at Etah, Peary came across Dr. Cook's trail. In fact, he found Cook's supplies — but not Cook, who had struck out northwestward, months earlier, into Ellesmere Land with several Eskimos. His goods had been left at Annoatok,[15] in the custody of a man named Rudolphe Franke, who had made the voyage in the *John R. Bradley* and had remained in the Arctic with Cook. When Peary arrived, however, Franke was despondent, suffering from an injured leg, ill with scurvy, and extremely eager to return to civilization. He showed Peary a letter from Cook authorizing a return trip that season on a whaler,[16] and asked for permission, which was granted, to return on Peary's auxiliary ship *Erik*. Before his departure Franke wrote a letter of instructions consigning to Peary all the supplies in his care, and he gave Peary a treasured possession — a large narwhal horn — in appreciation of Peary's "kindness and hospitality." [17] Peary loaned Franke fifty dollars for transportation from Sydney or Saint John's, wherever the *Erik* should call, to New York City[18] and drew for Franke from his own stores underwear, a shirt, a sweater, four pairs of socks, two blankets, and a mattress. He expected that John R. Bradley, as Cook's sponsor, would reimburse him later for this expense.[19]

Franke told Peary that Cook had said he intended to try to reach the North Pole, but neither Peary nor any other member of the expedition considered Cook's endeavor a serious one. Typical of the observations was one recorded by Chief Engineer George Wardwell in his diary: "I heard today that Dr. Cook hadn't got back to Etah. . . . Cook took only two Eskimos with him, so he couldn't have gone very far." [20]

The more Peary brooded on Cook's actions, the more indignant he became, even though he never believed that his former surgeon had the slightest chance of attaining the North Pole — or, actually, that the man really intended to try. Without question, however, was the fact of Cook's disturbing presence in that part of Greenland Peary considered his own domain: Cook had made off with some of the dogs Peary might have obtained for his own use, and he had employed Eskimos who might otherwise have worked for Peary. Should Cook's supplies fall into the hands of the natives, Peary feared, his own chances could be ruined: by possessing such luxuries the Eskimos would lose much incentive for working with Peary, no matter what rewards he offered.

To guard Cook's stores Peary ordered two of his men ashore: Boatswain John Murphy and Cabin Boy Billy Pritchard. Both were to remain there until the *Roosevelt* returned from Cape Sheridan the following summer. This action served two other purposes: he could also land some of his own supplies, ostensibly for sustaining Murphy and Pritchard but actually for emergency use in case he lost the *Roosevelt* — and without alarming other members of the expedition; and he could claim credit for an act of mercy, by landing a party for relief of Dr. Cook.

Peary read the following order for Murphy, whose seamanship considerably exceeded his literacy, then handed the order to him:

S. S. *Roosevelt*
Etah, North Greenland
August 17, 1908

Dear Sir:—

The following are instructions for your guidance while in charge of the station here for the relief of Dr. Cook.

You will exercise the utmost care and diligence in using and protecting all supplies and equipment left here.

Should Dr. Cook return or be brought back in bad condition you will take every endeavor to bring him around as speedily as possible.

You will take all possible care of his equipment and supplies, and on his return allow him to use them. Any of the supplies from the *Roosevelt* which Dr. Cook needs you will give him.

It will be advisable for you to use Dr. Cook's supplies, and particularly the broken packages first, in order to avoid loss, as these goods are already over a year old, and some of them doubtless improperly packed.

Very truly,
R. E. Peary[21]

Cook's prolonged absence from his Greenland base raised the possibility, of course, that he might be dead, but Peary never believed that this was the case. Instead, Peary felt certain that the doctor and his two Eskimos were in Ellesmere Land, and that they would return as soon as the winter ice closed Kane Basin. This possibility of Cook's returning while he was at Cape Sheridan, cut off from all communication with the world, further increased his concern, and before the departure southward of the *Erik* Peary wrote several of his supporters, warning them of Cook. One person he thus wrote was President Roosevelt, to whom he jotted down an additional note of incrimination: "John R. Bradley, Dr. Cook's backer in this enterprise . . . is a well known gambler, known in certain circles as 'Gambler Jim.' I have heard that he was formerly a card sharp on the Mississippi River until driven out, and it is a matter of actual fact that he runs a gambling hell at Palm Beach, where both men and women gamble." [22]

The day before the *Erik* left Peary also wrote his wife:

Everything thus far has gone well, too well I am afraid, and I am (solely on general principles) somewhat suspicious of the future.

The ship is in better shape than before; the party and crew are apparently harmonious. . . .

The Cook circumstances have given me a good deal of extra work and trouble; but have worked out satisfactorily.

I have landed supplies here, and leave two men ostensibly in behalf of Cook. As a matter of fact I have established here the sub-base which last time I established at Victoria Head, as a precaution in event of loss of the *Roosevelt* either going up this fall or coming down next summer. . . .

Tell Marie to remember what I told her; tell "Mister Man" [Robert, Jr.] to remember "straight and strong and clean and honest," obey orders, and never forget that daddy put "Mut" [mother] in his charge till he himself comes back to take her.

. . . In fancy I kiss your . . . eyes and lips and cheeks,

sweetheart; and dream of you and my children and my home till I come again. . . .

Your
Bert.[23]

Before the *Roosevelt* and the *Erik* left Etah, a wealthy sports-man who had taken passage in the *Erik*, Harry Whitney, asked permission to remain with Murphy and Pritchard. He wanted to hunt — for musk oxen and polar bear — during the coming year. Peary consented, and Whitney's belongings were landed. Then, on August 18th, the *Roosevelt* steamed northward again. The *Erik* headed south, and from the deck of the *Roosevelt* Peary watched his auxiliary ship disappear behind a thick veil of snow. Again his last link with civilization thus vanished, but he re-frained from brooding on that fact. "The ice in Robeson Chan-nel," he observed instead, "is more dramatic than any parting." [24] Once more the *Roosevelt* hammered her way through the ice to Cape Sheridan, where she arrived on September 5th. After the usual autumn crammed with activity — hunting, readying equip-ment, acclimatizing new Arctic hands, recording tidal and mete-orological observations, transporting provisions — by moonlight — to Cape Columbia, the point of departure from land, the over-whelming midnight began to wane. December 22nd signified the gradual re-emergence of the sun and called for a celebration:

> . . . The sun began its return early this morning (4:30). In the afternoon assembled all the Eskimos on deck . . . [and] told them the sun was now returning. Marvin rang ship's bell, Matt fired three shots, Borup turned loose some flashlight pow-ders. Then men formed in line, marched into afterhouse and each received two pounds of meat, a drink of grog, tobacco, and coffee. Women and boys followed.[25]

Peary concluded his preliminaries and, on February 22nd, left the *Roosevelt* for a final supreme effort. With him were two Eskimos, two sledges, sixteen dogs. The weather was thick, the air was filled with light snow, the temperature was 31 degrees below zero. He sped toward Cape Columbia, where Ellesmere Island drops abruptly into the Arctic Ocean. There were gathered the other members of his polar sea party, for a final rendezvous.

Six days after Peary had left the ship, he and Bartlett climbed a snow-veiled bluff at Cape Columbia and surveyed their prospects for travel on the ice. From their lookout point, located at latitude 83 degrees 7 minutes north, they peered intently northward, as if to penetrate the four hundred and thirteen nautical miles that separated them from the pinpoint that represented the top of the globe.

As far as the two could see in the dim morning light of Sunday, February 28th, 1909, the ocean appeared to be an appalling jumble of ice. The sight would have been a forbidding one to most persons, but it brought to Robert Peary a sense of comfort: he could see no open water. He commented to Bartlett that conditions appeared to be much more favorable than in 1906.

This was departure day for Bartlett's pioneer party, which had the job of breaking a trail, and when the light became sufficient for traveling they left. Peary walked beside Bartlett for a hundred yards or so, giving final instructions. Then the master of the *Roosevelt* and his Eskimos, dogs, and sledges disappeared behind the broken shore ice. The morning was clear and relatively calm, the temperature minus 50 degrees.

Bartlett had been given orders to limit his advance to about ten miles a day, because the heavy sledge loads would require careful handling on the rough ice inshore. He was to proceed at this rate until the main party overtook him.

Two hours later a division led by George Borup, the athletic young Yale man, followed Bartlett. Borup had been instructed to make three marches north, to drop his supplies, and to return to Crane City, his base at Cape Columbia, for another load. Again

Peary walked out of camp with the party for a hundred yards or so, giving final instructions. He was particularly careful to advise Borup, a newcomer to the Arctic, about expected ice conditions.

The men and dogs of the main party were to move out from Crane City the following day. That night the dogs enjoyed a double feeding, and the men also devoured a hearty meal before turning in for a long sleep.

Peary awoke before daylight on the morning of March 1st. He lay quietly for a few moments, and he heard the sound of a fierce wind blowing outside his igloo. He looked through the peephole and observed that the sky was clear — "the stars were scintillating like diamonds" — but that a powerful wind was blowing from the east, a direction from which he had never known it to come in all his years of experience in that region.[26]

After a quick breakfast Peary dressed in new, dry furs for the trip. Then he went outside.

"The wind was whistling wildly around the eastern end of Independence Bluff," he observed, "and the ice fields to the north . . . were invisible in that gray haze which . . . means vicious wind. . . . Some parties would have considered the weather impossible for traveling and would have gone back to their igloos." [27]

Peary's own Eskimos were discomposed by the weather. The east wind, they said, was the work of *Tornarsuk* — the Devil — and Peary's plans were doomed again. Wind would open leads of water in the polar sea, and wind usually meant bad weather.

Wind certainly inflicted acute distress on travelers. When it was extremely fierce, hurling ice particles and snow against a man's flesh, it was sheer torture. Under those conditions a man might put his hand to his face and find blood. *Tornarsuk* had made his presence known, however, even before the wind, Peary's Eskimos said, because two of the twenty-six natives who were to have traveled northward from Crane City had been incapacitated by the cold weather, and six of the hundred and forty dogs had died of distemper. Still another dog was left behind.

Peary broke up these somber ponderings with an order for everybody to dress in the new furs prepared for the journey. By 6:00 A.M. all the men in the main party were at the upstanders of their sledges, their backs to the wind, awaiting the command to start.

Henson and his Eskimos were the first to leave. They followed the trail made by Bartlett and Borup. Then the others started. Peary and his Eskimos left last.

Conversation was impossible. Voices could not be heard over the roar of the wind. Nevertheless, for the first quarter of a mile the going was fairly easy. Soon after leaving, however, men and dogs plunged into ice so rough that Peary's Eskimos were forced to chop a path with pickaxes, even though all other divisions of the main party had just preceded them over the same area.

One hour after Peary's division had left camp the entire polar expedition was on the ice of the Arctic Ocean — twenty-four men, nineteen sledges, and a hundred and thirty-three dogs. When they left the shelter of land they felt the wind at its fullest intensity, and a temperature of 50 below. Brandy in a bottle under Peary's deerskin coat froze solid. The trail was visible, however, and with heads bowed and eyes half closed the men soon were able to follow it without serious discomfort.[28]

Peary's greatest concern was the wind. He knew what its effect would inevitably be: to open leads of water in the ice ahead. Also discomforting was the pain in his leg, the one that had been broken in Greenland in 1891. Until now it had not bothered him for sixteen years.

After a few miles that took several hours to traverse, Peary reached the surface of some old floes, and traveling became much easier. He met one Eskimo, then another, hurrying back to Crane

City with empty sledges that had been smashed so badly on the rough ice that it was considered simpler to send back for replacements than to repair them. Peary admonished both Eskimos not to waste a moment.

Soon Peary came upon men who had been forced to halt to repair other broken sledges. Henson, after leaving Crane City first that morning, had been especially plagued by this misfortune. He dreaded the work, knowing that he would have to remove his gloves and risk frosting his hands. When he felt his fingers beginning to freeze he would pull his hand up through his sleeve and hold it in his armpit until a burning sensation told him his fingers were thawing.

After a full day of such interruptions the main party reached Bartlett's first camp. There they found two igloos — one built by Bartlett's men, the other by Borup's. Peary's division took one igloo; Ross Marvin and his men were assigned to the other. On this first night of the journey the other divisions wearily built their own shelters.

Some sledges, those undergoing repairs, remained behind on the trail when the main party halted for the night. By the time the last sledge reached camp, day twilight, which at that season lasted about twelve hours, had vanished. A frigid darkness had settled over the area.

The men in each division fed their dogs and retired to their snow igloos for supper. Once inside, they discovered that their breath had condensed and frozen to the fur hoods. Some cheeks and noses had to be carefully thawed. The shelters were, however, comparatively snug. Outside, the wind continued to shriek over the dark, rugged surface of the ice. Somewhere ahead, ten miles or so, the parties of Bartlett and Borup were similarly camped.

Peary was making himself comfortable when one of Henson's Eskimos ran over to report that *Tornarsuk* was in camp, for the alcohol in their new stove would not light. Peary hurried to investigate. The failure of even one stove was a serious matter and, considering the austere equipment allowance, might eventually impair the chances of the entire expedition.

A pile of burned matches lay on the floor of the igloo; Henson had used a whole box in his effort to light the stove. Peary realized immediately what was wrong: the temperature was so low there was no vaporization of the alcohol. He stuck a piece of paper in the alcohol and applied a flame to it, and Henson had his fire.

Although Peary was unaware of it, Bartlett and Borup had encountered the same problem twenty-four hours earlier at this same camp. They, too, had solved the problem — by warming the alcohol over a kerosene stove.

During the night one of the two Eskimos whom Peary had met returning to land with broken sledges, Kyutah, arrived in camp. The other, Kudlooktoo, failed to appear, and Peary found himself at the end of the first day another man short. Worse, the rough sledging had sprung leaks in several alcohol and petroleum tins, giving Peary reason to worry about his fuel supply. He resolved to ask George Borup to bring back an extra supply of fuel. He could do this when he met Borup returning to land.

The second day began cold and cloudy. The wind continued to blow furiously from the east. A breakfast of hot tea and frozen pemmican provided some cheer for the men, but the pemmican cut the roofs and sides of their mouths. This resulted in a resolution by Henson and several others to boil the pemmican in the tea at the next camp.

At 6:30 A.M. Henson's division departed. The others followed. Peary's group left last, for this was the plan. He was to save himself for the final dash, if it ever materialized. Also, the rear position was a better one for assuring himself that the expedition was making normal progress and that there were no stragglers.

The second march, over heavy rubble ice, was similar to the

first. Men with heads bowed, eyes half closed, strained to follow the trail broken by previous divisions. Henson's party, leading, was able to follow Bartlett's and Borup's trail, but Henson and his Eskimos were forced to hack out a fresh path. Again, even the divisions that followed Henson's had to use pickaxes frequently. While the men were thus engaged the dogs curled up in the snow, noses protected by tails, and waited. All the while, the wind continued to blow furiously from the east. Peary wondered that it had not yet ruptured the sea ice.

Three quarters of the second day's march had been completed when Peary saw on the northern horizon a dark cloud, the kind that hovers over open water on the Arctic Ocean. As he approached he could make out black spots on the ice — the men, dogs, and sledges of his various divisions. When he joined them he found a lane of open water about a quarter of a mile wide. The wind had been doing its mischief.

Bartlett and Borup were not there. They had been able to traverse the area before the lead appeared and were somewhere on the ice ahead — or at least Peary hoped so.

Making camp at this place was unavoidable, although slow progress over the roughest ice would have been preferable to the mental torture caused by such a delay. The Eskimos built four igloos, one for each division. Marvin and MacMillan made a sounding at the edge of the lead and reported ninety-six fathoms. Peary settled down to a restless sleep. When, he asked himself, would the lead close?

Before daylight the next morning he had his answer. A frightful grinding noise told him that the lead was crushing together. He grabbed a hatchet and pounded the ice floor of his snow igloo, signaling the division leaders in the other three shelters to get their men up at once. After bolting a meager breakfast they were out, at first daylight, hurrying sledges across the narrowing lead on raftering young ice, which was moving, crushing, and piling up as the lead closed.

It was like crossing a river on a succession of giant shingles, all afloat and moving. At any moment a man or a sledge and its team might plunge into the icy water. Such an accident could easily have proved fatal, for the air temperature was 20 below and the east wind continued to blow briskly.

Everyone crossed safely, but on the other side Peary discovered there was no sign of the trail broken by Bartlett's pioneer division. The lateral movement of the ice, he concluded, had carried the trail along with it.

In about two hours one of the Eskimos, Kyutah, signaled that he had found the track. Peary hurried over to the site and immediately noticed footprints of men and dogs traveling south. George Borup, ordered to carry his supplies three marches northward, to cache them, and to return to Crane City for more provisions, had apparently already passed, and Peary would now have no chance to inform him of the fuel shortage.

Peary told Ross Marvin to throw off his sledge load and to hurry back after Borup; Marvin could tell him about the shortage. Also, Peary thought, Borup might need a white companion of Marvin's experience.

As Peary had surmised, Borup was indeed headed landward. At first light on March 3rd, his division, having dumped the supplies as instructed, had turned south. Borup had been with Bartlett then, and before leaving he had asked Bartlett what he should do if he missed Peary. The captain had replied that Borup would surely meet him.

When Borup arrived at the second camp, however, he saw no sign of the main party. Either they had not been able to start on the day planned, Borup surmised, or they had lost the trail. Soon after that he lost his own trail, and when he picked it up again he observed the tracks of the main party heading north. He knew then that he had missed them, after all.

Lacking advice on what supplies to carry on the second trip, he decided that he should haul a standard load and trust to luck it would contain what Peary needed.

At Crane City Borup thus loaded his sledges on March 4th. He was drying clothes for the return trip when Ross Marvin and Kyutah arrived. Marvin told him about the leaking fuel tins and said it was vital to reach Peary with the additional fuel.

Peary now was forty miles out to sea, however, with much open water and a badly faulted trail between. To make additional speed, Borup and Marvin, who was also returning, decided to carry only three fourths of the usual sledge load each. After loading they turned in for the night.

With morning came a raging wind that held up their departure for three hours. Then they left, but from a pressure ridge at the end of the land ice they saw they could not go far. A lead of water four hundred yards wide stretched east and west as far as they could see. The Eskimos scouted in both directions, but they reported no way across. They knew they must wait for the lead to close or to freeze.

It did neither. The lead widened for five days. Had it remained stationary it would have frozen within twenty-four hours sufficiently for them to cross, but it grew wider; and from the ribbon of open water in the center poured a smoke like that from coke ovens.

March 6th provided some diversion, however, for Borup, Marvin, and their Eskimos. At midday they were sitting in their igloos enjoying a cup of tea when a cheer from the Eskimos startled Borup. They pointed excitedly at the ice wall and yelled, "*Suck-in-nuck!*" Borup, following their gaze, looked through a small peephole in the southern side of the house and saw the sun for the first time in five months. He whooped, and he and the two

Eskimos squirmed out of their igloo. Outside, Marvin and his men joined in the shouting.

Their glee was cut short, however, for while they were outside they saw that the lead was still widening.

On March 7th Borup observed the sea ice drifting eastward. "The Lord only knew where the trail was," he said later. "We didn't." [29] Then March 8th and 9th passed, accompanied by the gnawing agony of the long wait beside the black lead that refused to close.

By the end of the fifth day of waiting Borup and Marvin estimated that Peary was ninety miles out — unless he, too, had been held up somewhere by open water. Even if they should be able to cross the lead soon they could not be certain of recovering the trail. Considering the easterly drift of the ice, the trail might well be thirty miles away — "somewhere off Cape Colon," concluded Borup.[30]

Adding to their difficulties were the Eskimos, who wanted to return to their families aboard the *Roosevelt*. Marvin agreed that they could go, but he warned them that such a course would cause them and their families to lose their living space aboard the ship. The Eskimos considered the discomfort this would entail, and they decided to stay.

Still the lead did not close. Marvin and Borup spent hours pacing back and forth, becoming more impatient as each day passed.

". . . It looked as though we wouldn't get out to Peary again," Borup said later. "So, besides knowing the success or failure of the expedition might depend on our catching the others, we also [knew] that if we did not get out, we could never explain it, and at home there would always be the question of someone having lost his nerve." [31]

Many miles out on the ice, Peary had observed a change in the weather on March 4th, the day that Marvin had joined Borup at Crane City. "The sky was overcast, the wind had swung completely around to the west during the night, there were occasional squalls of light snow, and the thermometer had risen to only nine degrees below zero." [32]

The temperature seemed almost warm to Peary, who was even more concerned now that leads were numerous. As always, the dense, black vapor clouds, rising from the warmer water into the frigid atmosphere, indicated their presence.

A mile or two to the east a lead stretched far north, directly parallel to Peary's course. It did not create great apprehension. Ten or fifteen miles ahead, however, Peary could see an ominous black band of vapor extending east and west across the course. This caused him to worry. Nevertheless, Bartlett's trail was easy to follow, and the main party made good progress.

Peary's concern increased with each mile covered. The black cloud on the northern horizon grew larger until it seemed almost overhead. At that point the main party came upon an igloo erected by Bartlett. Inside was a note informing Peary that the captain was camped about a mile farther north, held up by open water. The main party soon reached Bartlett's camp.

"There I found the . . . unwelcome sight which I had so often before me on the expedition of 1905–06," Peary said, "— the white expanse of ice cut by a river of inky black water, throwing off dense clouds of vapor which gathered in a sullen canopy overhead." [33]

The lead had opened directly through the heavy floes, which sometimes attain a thickness of one hundred feet. The force that could open such a river, Peary meditated, was comparable to the forces that threw up the mountains and opened the channels between lands. The width of the lead was approximately a quarter of a mile, and it extended perpendicular to his course as far as Peary could see from the highest ice pinnacle in the area. The vapor pattern told him that two or three miles east, the north-south lead that had been paralleling his course intersected the lead that had stopped him. The east-west rupture had the appearance of what Peary called the "Big Lead."

Peary looked again at the water. The absence of lateral ice movement was a good sign. The shores of the lead were not moving in either direction; so it was simply an opening in the ice, caused by the force of the wind and the spring tides. It could freeze soon, he believed.

On the morning of March 5th — when Borup and Marvin had first been stopped by open water — Peary noticed the lead narrowing somewhat. Then it opened wider than ever, leaving a ribbon of black water in the center of the young ice that had begun forming. All day March 6th, then March 7th, Peary watched the lead. Three, four, and five days passed; still the lead blocked advance. Peary walked back and forth, deploring his luck and waiting for the lead to close, while Marvin and Borup were unconsciously duplicating his actions many miles away.

Peary wrote in his diary:

> Fourth day of helpless, irritating inaction; calm and mild but too thick to see sun. Lead changed less during night than any time since we have been here. Could have crossed today but shall not move until the rear party is heard from. Felt sure it would be in tonight. Four fine marching days lost. When the party arrives we shall have a storm. G — d — K — to h —.[34]

Whatever the "K —" stood for Peary never said, but the rest was obvious. His impatience increased daily, although he tried to hide it in front of his men, and he spent most of his hours pacing the floe in front of the snow igloos. Frequently he stopped and looked toward the north, across the open water. More often, however, he looked southward, straining his eyes to try to see through the dim light. Always he listened for the faintest sound of dog teams. An additional supply of fuel was vital, but Peary was determined to go ahead as soon as possible, whether or not it arrived.

"I could not turn back here," he concluded. While he paced the floe, he decided on a plan to use the sledges piecemeal as fuel in the cookers, to make tea after the oil and alcohol were gone. By the time the wood was exhausted, Peary guessed, the season's advance and his progress southward from the Pole would bring temperatures warm enough so that he and his men could suck ice or snow to quench their thirst. They could also get by on pemmican and raw dog, and without tea.[35]

The delay created still another problem: the Eskimos were becoming uneasy about their situation. Peary observed them talking quietly in groups of twos and threes, just out of his hearing. Without Eskimos Peary could not hope to reach the Pole.

He knew the peculiar Eskimo temperament, and he knew more about handling them than most men. They were like children, he had decided, and they should be handled like children — firmly but gently.

Peary also was aware of the Eskimos' strong belief in *Tornarsuk* and of their fear of the sea ice. He was not surprised, then, when two of the natives, Poodloonah and Panikpah, reported to him on March 7th that they were ill. Peary knew better ("I have had sufficient experience to know a sick Eskimo when I see one" [36]), but he instructed the two to take a sledge and dog team and return to land as quickly as possible — and, not incidentally, to carry a note to Marvin and Borup urging utmost speed. After that, Peary said, the two Eskimos could return to the *Roosevelt*.

At the same time, other Eskimos complained of ailments. Two of them had a solid reason for doing so: they had been rendered unconscious by the fumes of an alcohol stove. The accident could scarcely have occurred at a less opportune time.

It happened in MacMillan's division. One morning when he was preparing breakfast for himself and his two Eskimos his alcohol stove began to burn improperly, filling the snow igloo with fumes. Suddenly the two Eskimos fell backward. At first, however, MacMillan assumed they were taking a last-minute rest before beginning the daily chores; then he realized they were unconscious. He kicked out the snowhouse door and tried to revive the men, but he succeeded only in evoking groans and a few muscle twitches. He was thus engaged when Peary, approaching the shelter, inquired of MacMillan how he had rested during the night. MacMillan answered, somewhat excitedly, that he had fared well enough but that his Eskimos had passed out. Peary popped into the igloo with an anxious look on his weathered face that would have been laughable, MacMillan said, if the situation had not been so serious.

One of the Eskimos groaned again, and Peary quickly withdrew to see if any others were within hearing distance. Then, while Peary stood guard outside, MacMillan frantically tried to revive the two men. After they had regained consciousness MacMillan told them they had been asleep, but when he lighted the stove for supper some hours later both Eskimos dived for the door.

Efforts to keep the incident secret were unsuccessful, and it served to frighten the rest of the natives. MacMillan helped to calm the unrest by organizing games and athletic contests. Then, fortunately, young ice began forming over the lead. Peary might have crossed on March 9th or 10th by taking desperate chances, but he waited. One reason was that he thought Marvin and Borup must be near, and he needed the additional fuel they must surely bring.

The two men, however, were nowhere near Peary. In the late hours of March 9th they were still held up by their own lead. Both despaired of seeing Peary again. Adding to their dismay, Kudlooktoo's dog team broke away from its moorings and raced for Crane City, four miles away, with the annoyed Eskimo chasing after it.

At daylight the rest of the stranded party emerged from their snowhouses and were astonished to find the lead closed. Hastily they broke camp and prepared to depart; then one of the Eskimos reported hearing a rifle shot. They thought this signified Kud-looktoo's return with the recaptured dog team, but, instead, they saw two Eskimos, with sledges and dogs, approaching from the north.

Marvin and an Eskimo harnessed a double team of dogs and dashed off to intercept them. They encountered Panikpah and Poodloonah, the "ailing" natives sent back by Peary on March 7th. The two Eskimos said they had been camped on the other side of the lead, and that — surprisingly — the trail was within a mile of the camp, to the west.

Panikpah handed Peary's note to Marvin. It declared that the main party, four marches out, had been held up by open water for three days, that Panikpah had an ailing shoulder and a case of nerves, and that Poodloonah had a bad case of cold feet. Peary ended the note with an urgent appeal to Marvin for speed in delivering the fuel.

Marvin hurried the men for a speedy departure. Between the land and the sea ice, however, they encountered a long stretch of rubble ice and pressure ridges and were able to make progress only by using pickaxes every foot of the way.

Finally they struck the old trail. They reached the first camp in darkness. The sky was overcast and a brisk wind howled across the ice, but the snow igloo was cozy. They bedded down, reflecting that even if Peary had crossed the lead March 7th, the day his note had been written, he could not be more then seventy miles ahead. They had a chance to catch him.

Even as Marvin, Borup, and their Eskimos dropped off to sleep, Peary — still blocked by the lead — was giving orders to get under way in the morning, March 11th. The lead had nearly closed. That night he wrote in his diary: "Lead crushing slowly together all day. Still no rear party. Shall push on tomorrow and take chances." [37]

Later he elaborated: "The delay had become unendurable, and I decided to take the chance of Marvin's overtaking us with the oil and alcohol. Of course, there was the alternative of my going back to see what was the trouble, but that idea was dismissed. There was little attraction in ninety miles of extra travel, to say nothing of the psychological effect on the members of the expedition." [38]

Peary was relieved to observe that the morning of March 11th came accompanied by clear, calm weather. A temperature of 40 below meant that all open water probably would be frozen. He ordered an early start; then he wrote and signed this note to Marvin:

> Have waited here six days. Can wait no longer. We are short of fuel. Push on with all possible speed to overtake us. Shall leave note at each camp. When near us rush light sledge and note of information ahead to overhaul us.
>
> Expect send back doctor and Eskimos three to five marches from here. He should meet you and give you information. . . .
>
> We go straight across this lead (E.S.E.). There has been no lateral motion of the ice during seven days, only open and shut. *Do not camp here. Cross the Lead.* Feed full rations and speed your dogs. It is vital you overtake us and give us fuel.
>
> Leaving at 9 A.M., Thursday, March 11th. [39]

Peary left the note in his igloo and joined his men. They crossed the lead — after a delay of nearly one week — without difficulty. Then they crossed seven more leads, varying in width from half a mile to a mile, all covered with barely negotiable young ice. They also passed the 84th parallel and covered a total of at least twelve miles during the march. [40] Exhausted, they camped and slept soundly, despite the raftering of ice nearby that caused a continual grinding, groaning, creaking as the pieces crunched together.

On the following day Peary estimated a march of another twelve miles, despite frequent delays caused by cracks, narrow leads, and rough ice. That night, before he dropped off to sleep, his thoughts were with the men carrying the oil and alcohol.

"We hoped that Marvin and Borup, with their men and vital supply of fuel, would get across the Big Lead before we had any more wind; for six hours of a good fresh breeze would utterly obliterate our trail, by reason of the movement of the ice, and their search for us in the broad waste of that white world would have been like the proverbial search for a needle in a haystack." [41]

March 13th arrived without wind, but the temperature was 53 degrees below zero. Peary's brandy had again become solid, and even the kerosene, normally colorless and fluid, appeared white and viscid. When the main party left camp the dogs were enveloped in a white cloud created by their own breath. Peary, walking ahead of his division, looked back and saw neither men nor dogs — "only a low-lying bank of fog glistening like silver." [42]

A five-mile stretch of exceptionally rugged ice slowed Peary during the morning, but about noon the surface became smoother. He ordered a halt for camp, having covered twelve miles. His division had just completed building their snowhouse when one of the Eskimos shouted, *"Kling-mik-sue!"* — "Dogs are coming!"

Peary scrambled up a nearby hummock and peered southward. In the distance he saw a small veil of silvery mist, unmistakably created by the breath of running dogs. While he watched, the dogs drew nearer, and soon he recognized the figure of Seegloo,[43] sent ahead by Marvin with a note saying that Marvin, Borup, and the others would overtake the main party the following day. The note also informed Peary that they were carrying thirty gallons of alcohol in addition to the usual provisions.

Peary read the note with profound relief: the danger of a fuel shortage, which surely would have defeated him, was now over.

He was able to concentrate again on the progress of the expedition.

The main party had been on the ice about two weeks when the supporting divisions finally began turning back. First to return was a party commanded by Dr. Goodsell, who left from about latitude 84 degrees 29 minutes north, on March 14th. On the way back Goodsell met Marvin and Borup, and the three exchanged the latest news. A few hours later, Peary noted, Marvin, Borup, and their four Eskimos came "swinging in, smoking like a battleship squadron" [44] — and carrying the precious fuel.

MacMillan, suffering from a frozen heel, proceeded only a short distance farther before turning back — on March 15th — with another party.

It was a tribute to Peary that these two novices, MacMillan and Goodsell, along with a third tenderfoot, Borup, had already surpassed the "farthest north" of every preceding Arctic explorer but two — Fridtjof Nansen and Umberto Cagni.

Left in the main party now were sixteen men, twelve sledges, and one hundred dogs. A terrifying accident, which occurred on the same day that MacMillan departed, nearly decreased the numbers further. Borup, urging his dog team across an open crack between two pieces of floating ice, was horrified to see the animals slip and splash into the water. He leaped forward, steadied the sledge, and kept it from following the dogs; then he grabbed the traces and hauled the struggling animals out of the water. Without his quick thinking five hundred pounds of irreplaceable supplies would have gone to the bottom of the Arctic Ocean, and the dog team would surely have been carried along with the load.

On March 20th, five days after this harrowing incident, Borup's division went back from latitude 85 degrees 23 minutes north. As Borup left camp Peary walked beside him, giving advice for the return journey. He warned Borup to be especially careful of the leads and under no circumstances to let the Eskimos get ahead of him. They were homeward bound, Peary emphasized, and they would not come to his rescue if he encountered any difficulty.

Next, Ross Marvin led a group back to land, on March 26th. The day before departing Marvin took a latitude observation, then wrote out and signed a memorandum for Peary. It was to be the last communication from Marvin:

This is to certify that I turned back from this point with the third supporting party, Commander Peary advancing with nine men in the party, seven sledges with the standard loads, and sixty dogs, men and dogs all in first-class condition. The captain with the fourth and last supporting party expects to turn back at the end of five more marches. Determined our latitude by observation on March 22nd and again today, March 25th. A copy of the observation and computations is herewith enclosed. Results of observations were as follows:

Latitude at noon March 22nd   85 degrees 48 minutes north.
Latitude at noon March 25th   86 degrees 38 minutes north.

Distance made good in three marches, 50 minutes of latitude, an average of 16⅔ nautical miles per march.

The weather is fine, going good, and improving each day.[45]

When Marvin left, the morning was clear and crisp; sunlight glittered on ice and snow. Despite this aura of cheerfulness, however, Peary felt obliged to give Marvin some parting advice. "Be careful of the leads, my boy," he said. Then he shook Marvin's hand and the two men exchanged farewells.

The divisions led by Peary and Henson went on northward, following the trail made several hours earlier by Bartlett's pioneer party. At the end of their march they reached Bartlett's camp — just as he was departing for another pioneering stint — after covering fifteen miles more.

The next day, March 27th, brought dazzling Arctic sunshine, of such brilliance that everybody would have been struck by snow blindness had not goggles been worn continually. The sunshine, however, did not herald more comfortable traveling. A cutting northeasterly wind intensified the minus-40-degree temperature, and the ice surface grew broken and raftered, jagged and sharp. Midway through the march the two divisions struck heavy rubble ice covered with deep snow. Men and dogs plowed their way through, with the men pushing the sledges until their muscles ached and utter exhaustion seemed imminent.

Providing some diversion were the tracks of two itinerant foxes, more than two hundred and forty miles from land. Peary wondered where they were going and how they had ever reached a point so far north.

At the end of that march Peary wrote:

Reached captain's camp in six hours among small, very heavy old floes raftered all along edges (twelve miles). As he had been in his igloos only some three hours when I arrived I told him to turn in and sleep more and get under way about midnight. Lightened the sledges of his men over one hundred pounds each by taking some of their pemmican on to my sledges.

I am glad of the drop in temperature. Hope it will continue. Do not like the [temperatures] in the "teens" and minus twenties. These mean open water.

We are over the 87th parallel at this camp.[46]

In 1906 Peary had proceeded only a few miles farther, to 87 degrees 6 minutes, before retreating. This time his divisions were in much better condition — and the Pole was fewer than one hundred and eighty miles away.

On March 28th Peary awoke, wriggled through the igloo entrance, and saw that Bartlett had left. Then, as usual, he scanned the horizon. The sky was brilliant blue, but to the north he saw, with a feeling of despair, a thick, smoky haze, and he felt a wind strong from the northeast. It all spelled open water ahead.

For six hours Peary's and Henson's divisions toiled northward before coming upon Bartlett's camp, beside a wide lead. To the northwest, north, and northeast Peary saw a dense water-sky. Without waking the pioneer party, Peary ordered his men to build their igloos one hundred yards distant from Bartlett's, to avoid disturbing him. Then, after devouring a supper of pemmican, biscuit, and hot tea they all turned in.

As Peary dozed he heard ice groaning nearby. It was not a loud noise, and he cheerfully attributed it to the closing of the lead. Nevertheless, he was cautious enough to feel for his mittens in the dark. Satisfying himself that they were nearby, he rolled over on his deerskins and slept. A distant shout from somewhere outside awoke him.

He leaped to his feet and peered through the peephole. He was aghast to see a wide, black lead between the two igloos and Bartlett's. On the opposite shore one of Bartlett's Eskimos yelled and waved in terror.

Peary shook his Eskimos awake and kicked out the snow door. Rushing outside, he discovered that the ice break had occurred within a foot of the "anchor" to which a dog team had been secured. Another team had barely escaped burial under a pressure ridge.

The ice raft that supported Bartlett's igloo was slowly drifting eastward, into an expanse of open water. As it moved, however, it came nearer the floe on which Peary stood. He shouted to Bartlett's men to hitch up their teams and be ready to dash across.

Then he was able to survey his own position, which was precarious indeed. His and Henson's igloos were situated on ice that seemed ready to separate from a large floe. Quickly he roused Henson's party and instructed them to load and hitch their teams.

After all the sledges had been safely hauled across an alarming crack to the larger floe Peary returned to the edge of the lead to help Bartlett. He thought to himself that if the drifting ice raft failed to make contact he might never be reunited with the captain.

Gradually the floe approached; then it crunched against the ice near where Peary stood. The two edges were fairly even, so that the ice raft lay alongside like a boat against a wharf. Bartlett and his men wasted no time debarking, and everyone retreated to the large floe.

Peary realized there was a possibility that even this floe would break up, but he reasoned, "We couldn't waste our sleeping hours sitting up to watch for it." [47] The men constructed three more igloos, and they all turned in for a few more hours of sleep. During the rest of that night, however, they slept with mittens on.

All next day, March 29th, the lead blocked progress. Peary could not even see the other side. It was hidden behind a dense cloud that reminded him of a prairie fire. The men spent the time overhauling sledges and drying clothes over oil lamps. That night, after Peary had retired to his igloo, he heard a sound like a distant surf.

"To the inexperienced it might have seemed . . . ominous . . ." he said later, "but to us it was cheering . . . because we knew it meant the narrowing, and perhaps the closing, of the stretch of water that barred our way." [48]

Then he dozed, but at 1:00 A.M. he awoke. The surflike roar from the closing lead had become louder. He looked through the peephole and saw that the cloud caused by the lead was much less dense. Farther on, however, he saw still another cloud, suggesting more open water. Disappointed, he went back to sleep.

When he awoke again he realized that the groaning of the ice had ceased. No low clouds were visible; the leads had vanished. The temperature was 30 below.

He hurried his men across the ice before it reopened. All that day, March 30th, Bartlett's pioneer party traveled in company with Henson's and Peary's divisions. They crossed many cracks and narrow lanes of young ice, which had only recently been open water. During that same march they also crossed a six-mile-wide "lake" of young ice so thin that it rippled under their feet. Despite these perils Peary pushed on for at least twenty miles before he ordered a halt for camp; he was anxious to make up for the recent delay.

Bartlett, too, now became anxious about his progress. The next march was to be his last one, and he put all his energy into it. So good was his pace that Peary was "obliged repeatedly to jump on sledges to keep up." [49]

> If the captain's observations tomorrow do not place us on the 88th parallel [Peary wrote] it will be because this north wind has set us south some by crushing up the young ice behind us. [50]

Bartlett was in a somber mood. Had the decision been left to him he would have proceeded northward, but Peary had concluded this was not feasible.

"The food which he and his two Eskimos would have consumed between this point and the Pole on the upward and return journeys might have meant that we would all starve before we could reach the land again," Peary reasoned later. [51] Nevertheless, Peary's decision to send Bartlett back at this point was, in time, to be subjected to violent criticism.

At the end of Bartlett's last march he and Peary guessed they had made at least twenty miles, which would have put them near the 88th parallel, as Peary hoped. To make certain Bartlett reached that latitude, however, Peary suggested that he walk northward for a few miles when he rose the next morning. This Bartlett did, after a sleep of four hours and a 5:00 A.M. breakfast. A five- or six-mile trek toward the Pole gave him a temporary "farthest north" among Arctic explorers, but when he returned and took a meridian observation he was disappointed to find that the camp was at 87 degrees 46 minutes 49 seconds.

This latitude is a direct result of the north wind of the last two days [Peary wrote]. We have traveled a good twelve miles more than this in the last five marches but have lost them by the crushing up of young ice in our rear, and the closing of the leads.[52]

Bartlett had taken this observation — and, with Marvin, previous ones — for two reasons: to spare Peary's eyes and to provide a set of independent observations. After Bartlett had figured the latitude he gave Peary one copy of his calculations and kept the other for himself. With Peary's copy was a note from Bartlett:

I have today personally determined our latitude to be by sextant observations . . . 87 degrees 46 minutes 49 seconds north. I return from here in command of the fourth supporting party. I leave Commander Peary with five men, five sledges with full loads, and forty picked dogs. Men and dogs in good condition. The going fair, the weather good. At the same average as our last eight marches Commander Peary should reach the Pole in eight days.[53]

At 3:00 P.M. on April 1st, Bartlett departed for land with two Eskimos, one sledge, and eighteen dogs. One other sledge had been smashed, and two of the poorest dogs had been killed.

Bartlett called out a "good-by, good luck," before he left. Peary watched him head southward, until the captain and his party disappeared behind ice hummocks. Then he turned away, toward the north. "I felt a keen regret as I saw the captain's broad shoulders grow smaller in the distance," Peary said later.[54]

In his diary Peary jotted down a few remarks on the man's effectiveness:

Bartlett has done good work and been a great help to me. I have given him this post of honor because he was fit for it, because of his handling of the *Roosevelt,* because of his saving me hundreds of petty annoyances, and because I felt it appropriate, in view of England's magnificent Arctic work . . . that it should be a British subject who could boast that next to an American he had been nearest to the Pole.[55]

One month exactly had passed since Peary had left land. Remaining with him now were the two Eskimos he had chosen to comprise his own division for the final dash, Egingwah and Seegloo; his long-time manservant, Matthew Henson; and Henson's two Eskimos, Ootah and Ooqueah. As Bartlett had noted, they had five sledges and forty of the best dogs. Peary planned to kill the poorest of these along the way and feed them to the others.

Peary mused over his final plans while he paced the lee of a pressure ridge near which the snow igloos had been built. "Every nerve must be strained to make five marches of at least twenty-five miles each," he concluded, "crowding these marches in such a way as to bring us to the end of the fifth march by noon, to permit an immediate latitude observation."[56] Weather and leads permitting, he believed that he could do this.

If for any reason he fell short of these proposed distances he had two methods in reserve for making up the deficit. One was to double the last march — "that is, make a good march, have tea and a hearty lunch, rest the dogs a little, and then go on again, without sleep." The other was to push on with one light sledge, a double team of dogs, and one or two of the party at the conclusion of the fifth march, leaving the others in camp. Even should traveling be worse than anticipated, eight marches like the three from 85 degrees 48 minutes to 86 degrees 36 minutes, or six similar to the last one, would bring triumph.[57]

Clouding Peary's thoughts, even while he planned for success, was the realization that a gale lasting several hours would open leads that could prove to be impassible. Such open water might appear south of him, preventing a return to land.

Various terse diary entries from April 1st through April 6th, never before published verbatim, described his success:[58]

Thursday, April 1st

. . . We are ready now for the final lap of the journey, sledges thoroughly overhauled and strengthened, dogs the pick of 133, and dogs and men in training. It is the time for which I have reserved all my energies, and I feel tonight as if I was in trim, and equal to the demands upon me of the next few days. Assuming the captain's figures to be correct we are 133 [nautical] miles from the Pole. . . .

Friday, April 2nd

Eight hours sound, warm, refreshing sleep. Left camp 5:00 A.M., leaving others to break camp and follow. A fine morning; clear, temperature minus 25 degrees, wind of last days subsided. Going the best and most equable of any day yet. Large old floes, hard and level, with patches of sapphire blue ice [the pools of last summer], and surrounded by pressure ridges, some of which almost stupendous, yet easily negotiable either through some convenient gap or up the slope of some huge drift. Came on at a good clip for nearly four hours, when the sledges overtook me. After that obliged to sit on sledges most of the time . . . or else run to keep up. Kept the pace for ten hours.

Have no doubt we covered thirty miles but will be conservative and call it twenty-five. My Eskimos say we have come as far as from the *Roosevelt* to Porter Bay. This by our winter route scales thirty-five miles on the chart. Whatever the distance is, we are likely now that the wind has ceased to retain what we have made. It is possible that with release from wind pressure the ice may rebound some and return us some of the hard-earned miles it stole from us yesterday and day before. In any event we are now beyond the 88th parallel, and I am a tired and satisfied man.

A brilliant day and as we camp late in afternoon near a huge pressure ridge, the sun almost seems to have some warmth. Got in above my knees twice today in the narrow cracks. While building igloos a long lead forms east and southeast of us some miles distant as shown by the water clouds. Dogs show effects of yesterday's rest.

Saturday, April 3rd

Got on the trail three hours earlier this morning after a small sleep. Am going to try and work in an extra march. Am train· ing down. Took up another hole in my belt this morning. Weather fine, clear, and calm. Ice as yesterday except at beginning of march it was rougher, requiring use of pickaxes. This and a brief delay at a narrow lead cut down our distance some. Ten hours (twenty miles) halfway to 89 degrees. Dogs frequently on trot. Some gigantic rafters but not in our path. Ice grinding audibly in various directions but no visible motion. Either twisting into equilibrium after the wind, or else the spring tides (full moon about tomorrow). Yesterday's lead to east and southeast closed up or crusted over. A similar one visible west and northwest during early part of march.

Sunday, April 4th

Hit the trail again before midnight, after a short sleep. If weather holds good shall be able to get in the extra march. The day a duplicate of day before yesterday as to weather and going. The latter even better. The surface is as even (except for the pressure ridges) as the glacial fringe from Hecla to Columbia, and harder. Something over ten hours on a direct course, dogs often on the trot, occasionally on the run. Twenty-five miles. Near end of march crossed a hundred-yard lead on thin young ice.

As I ran ahead to guide the dogs obliged to slide my feet and travel wide, bear style [to distribute weight]. One runner of one sledge cut through for some distance, but the sledge kept up. The men let sledges and dogs come on by themselves, and come gliding across [themselves] where they could. The last two came over on all fours. Sledge ran over side of my right foot today as result of my stumbling while running but think it will give me no trouble. Am tired but satisfied with our progress. We are inside 89 degrees. Give me three days more of this weather! Temperature at beginning of march minus 40 degrees.

Monday, April 5th

Over the 89th!! Started early last evening. The march a duplicate of previous one as to weather and going. Temperature at starting minus 35 degrees. Sledges appeared to haul a little easier, dogs on trot most of the time. Last two hours on young ice of a north and south lead. They were often galloping. Ten hours, twenty-five miles or *more*. Great. A fifty-yard lead open when I reached it, moved enough by time sledges came up to let us cross; still this biting cold, the face burning for hours. (Like the inland ice.) The natives complain of it and at every camp are fixing their clothes about the face, waist, knees, and wrists. They complain of their noses, which I never knew them to do before. It is keen and bitter as frozen steel. Light air from south during first of march, veering to east and freshening as we camp. Another dog expended here. Tomorrow if ice and weather permit I shall make a long march, "boil the kettle" midway, and try to make up the five miles lost on the 3rd. We have been very fortunate with the leads so far, but I am in constant and increasing dread of encountering an uncrossable one. Six weeks today since I left the *Roosevelt*.

Tuesday, April 6th

On the trail again before midnight though I gave the party more sleep at this camp than at the previous ones, as we were all needing it, but I wanted to make the next camp in time for a noon sight if the sun was visible. Weather thick, like the march

after Marvin turned back. A dense, lifeless pall of gray overhead, almost black at the horizon, and the ice ghostly chalky
white with no relief. Like the icecap, and just the thing an artist
would paint for a polar icescape. Striking contrast to the glittering sunlit fields over which we have been traveling for four
days, canopied with blue and lit by the sun and full moon. The
going better than ever; hardly any snow on the hard granular
last summer's surface of the old floes, the blue lakes larger. The
rise in the temperature to minus 15 degrees has reduced friction
of the sledges 25 per cent and gives the dogs appearance of having caught the spirits of the party. The more sprightly ones as
they trot along with tightly curved tails, repeatedly toss their
heads with short barks and yelps. Two hours on a direct course
(thirty miles). Can I wait to cover those other five? Not a sign
of a lead in this march. The thick weather gives me less concern than it might, had I not been forehanded yesterday, and
fearing a cloudbank in the south took a latitude sight (89 degrees 25 minutes). This is two miles ahead of my dead reckoning and indicates that I have been conservative in my estimates,
as I intended, or that the ice has slacked back, or both.

The last march ended at 10:00 A.M. April 6th, 1909. Henson
and the Eskimos secured the dogs and commenced building igloos, while Peary began unloading and unpacking several bundles.
From under his coat Peary retrieved a small package, Henson noticed,[59] then opened it to reveal the silk taffeta flag that Jo had
made for him years ago. This was indeed to be a camp of importance, Henson concluded, and he asked Peary what name it would
be given.

"This, my boy, is to be Camp Morris K. Jesup," Peary answered,
"the last and most northerly camp on earth." [60]

Peary fastened the flag to a staff and planted it firmly atop his
igloo. There it hung limply for a time in a dead calm; then a
slight breeze caused the folds to straighten out.

Peary asked Henson and the four Eskimos to build a snow

shield to protect him from the flying drift of surface snow while he took an observation. This structure consisted of a semicircular arrangement of snow blocks, two tiers high, opening toward the sun. It was ready in time for an observation at local noon (Cape Columbia meridian time).

An artificial horizon was to be used for the sight. Moments before Peary engaged himself in this observation Henson heated a pan of mercury and brought it to him. Peary filled a trough with the mercury, lay on his stomach, and held the sextant to his eye. Using the reflection of the sun in the mercury, he got the elevation and wrote down the figures.

Such observations were hard on his eyes, and they blinded him temporarily. He was able, however, to complete the calculations and figure his latitude as 89 degrees 57 minutes 11 seconds, about three nautical miles from the Pole.

Henson saw Peary square his jaw.

"I was sure that he was satisfied," Henson said. "Feeling that the time had come, I ungloved my right hand and went forward to congratulate him." [61]

At that moment, however, Peary pressed his hands over his closed eyes, which ached and burned after the observation and the lack of sleep. He did not see Henson's extended hand. Instead, Peary said he was going into his igloo for a nap. He asked Henson to awake him after four hours, because he wanted to get other sights from various locations.

"The accumulated weariness of all those days and nights of forced marches and insufficient sleep, constant peril, and anxiety, seemed to roll across me all at once," Peary said later. "I was actually too exhausted to realize at the moment that my life's purpose had been achieved." [62]

Fatigued as he was, he nevertheless awoke without a call before his four hours had elapsed. His first act was to take out his diary, recently neglected because of hurried marches, and to write:

The Pole at last!!! The prize of three centuries, my dream and ambition for twenty-three years. *Mine* at last. I cannot bring myself to realize it. It all seems so simple and common-place. . . . I wish Jo could be here with me to share my feelings. I have drunk her health and that of the kids from the Benedictine flask she sent me.[63]

When Peary went outside he saw that the sky was overcast, preventing a 6:00 P.M. observation. Indications were, however, that the weather might clear soon. Hopefully, he loaded a sledge with instruments, a tin of pemmican, and a few skins, hitched up a double team of dogs, and departed camp with Egingwah and Seegloo for a midnight reading ten miles farther on. It showed him to be beyond the North Pole.

He returned to Camp Jesup and took another series of observations — at 6:00 A.M. April 7th — at right angles to those already made there. Again he calculated that the camp was within four or five miles of the Pole.

Once more Peary left camp. This time he sledged eight miles toward the Pole, to be sure of passing near it, but he returned in time for another series of observations at noon (Cape Columbia meridian), April 7th. These observations resulted in a latitude of 89 degrees 58 minutes 37 seconds — little more than one nautical mile difference from the ones of twenty-four hours earlier and this time closer to the Pole.

Peary satisfied himself. He had indeed achieved his goal.

"I had now taken . . . thirteen single, or six and one-half double, altitudes of the sun, at two different stations in three different directions at four different times," he said. "In traversing the ice in these various directions . . . I had allowed approximately ten miles for possible errors in my observations, and at some moment during these marches and countermarches I had passed over or very near the point where north and south and east and west blend into one." [64]

Before Peary left the vicinity of the Pole he posed his men for a photograph. Each man held one of the five flags Peary had brought.

Henson held Peary's polar flag, made by Jo. Peary had left a fragment from it at each of these places: Cape Morris Jesup, northernmost point of land in the world; Cape Thomas Hubbard, northernmost point of Axel Heiberg Island; Cape Columbia; on the sea ice at latitude 87 degrees 6 minutes north, Peary's 1906 record; and now, the North Pole.

Ooqueah held a Navy League flag; Ootah, the colors of Delta Kappa Epsilon fraternity; Egingwah, a Daughters of the American Revolution peace flag; and Seegloo, a Red Cross flag.

Peary himself planted a United States flag in the ice, and Henson led the Eskimos in three cheers. Peary observed that the Eskimos joined in with great enthusiasm, but he doubted that they really understood the meaning of the occasion.

Then he cut a diagonal strip from his polar flag and deposited it in a glass jar with two notes carrying the date of his arrival:

> 90 North Latitude, North Pole
> April 6, 1909

Arrived here today, twenty-seven marches from Cape Columbia.

I have with me five men, Matthew Henson, colored, Ootah, Egingwah, Seegloo, and Ooqueah,[65] Eskimos; five sledges, and thirty-eight dogs. My ship, the S. S. *Roosevelt*, is in winter quarters at Cape Sheridan, ninety miles east of Columbia.

The expedition under my command which has succeeded in reaching the Pole is under the auspices of the Peary Arctic Club of New York City, and has been fitted out and sent north by the members and friends of the club for the purpose of securing this geographical prize, if possible, for the honor and prestige of the United States of America.

The officers of the club are Thomas H. Hubbard, of New

York, president; Zenas Crane, of Massachusetts, vice-president; Herbert L. Bridgman, of New York, secretary and treasurer.

I start back for Cape Columbia tomorrow.

Robert E. Peary,
United States Navy

90 North Latitude, North Pole
April 6, 1909

I have today hoisted the national ensign of the United States of America at this place, which my observations indicate to be the North Polar axis of the earth, and have formally taken possession of the entire region, and adjacent, for and in the name of the President of the United States of America.

I leave this record and United States flag in possession.

Robert E. Peary
United States Navy[66]

Next, Peary took out a postal card that he had brought from the *Roosevelt*. He wrote his wife a twenty-four-word message from "90 North Latitude," put the card away for mailing at the first opportunity, and tried to sleep before starting for Cape Columbia. He and the two Eskimos — Seegloo and Egingwah — who occupied his igloo were restless despite their fatigue, however, and they could not sleep. Peary arose, and he found three men in the other igloo also awake. He instructed the men to hitch up; perhaps, he thought, they could reach the last camp, which was thirty miles away, before sleeping.

"It seemed unwise," he said, "to waste such perfect traveling weather tossing about on the sleeping platforms of our igloos."

About 4:00 P.M. (Cape Columbia time) April 7th they started south. Peary looked backward one time; then he did not look again.[67]

"I left it," he said, "with . . . that tinge of sadness that sometimes flashes over one at the thought, 'This scene my eyes will never see again'."[68]

During Peary's race back for land, his arduous upward journey, his age, and the strain told on him, and he apparently rode frequently: "After the first two marches back," Henson said later, "[Peary] was practically a dead weight, but do not think that we could have gotten back without him, for . . . he was still the heart and head of the party." [69] The fatigue on Peary's lined face, now covered by an inch-long beard, was accentuated by a pair of inflamed eyes.

Furthermore, Peary continued to be plagued by mishaps and by doubts. He lost a large portion of his sounding wire five miles from the Pole after reeling it out to fifteen hundred fathoms and finding no bottom. He worried about leads of open water ahead, about gales, about keeping the previously broken trail. He fell ill with a severe attack of quinsy.

Still, he had his success. When he and his men returned to the camp where Bartlett turned back he wrote in his diary:

. . . From here to the Pole and back has been a glorious sprint, with a savage finish. Its results [are] due to hard work, little sleep, much experience, first-class equipment, and good fortune as regards weather and open water.[70]

For a change the good fortune held. Leads posed a minor problem, gales held off, and they were able to follow the trail to within fifty miles of land. Shortly before midnight on April 22nd they reached firm ice of the Grant Land glacial fringe, and the four Eskimos shrieked and danced with delight. Peary later recalled that Ootah flopped on his sledge and exclaimed, in Eskimo, "The devil is asleep or having trouble with his wife or we should never have come back so easily." [71]

The following day Peary relaxed in a snow igloo at Crane City, with the sea ice and all of its perils behind him, and he wrote:

My life work is accomplished. The thing which it was intended from the beginning that I should do, the thing which I believed could be done, and that I could do, I have done. I have got the North Pole out of my system. After twenty-three years of effort, hard work, disappointments, hardships, privations, more or less suffering, and some risks. I have won the last great geographical prize, the North Pole, for the credit of the United States, the service to which I belong, myself, and my family. My work is the finish, the cap and climax of three hundred years of effort, loss of life, and expenditure of millions, by some of the best men of the civilized nations of the world; and it has been accomplished with a clean-cut dash, spirit, and I believe thoroughness, characteristically American. I am content.[72]

For two days he and his five companions tarried at Crane City, sleeping and eating. There Peary thought over the recognition and honors he felt were now due him. Several notes in his North Pole diary suggested a variety of possibilities: "Present sextant and horizon to the Navy Museum" — "Have my North Pole eyeglasses gold mounted for constant use. Have extra pair ditto as a present to someone?" — ". . . monument for mausoleum? Faced with marble or granite, statue with flag on top; lighted room at base for two sarcophagi? Bronze figures, Eskimo, dog, bear, musk ox, walrus, etc. etc. Or bronze tablet of flag on North Pole and suitable inscription. Bust." [73]

After their brief period of recuperation they hurried on to the *Roosevelt*, where they arrived April 26th, only two days after Bartlett. There Peary learned of the death of Ross Marvin, who had, said his Eskimos, broken through young ice of the treacherous Big Lead on the return journey. "The news staggered me," Peary remarked, "killing all the joy I had felt at the sight of the ship and her captain." [74]

Even his sleep was troubled. "For nearly a month after my return," he wrote, "as soon as I feel asleep I was on the ice picking a trail, or seeking a way across a lead. Marvin's fate emphasized very clearly the risks that we had all been exposed to. Nearly everyone of the party was into the water more or less completely." [75]

Late in July the *Roosevelt* began nudging her way southward. On August 8th, at Cape Chalon on the Greenland coast, Peary first came into contact with natives on his return journey and heard that Dr. Cook had returned to Greenland. That night Peary wrote:

> Learned Cook returned this spring, on foot, no dogs; had been south to Jones Sound. He went to Upernavik with Koo-loohngwah, Etookashoo,[76] and Pewahto, before my two men Panikpah and Poodloonah [who had been sent back from the sea ice because of "nerves" and "cold feet"] came down.[77]

At Etah Peary heard more talk of Dr. Cook: that he had told the Eskimos he had been to the North Pole. Peary instructed his assistants to question the two Eskimos, Etookashoo and Ahpe-lah,[78] who had been with Cook. George Borup wrote up the interviews: Etookashoo, he reported, "states that Cook said he went a long way [on the sea ice] but that he lied. They went for a short distance and made poor progress." Ahpelah corroborated this, declaring that they were never out of sight of land and that Cook was a poor traveler over the ice.[79] Both Eskimos said that instead of proceeding a great distance northward they turned southwestward from the northern end of Axel Heiberg Island, circled around to North Devon Island, and wintered there, at Cape Sparbo; Ahpelah pointed out this place on a map.[80] In the spring they crossed over to Ellesmere Island and followed the coastline north to Cape Sabine, from where they returned, over the ice of Smith Sound, to Annoatok. They arrived without sledges or dogs.[81] Both Eskimos gave as the reason for staying with Cook the expectation of receiving rewards he had promised them.[82]

If Peary had any desire to rush back to civilization to satisfy his curiosity regarding Cook's actions there, he stifled it. Instead, he conducted his usual walrus hunt, to provide a winter meat supply for the Eskimos.[83] Then he took the *Roosevelt* southward, and at Indian Harbor, Labrador, he and Bartlett went ashore to the tiny telegraph station, the first one they came upon. Peary wired his wife, "Have made good at last. . . ."[84] Then he turned to Bartlett and asked, "Where's your telegram to your mother?" Surprised, Bartlett produced the message; he had not expected to get it off "for some time."[85] Peary then sent his other messages, to news media and to his backers, including an often-repeated one in language so typical of him: "Stars and Stripes nailed to the Pole."[86]

When his year's accumulation of mail was delivered Peary read a letter from Jo, written six weeks before he sent his exultant telegram from Indian Harbor:

> If you have succeeded then you are happy and nothing will matter to you, but if you have not, oh, my dearest, . . . try to content yourself with us. We will try our best to make up in a measure for your disappointment. . . . My nerves are all gone. You must, *you must come home*. . . .[87]

Now Peary was coming home, successful at last. The man who as a boy had become enthralled with the Arctic after reading Dr. Kane's accounts, who as a youth had yearned for fame, who as a young man had compared Columbus's landing at San Salvador with the attainment of the North Pole, and who as an experienced explorer had not been satisfied with less than reaching 90 degrees north latitude — this man had finally reached his goal.

A poem composed in Peary's honor by Richard Le Gallienne eleven years earlier had foreseen this. No matter how the lines might be judged on literary merit, they had the ring of truth:

> . . . I care not much that Peary find the Pole!
> And perhaps the wish were kind

He ne'er may find
What with its finding
Means a dream at end,
For whoso finds a dream,
Strange though it seem,
Must lose it as he finds —
'Tis so with dreams.[88]

Part V

AFTERMATH

Cook controversy

Aviation and military preparedness

Death

Chapter 12

WHEN ROBERT PEARY returned to civilization he was caught in a frenzy of excitement over the attainment of the North Pole after four centuries of human effort, including twenty-three years of his own toil. To his shocked disbelief, however, he found that this triumph was not credited to him. The glory belonged to his affable former surgeon, Dr. Frederick A. Cook, who had telegraphed his claim of attainment from Lerwick, in the Shetland Islands, five days before Peary had reached the wireless station at Indian Harbor. Cook had been en route from Greenland to Copenhagen at that time, and upon his arrival at Copenhagen Cook was given a tumultuous welcome. On the following day he was received by the king.

Not until this moment did Peary vent his supreme fury on Cook. In several telegrams to news media Peary pronounced Cook a liar, basing his statement on what Cook's own Eskimos had said — that they had never been out of sight of land. Cook replied that he had asked his Eskimos to keep his trip secret.

The reaction of American newspaper readers was an almost universal denunciation of Peary, whose unfairness appeared to be despotic. This attitude dismayed, then enfuriated Peary, who could not understand how his fellow citizens could stumble to such gullibility, even though he realized that the mass level of Arctic knowledge was extremely low. "I know what I know," [1] Peary reiterated, but his arrogant manner and his fierceness only further antagonized the public and, in fact, surprised his friends. Cook, on the other hand, was a mild, friendly man — almost self-effacing — whose sportsmanlike attitude under the circumstances was remarkable, his public reflected. From Copenhagen Cook was quoted in various newspaper accounts as being delighted that Peary had reached the North Pole, because Cook said, "Two records are better than one."

"Cook was a liar and a gentleman," remarked an explorer of later renown, Peter Freuchen. "Peary was neither." [2]

Furthermore, Peary's previous bluntness had already alienated a good many persons: General Greely, because Peary had been quoted as saying Greely's lack of leadership and enterprise in searching for game at Cape Sabine had caused the deaths of some of his men; explorer Otto Sverdrup, at least partly because Peary had regarded him as a poacher and had refused to stop in Sverdrup's Arctic camp for a cup of coffee; Dr. Thomas Dedrick and certain other disgruntled members of Peary's past expeditions, for a variety of reasons. Now these individuals and others joined happily in hailing Frederick Cook as the "discoverer" of the North Pole. The availability of Cook's proof was of minor importance to them — and certainly to the public, which was generally unaware of the rumors of Cook's Mount McKinley hoax. Later some of these persons, notably General Greely, repudiated Cook, but their antipathy toward Peary remained.

Typical was a poll of newspaper readers in Pittsburgh. Of those who voted, 73,238 favored Cook as the victor in the polar controversy; only 2814 sided with Peary. All 2814 Peary advocates expressed disbelief, of course, that Cook had reached the Pole; and of the others 58,009 did not believe Peary. Commented the editor, ". . . The curious thing about it is that 58,009 persons should believe that Peary did not reach the Pole merely because he had treated ungraciously a man who was trying to rob him of his glory. . . ." [3]

The abuse poured in upon Peary. When he released for newspaper use a story of his interview with Cook's Eskimos and a map showing their plotting of Cook's route he received the following letter — reprinted with its original errors — along with hundreds of others like it, many of them unsigned.

Those who read today your "Cook Proof" with map — and I have met scores of men and all of them, but one — denounce you as a man not capable of giving the truth, and not one will believe you ever reached the goal — the North Pole.

And I heard many of them call you a "s of a b" and a "b" and I approved it.

Your selfish motives . . . has cost you 95 per cent of your former admirers, and I was one of them. . . .

Dr. F. A. Cook is the only man who ever reached the fartherest [sic] north.

No one will believe you did; not even Mrs. Peary — though she will endorse you. The world however has little respect for her.

Neither of you two are worthy the respect of the American reading public.

All agree with me — and there are few better known.

I remain without any respect for you.

A. D. Reader[4]

Even the membership of the National Geographic Society, which had helped sponsor Peary's 1908–1909 expedition, had been largely antagonized. When the society solicited contributions, over the signature of Peary and others, for an Antarctic expedition response was disappointing: "For every letter we received containing a subscription we received one abusing our friend Peary," said Henry Gannett, president, "and refusing to have anything to do with the expedition because he was associated with it. . . . Of course Peary must never hear of this matter. for he would break his heart." [5]

Peary had already heard enough from other sources, however, and he withdrew to his home on Eagle Island. There he remained for several months, refusing to make appearances and refraining from further public comment on Cook. None of his actions seemed to placate his fellow Americans, however; for some of them now grumbled that Peary was "sulking in his tent like Achilles." [6] A few of his friends urged him to come out and fight some more; others advised him to let Cook talk and incriminate himself. Thomas Hubbard, Peary's most trusted adviser, urged Peary, "Let him alone," [7] reasoning that debate with Cook would only appear ridiculous. This advice Peary followed, but he had still another reason of his own: "I do not care to lecture and tell the real story of the discovery of the North Pole for terms that are entirely insignificant in comparison with those that have been paid the sordid imposter for a fake story." [8]

Privately, Peary indulged himself in abundant emotion. To an English geographer he wrote:

. . . I have put my life into the effort to accomplish something which seemed to me a thing worth doing, and because it had the great attraction of being a clean, manly proposition.

I pulled the thing off finally, and then have the whole matter soiled and smirched by a cowardly cur of a sordid imposter; am blackguarded by my own people because I attempt to warn them and keep them from making damned fools of themselves. . . . [9]

". . . My feeling at present," he said on a later occasion, "is that I never want to hear anything more in regard to Arctic or Antarctic explorations." Then, as he had in his younger days, he qualified his emotional outburst: "Perhaps this feeling may wear off." [10]

To his old shipmaster, Bob Bartlett, Peary sent this gloomy

thought in admonition of Bartlett's tentative plan to lead an expedition of his own toward the South Pole:

. . . Frankly I do not think there is one chance in a hundred of your success at present, as I believe that your efforts are premature.

The country is still sick of Arctic and Antarctic matters and discussions; more than this Scott is down there with everything in his favor, and most people will hardly care to go into a thing which they think he is likely to accomplish.

. . . Your plan is first rate but, my boy, you must prepare yourself for numerous and continuous disappointments before you get the money, and you must make up your mind that you are doing the thing solely for the satisfaction of doing it, because if you go and win and come back you will get nothing for it, from the people of this country at least.[11]

At the annual dinner of the Ends of the Earth Club in New York Peary read with particular interest this quotation from James Russell Lowell, which was printed on the menu:

> And disappointment's dry and bitter root,
> Envy's harsh berries, and the choking pool
> Of the world's scorn, are the right mother-milk
> To the tough hearts that pioneer their kind,
> And break a pathway to those unknown realms
> That in the earth's broad shadow lie enthralled.

With a pencil he encircled the quotation, folded and pocketed the menu, and kept it with his memorabilia.

Peary was absolutely incapable of regarding the polar controversy with any emotion other than rage. He would not permit any jesting about it in his presence. While Cook, with engaging benevolence, was offering to share honors of attainment, Peary was refusing to be associated in any way with Cook, and most emphatically not on the lecture platform or in other public appearances.

Once, after accepting an invitation to the annual dinner of the Washington, D.C., Gridiron Club, Peary canceled after having been warned by his foreseeing friend Bill Reick of the New York *Times* that Cook, also invited, had accepted too.[12] The invariable barbs certain to have been tossed by fun-loving members would have been brutal to Peary, although Cook could have survived handsomely — as had already been shown.

Backers of Peary were eager to have Cook submit his proof, but Cook delayed, offering as one excuse that he had left his navigation instruments in Greenland, after his return from the polar journey, with the sportsman Harry Whitney, and that Peary had not allowed Whitney to bring the equipment back aboard the *Roosevelt*. Later, however, Cook agreed to submit his observations to a committee of authorities appointed by the University of Copenhagen, but he asked for a month or two to get them in shape. Peary, at his Eagle Island residence, heard of this development and seethed again, but he said nothing publicly. Privately, he observed in a letter to Herbert Bridgman that if Cook indeed had any observations at all he did not need two months, or even one month to get them in shape for examination. Peary added, "If I make the statement it will be simply a continuance of the jealous blackguard abusing the perfect gentleman." [13]

Finally, when Cook delivered his evidence to Copenhagen, the committee ruled against him, announcing that the only material received consisted of a typewritten report of Cook's journey to the North Pole and a typewritten copy of notebooks comprising the period from March 18th, 1908, to June 3rd, 1908. The report of Cook's journey to the Pole, sixty-one folio pages in length, was similar to the story that had appeared in the New York *Herald*. The typewritten copy of the notebooks contained no original astronomical material whatever, only results. There was no accompanying letter from Cook, who had disappeared, apparently having gone into seclusion. The committee reasoned that this was insufficient proof,[14] and the members did not change their minds later when letters from Cook and his original notebooks arrived.

Still Cook retained a large following, including many underdoglovers who seemed to be attracted to him by his defeats. Three days after the Copenhagen decision was announced, the Explorers Club of New York dropped "the name of Dr. Cook . . . from the rolls of the club" for failure to supply a committee investigating Cook's Mount McKinley claim "with the data promised, or any other data, ignoring the committee's further request made six weeks later." [15] Fourteen years later, in 1923, Cook was to suffer a still greater defeat, this time in a Fort Worth, Texas, courtroom, where he was sentenced to more than fourteen years in the penitentiary for mail fraud in connection with an oil promotion.[16] Cook was to die, however, without retracting his polar claim, and for the rest of his life he maintained that his troubles were caused by the Peary faction hounding him.

Peary himself, for the rest of his life, was hounded by the enemies he made during the ridiculous controversy that had been forced on him — and by several former expedition members who had been antagonized for one reason or another, by Peary's treatment. Had there been no controversy and no demands by Peary adherents for Cook to produce his proof of attainment, the pressure on Peary for positive authentication of his own claim would not have been so great, nor would the doubt of its finality, after it had been provided, have been so widespread.

For a time during the controversy Peary himself refused to produce his own records for study, even by experts, reasoning that Dr. Cook might somehow obtain the information they contained and use it to fake data in his own behalf. Eventually he did deliver his records and instruments to an examining "subcommittee on research" appointed by the National Geographic Society, and the three-man group decided in Peary's favor. Many people distrusted this verdict, however, because the society had helped sponsor Peary's 1908–1909 expedition. Nevertheless the committee members were authorities of commanding stature: chairman was Henry Gannett, geographer of the United States Geological Survey, and the other two members were Admiral Colby M. Chester, one of the foremost navigators in the United States Navy, and O. H. Tittmann, from the Coast and Geodetic Survey.

Later the Royal Geographical Society of London was to scrutinize Peary's records, after having already awarded him a special gold medal for reaching the North Pole, and reported to him that their opinion of his success remained unchanged.[17]

Another examination of Peary's records was conducted by two computers with the Coast and Geodetic Survey: Hugh C. Mitchell, a mathematical analyst who later was to evaluate similar data for Richard Byrd, and Charles R. Duvall. They undertook the work at Peary's request, and they were paid by Peary.[18] Their examination was intensive, and they both agreed that Peary "probably passed within one and six-tenths geographic miles of the North Pole, and when we consider that the errors of position may have amounted to as much as two miles, and that the chances are even for these errors being in any one direction as in another, it is possible that the march of the forenoon of April 7th, 1909, carried Peary within a stone's throw . . ."[19]

Less formal investigations also upheld Peary. One was conducted by the Danish explorer and anthropologist Dr. Knud Rasmussen, who had been a passenger on the same ship that brought Cook from Greenland to Copenhagen. Rasmussen had sponsored Cook at first; then, after he had seen Cook's observations as submitted to the University of Copenhagen, he had abandoned his position. "I realized it was a scandal," Rasmussen said of Cook's data. ". . . The papers which Cook sent to Copenhagen are most impudent." [20] Later Rasmussen, part Eskimo himself, talked with Cook's Eskimos and corroborated Peary's statements based on their testimony — the "never out of sight of land" declarations that Cook explained as being a temporary cover story for his actual accomplishment. Rasmussen also talked with Peary's own Eskimos, Egingwah and Ooqueah, and quoted them in substantiation of Peary's story. Describing the journey beyond the Big Lead, they said, as Rasmussen recorded the interview:

The weather was fine during the entire journey; only three days journey from land we were detained by open water.

After safely having crossed this, we were not detained during the whole journey. The ice was excellent; only now and then we came across pack ice, where we had to cut our way. Our way was at a straight angle to the packing of the ice. After leaving Captain Bartlett we made five day's journey; before we left Bartlett, Peary had taken several observations. Now as we were alone he took observations more frequently than ever.

We had sufficient provisions for men and dogs when Peary stopped; we were now so far to the north that the sun, even during the night, stood high in the sky, moving in a circle without rising or setting.

After Peary had ordered the stop, he continued from this place together with two men, and returned the same day, making the journey forward and backward without stopping.

"At last," said Peary to us, "I have obtained what I wanted."

In this place we slept two nights, Peary being much occupied with observations; the last night Peary did not sleep at all.

On the way home we had again fine weather without fog. How much distance we covered in a day's journey going out and coming back we do not know, as it was even and easy ice we had to drive on, and on account of this, each day-journey [was] long. On the entire way home we stopped only one day, and that was when we had reached land.

. . . At the North Pole we did not notice any joy on the part of Peary; after his arrival on ship he prepared a fete for the Americans and for us Greenlanders.[21]

Whether or not this testimony from unschooled natives impressed the masses, it was an effective argument to those few persons who knew the Eskimos. Explorer Vilhjalmur Stefansson commented, ". . . There are two things I know about Eskimo character — they seldom lie, and they never keep a secret, no matter how solemnly they promise to do so. Keeping a thing secret is in fact the deadliest sin of which the Eskimo knows — this is true of those Eskimos I know, for they generally attribute famine, epidemics, etc., to some member of their tribe having kept something of importance secret." [22]

In Congress less weight was accorded this Eskimo talk. There Peary's influential backers — and, though not openly, Peary himself — were working at getting through the House of Representatives a bill recognizing Peary's attainment of the North Pole — by retiring him as a rear admiral effective April 6th, 1909, the day he reached the Pole. The Senate had already passed a similar measure, but in the House an outspoken minority opposed the campaign either because they favored Cook or because they shared the attitude of line officers in the naval establishment.

In hearings on the bill, Peary was subjected to numerous indignities. Early in January, 1911, a group of representatives grilled him about his polar journey, about his records, and about a number of subjects on which they seemed to be entirely ignorant. The questioning was recorded in the *Congressional Record,* beginning here with a query by Representative R. B. Macon of Arkansas, whom Peary later claimed, in a letter to a friend, was acting in the interest of Navy line officers.[23]

Mr. Macon. Did you find any evidence of increase or diminution of weight at the Pole?

Peary. I did not, except the weight of the members of the party and the dogs.

Mr. Macon. I mean changes of weight except for lack of foodstuffs.

Peary. I beg your pardon?

Mr. Macon. Did they change except for lack of foodstuffs?

Peary. Not that I noticed. No.

Mr. Macon. Did the needle answer to the primary or the secondary magnetic pole?

Peary. The direction of the compass was fairly constant there.

Mr. Butler. Will you tell me, please, what that means?

Mr. Macon. I asked him whether the needle answered to the primary or secondary magnetic pole.

Mr. Butler. What are they?

Mr. Macon. Oh, they're known in science.

Mr. Bates. Where did you find that question?

Mr. Macon. They are known in science.

Mr. Bates. But I'm not a scientific person.

Mr. Dawson. I would be glad if the gentleman from Arkansas would explain.

Mr. Macon. The gentleman from Arkansas is going to ask questions and he is not going to ask any foolish ones, either.

Mr. Englebright. Is he trying to test [Peary's] knowledge on science by asking such questions — ridiculous questions?

Mr. Macon. I have asked no ridiculous questions.

Mr. Englebright. Did you ever hear of a primary or secondary magnetic pole?

Mr. Macon. Yes, I have.

Mr. Englebright. Where? In Arkansas?

Mr. Macon. Where I have heard of anything else. No; in Washington. And I want to say to the gentleman from California if he intends it as a slur in regard to Arkansas then it's unworthy of him.

Mr. Englebright. I withdraw the remark.

Mr. Macon. I want it understood that Arkansas is the equal of California in everything in the world except a little gold in the earth and a few hungry fellows for an exposition.

Mr. Butler. I will ask the members of the subcommittee not to further interrupt you.

Mr. Macon. I am advised by a school of scientists that it is a physical impossibility for man or beast to reach the North Pole for the reason that the diminishing centrifugal action — Did you ever heard of that?

Mr. Butler. I never did. I've heard of dogs and sledges though.

Mr. Macon. — For the reason that the diminishing centrifugal, and in proportion the increasing center of gravity near the Pole, causes a complete failure of man and animal energy that produces a kind of paralysis of the senses and of motion. A paralysis of sensation in any part of the body, including the exercise of the faculty of the mind. Do you know anything about that contention on the part of scientists?

Mr. Butler. That is an indication of lunacy, is it not, or feeble-mindedness, or a combination of the solids and fluids?

Mr. Macon [continuing]. — So that it would be almost impossible for them to exercise their independent functions so that anybody could ascertain a real fact — intelligently ascertain a fact.

Mr. Butler. What was your observation?

Peary. I've never heard of the matter.

Mr. Butler. You never did?

Peary. I never heard of the subject matter of the question.

Mr. Macon. You never heard of that before?

Peary. Never heard of it before.

Mr. Butler. Never heard of the theory?

Peary. And I have not noticed any such condition or effect or circumstance.

Mr. Butler. On either man or dog?

Peary. On any member of my party or dogs.

Mr. Macon. You remember, I reckon, to have read when you were a school child about the inhuman drubbings that had to be given to Arctic travelers to keep them from falling asleep, have you not? — When their energies would be so dissipated that they could not exercise them?

Peary. I have read of that kind of treatment being given to men who were on the point of succumbing to the effect of cold in order to keep them moving, but I never saw the thing — never had the experience on any of my own expeditions.

Mr. Macon. Then it did not affect your party that way? You were in as cold a latitude as the other explorers?

Peary. I have seen the thermometer 73½ degrees below zero.

Mr. Macon. And it did not have that effect on you or on anybody with you?

Peary. It did not. . . .

With persistent effort Peary publicly masked his emotion at being subjected to this additional harassment, but to his friend Thomas Hubbard he wrote, "God knows the winning of the Pole that day was less trying than this continued suspense, irritation, disgust, and fighting against cowardly and unseen enemies.[24]

Peary's wounds were further aggravated by Cook, to whom Peary often referred, icily, as "the perfect gentleman." Surprisingly, Cook now sent a letter supporting the Peary bill to the chairman of the House Committee on Naval Affairs, George Edmond Foss:

Dear Sir:

From various sources I am informed that my prior claim stands as a bar to Mr. Peary's demand for national honor. My object in writing you is to clear the way for Mr. Peary.

My claim of the attainment of the Pole is a personal one. I was not in the government pay; nor has the government or any private society advanced my cause in any way.

I ask for nothing. Within my own bosom there is the self-satisfying throb of success. In spite of unlimited funds to discredit me in a persistent campaign of infamy waged against me, that throb remains; it always will remain, and it is the only reward I expect.

Give Mr. Peary the honors — the retirement with increased pay. His long effort in a thankless task is worthy of such recognition. My reward will come with the reward that our children's children will give.

Very sincerely yours,
Frederick A. Cook.[25]

Finally, on March 3rd, 1911, the bill passed the House of Representatives by a large majority [26] Peary received the "Thanks of Congress" and retirement pay, as rear admiral, of $6500 annually. With the bitter campaign ended, Peary finally could see some small mirth in the situation, particularly in the reaction of certain old-time Navy men. "It would amuse you," he wrote Thomas Hubbard, "to see how some of the older line officers with whom I have had a speaking acquaintance for years fail to recognize me now when they meet me on the street." [27]

Elsewhere, recognition of Peary's North Pole feat had been bestowed more freely. This was particularly true in foreign countries where acceptance of Peary was more immediate and widespread than in his own nation. Toward the end of April, 1910, Peary and his family left on a European trip to visit London, Berlin, Rome, Vienna, Budapest, Saint Petersburg, Paris, Brussels, Antwerp, Dublin, and Edinburgh in response to invitations to receive awards or to lecture. In London he received the special gold medal of the Royal Geographical Society "not solely for the last journey of his in which he reached the Pole, but also for all the long years of toil and trouble which he has devoted to polar exploration." [28] Other awards followed: medals from the Geographical Society of Berlin, Italian Geographical Society, Royal

Imperial Austrian Geographical Society, Royal Hungarian Geographical Society, Royal Belgian Geographical Society, Royal Scottish Geographical Society, Paris Academy of Sports, Eastern Switzerland Geographical Society, and geographical societies of Marseilles, Geneva, and Paris. He was also presented the Legion of Honor by France, and honorary doctor of laws degrees from the University of Edinburgh in Scotland, Bowdoin, and Tufts.[29]

The travel was exciting, but Peary was most eager to enjoy his remaining summers at his Eagle Island home — he called it his "Promised Land" — the one place where he could invariably forget anxieties. From his secluded home he once wrote Gilbert Grosvenor of the National Geographic Society, at the peak of the Cook controversy:

> The quiet, undisturbed time which I am now having is very pleasant to me. It is particularly agreeable to have this opportunity after so many years of effort, of being with my wife and children in our little island home, with no thought of the future to disturb either of us, and with the feeling of intense satisfaction and content that results from having done the thing that one has started out to do, and has put one's whole life into.[30]

Now he was able to devote more time to Eagle Island. Each year he hastened there from his residence in Washington about the first of May and remained until the arrival of deep Maine winter, in November or December. On the island Peary lived the life he cherished: a freedom from society, and in the intimate company of nature. Once he was approached by a man who offered to provide him with an instantaneous link with the mainland, by laying a telephone line.

"What would it cost?" Peary inquired.

"Oh, about five thousand."

"I'd pay ten thousand any day to keep us free of telephones forever!" Peary answered sharply.[31]

A rapturous feeling warmed Peary whenever he tramped over his seventeen-acre island — along paths that cut through thick woods of spruce, maple, birch, oak, and fir; then out to wooded slopes overlooking a blue ocean, where was reflected a myriad of diamonds in the bright sunlight; and finally back to his spacious frame cottage, which faced the sea from a northern promontory.

Peary was especially proud of the house, a result of his own planning. He had begun constructing it in 1904, after his discouraging four-year expedition. Earlier he had not felt able to spare any money for building a home; but after his ordeal of 1898–1902 he had determined to waste no more time in preparing his "Promised Land."

The cottage reflected Peary's ingenuity. Dominating the living room was a giant stonework that seemed to divide that large room into two smaller spaces. Actually it was a chimney servicing three fireplaces arranged in a triangular form, to throw warmth across the room in three different directions. Each fireplace had a distinctive face, of white, brown, and black rock — all obtained on the island. Ornamenting the floors and walls were Peary's Arctic trophies, all tastefully arranged — polar maps, foxskins, mounted heads of bear, seal, musk ox. Next to the living room, and located so that it faced the Atlantic Ocean to the east, was a sunroom, where large glass windows afforded a spectacular view of the unchained sea. Elsewhere in the house were located a large dining room, kitchen, bathroom, and cozy sleeping apartments. Beyond the sunroom and stretching eastward to the heights overlooking the tossing waters was a broad piazza, which also extended, in smaller dimensions, around the house.

One other feature was distinctive: Peary had built beneath the piazza two turretlike rooms whose rounded exterior protuberances contrasted in shape but not in color with the jagged edges of the rocky cliffs below. Peary built these "bomb proofs," as he called them, of rock cut from the island, and from a distance these bastions blended into the dark cliffs. One "bomb proof" Peary used as an office; the other he made into a storeroom for his papers, trophies, instruments, and other gear. From each of these spaces easy flights of steps led upward to the piazza.

Visitors to Eagle Island found a warm, relaxed Peary — quite a different man from the reserved exclusive figure often seen elsewhere. There, where he was on his own ground and loved every foot of it, he was "the most companionable of men," as one visitor commented,[32] going about the island with almost boyish abandon. "To see Peary as I saw him last week," the same visitor continued, "is to understand the man. Tall, big of frame, he seems the very personification of American manhood. When he met me on landing . . . he wore a gray flannel shirt, dark trousers, and ordinary low shoes.

"No coat or vest hampered his movements, and he did not don them during the whole day. Dressed in this attire he immediately impressed me with the hugeness of his frame. Every inch of it from the great barrellike chest to the squarely planted feet indicated strength of body and character.

"When Peary smiles, he smiles with his whole countenance. His great reddish mustache seems to bristle with delight, his face wrinkles, eyes twinkle. As a companion, none better than Peary could be found, whether for a stroll or at the dinner table. He appreciates a joke and can tell one with effect.

"In the midst of fun, [however,] there may arise something of a serious nature — some allusion to the hardships of the North or some thrilling adventure. Then there is a change in Peary and one can see the stern commander, able to conquer the Arctic and achieve his ambition after years of work. This rapid change from smiles to sternness, a reflection of the talk going on about him, makes Peary most interesting." [33]

At Eagle Island, as nowhere else, Peary finally was able to enjoy the life of comfortable fame he had yearned for when a youth and a young adult, although it might have struck him now as being somewhat like his attainment of the North Pole: "all so simple and commonplace." Nevertheless, he relished it. From Charles and Company in New York he ordered cigars and fine wines for festive occasions; from Annapolis he obtained by mail tickets for the greatest sports event of the fall, the Army-Navy game; from the New Willard Hotel in Washington he was sent the chef's own instructions for preparing crab flakes, a favorite of Jo's, for use at Eagle Island.

Moreover, people had begun to seek him out, for a variety of reasons. Publishers wanted books and articles: Frederick Stokes gave him a fifteen-thousand-dollar advance[34] for a narrative of the North Pole journey — a book that Peary, pressed for time, paid to have ghost-written by A. E. Thomas — and it appeared with several unfortunate inconsistencies in the text.[35] *Hampton's* magazine promised Peary forty thousand dollars for a magazine series on the attainment and took out a short-term insurance policy on his life.[36] Still other magazines and newspapers offered to pay him well for articles; and his lectures brought considerable sums too — seventy-five hundred dollars for a talk at the New York Civic Forum, where Peary was introduced by Governor Charles Evans Hughes, and one thousand dollars, frequently, for other lectures.

A young publisher, Alfred Knopf, sought a statement from Peary for promotion in behalf of a British writer, Joseph Conrad.[37]

Others requested Peary to speak or to write on the qualities he valued in man, and he was always glad to answer on this. Once he replied to a college president: "I consider *persistence* and preparedness the essentials of success: Preparedness, to seize opportunity, preparedness to meet every contingency that can be thought of."[38] On another occasion he spoke of the value of experience: "The deciding factor in the winning of the Pole was experience. If it could have been won by inexperience and fortuitous circumstances, it would have been won long before. Nor could it have been won by courage or endurance alone. England would have won on that — and Italy, in 1900, by [the Duke of the] Abruzzi." [39]

He was even sought for a speech at the United States Naval Academy, a stronghold of line officers, and at the request of the midshipmen he spoke on his trip to the North Pole. The Academy superintendent was Peary's host during the visit.

Once he sat for a portrait bust, and the artist, William Couper, made an interesting comment on Peary's eyes: "They distinctively show the effect of bitter and intense cold which caused the upper lids to become strongly creased, and I also noticed a tendency to partly close them, which I imagined came greatly through the habit of squinting them — caused by the bright glare, the cutting winds, and intense cold." [40]

Toward the close of 1911 Peary's name was included among a distinguished list of Americans whom the New York *Times* asked for observations as to the five greatest achievements of that year. Peary wired his answer: "Passing in review the occurrences of the year 1911 as I recall them now, I should select the great advance in aviation, the improvements in wireless telegraphy, the enormous amount of work done on the Panama Canal, the revolution in China, the abrogation of the Russian Treaty, as five of the salient things which will mark the year in history." [41] Peary's choice of "the great advance in aviation" was significant, for Peary was to become a leading advocate of air power. In this he preceded even General "Billy" Mitchell, who did not make headlines for his espousal of air warfare until after the First World War — in the 1920's. Peary was to urge an air build-up a whole decade before that, and because of his interest in aviation he was to be elected an honorary member of the Aero Club of America on November 10th, 1913.

In 1912 Peary was a man particularly sought after for comment when the South Pole was reached. As it happened, confusion arose in this "discovery" also. Two men were after the South Pole: the Englishman Robert Scott and the Norwegian Roald Amundsen, whose venture into the Antarctic had come as something of a surprise, for he had announced plans for Arctic work.

On March 7th, 1912, Peary's newspaperman friend Bill Reick, who had been with the New York *Times,* wired Peary in behalf of the *Sun,* where he was then employed, a report that Amundsen had returned to civilization reporting that Scott had reached the South Pole before him. Reick based his dispatch on erroneous reports; but Peary telegraphed a reply that carried an unconscious premonition:

> Sincerely hope Scott's reported attainment South Pole is true. Scott deserves the fullest measure of success, and if he has won, he has my heartiest congratulations. Have always had faith that he would win in this last expedition; barring some entirely unforeseen and unavoidable catastrophe.[42]

Later, when other dispatches told of Amundsen's denial of seeing any sign of Scott at the South Pole, Peary wrote his friend Thomas Hubbard a letter reminiscent of his own situation of three years earlier: "I sincerely hope we shall hear soon that Scott got there, and got there first. That route was his, and he deserves to win the Prize. Whatever may be said, Amundsen's action in secretly entering Scott's field of work was not honorable. . . ."[43]

In the same letter Peary compared Amundsen's expedition with his own. Both Peary and Amundsen had been endowed with exceptional tenacity, and both looked after small details. Now Peary wrote:

> If you have had time and sufficient interest to read in detail the South Polar news, you have perhaps been struck by the various points of similarity between Amundsen's work in the South, and ours in the North.

Amundsen relied entirely for his tractive force on dogs, as we did.

Amundsen and his party appear to have been clad in furs, as we were.

Amundsen's instruments for determining his positions were a sextant and artificial horizon, as with us.

Amundsen's method of determining his ultimate position by a series of observations and by quartering the immediate vicinity was identical with ours.

Amundsen's temperature of nine degrees below zero Fahrenheit at the South Pole was comparable with ours of twelve degrees below at the North Pole.

Amundsen's speed on the return was something over twenty-four miles per day for thirty-nine days. Ours a little over twenty-six miles per day for sixteen days. This without any deductions for days they did not march, if any.

Points of difference are that Amundsen had a fixed surface, a smooth snow-covered surface; and with the exception of his climb from the surface of the ice barrier to the surface of the interior icecap, an essentially level surface over which to travel.

Amundsen traveled the latter part of his journey at elevations of 7,000 to 10,500 feet; our route throughout was at sea level.

Amundsen at the South Pole was on the surface of the interior snowcap, two miles above sea level; we at the North Pole had an ocean two miles or more in depth beneath our feet.[44]

Later, when Amundsen's South Pole attainment before Scott had been established and the details had been reported, Peary added his hearty congratulations. "Reading [Amundsen's] experiences has carried me back to my days in the Greenland icecap," Peary remarked. ". . . I am glad that Amundsen developed for himself a new and independent route the entire distance to the Pole."[45] When the National Geographic Society presented its gold medal to Amundsen, Peary served as toastmaster and made the actual presentation.

Then came the tragic news of Scott's death, after the Englishman had reached the South Pole January 18th, 1912, only to find
Amundsen had been there more than a month earlier. Scott and
his men, on their return from the South Pole, had been racing
against starvation when they were suddenly halted by a roaring
blizzard that lasted for days. Scott died on March 29th, but until
the last day he made diary entries that were remarkable for their
calmness — and poignance.

The Englishman's death naturally affected Peary deeply. Privately, he speculated that the tragedy stemmed from Scott's
finding Amundsen's records at the South Pole;[46] had Scott been
victorious, Peary reasoned, he would have survived. Perhaps this
feeling was somehow responsible for Peary's declining to review
the book *Scott's Last Expedition*, which utilized Scott's diary. Re-
plying to the request, which came from *The Bookman* of New
York, Peary offered as a substitute his eulogy of Scott released to
the press soon after the tragedy had become known.[47]

Thus was Peary sought out as an authority on many topics, and
another of his youthful desires had been fulfilled. On the subject
of exploration, at least, he had no superiors.

The rest of the decade following his retirement Peary devoted
to the sort of routine from which he had fled when a young man.
Now, in his later years, he found pleasure in much of this everyday life. There were, for instance, satisfying hours with the children. On Eagle Island he built for them a naturally heated swimming pool, constructing an ingenious system of retaining walls
near the beach so that the high tide filled an artificial basin, which
held the water for the sun to heat. Moreover, he devoted a good
deal of time to their education. He encouraged Marie to read
widely, and he studied with her. In literature, they would discuss
renowned writers, first reading a standard biography of each
writer, then reading his individual works.[48] His son Robert received similar attention: Peary spent hours encouraging the boy

with schoolwork — and on one occasion this help broadened to benefit many other youths besides his own son. One day while working with Robert on a study of the Arctic Peary noticed that the textbooks in use were badly outdated, and he instructed his secretary to write the publishers an offer to provide current textual matter and illustrations without charge.[49]

Other hours were less satisfying. He attended to correspondence which continued to be voluminous as long as he lived. He wrote to the Navy Department required routine letters, like notifications of address changes, and once, in a rough draft of a letter to the chief of the Bureau of Navigation, he delighted in crossing out the "Respectfully" preceding his signature.[50] He maintained a correspondence with his old friends and backers like former President Theodore Roosevelt, to whom he once wrote, "I know little and care less about politics";[51] then proved he supported issues and personalities, not parties, by writing another Roosevelt of a more liberal hue — Franklin, then assistant secretary of the Navy — "Though the Navy Department needs you, it has no right to keep you from a higher sphere." [52] He answered, with admirable patience, numerous ill-informed but sincere persons like the man in Florida who proposed eliminating winter by building a dam, with gates, across narrow Robeson Channel; this would allow the Arctic Ocean ice to flow out at high tide and block its return on the ebb, thus melting the ice and warming the Arctic region and, eventually, the whole earth.[53] Finally, Peary kept up a correspondence with numerous valued members of past expeditions, like Matthew Henson — who invariably used the salutation, "Dear Sir," when writing Peary — and Bob Bartlett.

Peary wrote a foreword for Henson's book, *A Negro Explorer at the North Pole*, then, without telling Henson, gave the publisher five hundred dollars for use in advertising the book[54] — this despite his feeling that Henson had broken faith with him by lecturing and writing on the polar journey and using photographs depicting it without Peary's specific approval, as called for in the contract.[55] Peary also wrote several job recommendations for Henson, although critics contended — and some still say — that Peary abandoned his manservant after 1909.

One outstanding characteristic of Peary was that he returned loyalty in full measure; he did not turn his back on persons who had stayed with him. If he impressed some strangers as being coldly aloof, he surprised others with warm thoughtfulness — as at the thirty-fifth reunion of his college graduating class.

Peary invited everyone in attendance to spend a day with him on Eagle Island, and at an elaborate dinner that evening he amazed them all.

One of his classmates, not a close friend, described it: "We found at each plate the class pictures taken at graduation, as placecards. This made a great impression on me. Here was a man whose work had literally taken him all over the world, yet when his classmates visited him he had their pictures, taken thirty-five years before, where he could easily get them. And yet they say he was cold." [56]

At another dinner Peary again displayed his competence as a host, but in a different way. In 1915, as the sixth anniversary of his polar feat neared, the Department of Commerce announced the purchase of Peary's expedition ship *Roosevelt* for government work in Alaska. Peary mused on the possibilities of some sort of dual commemoration and hit upon the idea of giving a dinner, on the evening of April 6th, 1915, at the New Willard Hotel in Washington, "in honor of [Secretary William C. Redfield's] purchase of my North Pole ship . . ." [57]

Peary was a man never really adverse to publicity, as long as it was favorable, and he invited several influential newspapermen along with government officials. He ended each invitation with the statement, "Sincerely trust you will not refuse me." [58]

Not many refused, and the dinner was an all-round success. Complete information on the guest list went to city editors of the Washington *Post* and the *Star;* it included cabinet members, senators, Department of Commerce officials, and newsmen. These guests were received by the two "most charming" Pearys, Jo and Marie, who seated them at tables where could easily be seen colored pictures thrown from a hidden stereopticon on an overhead ground-glass plate. The centerpiece was a model of the *Roosevelt* in winter quarters at Cape Sheridan.

Peary rose to address his guests after they had dined on such delicacies as tomatoes à la Russe, green turtle soup, crab meat à la Maryland, Smithfield ham glacé, spinach à l'Anglaise, Bermuda potatoes, new asparagus in sauce mousseline, boneless stuffed squab chicken, brandied peach savarin, and fancy cakes and coffee. He was to introduce other speakers, who were to talk on the future of Alaska, where the *Roosevelt* would be stationed. Before his introductions, however, he spoke briefly of the *Roosevelt* as it had figured in his own triumph; for this was, after all, Washington, from where Peary had written his mother thirty-four years earlier a plea for permission to go to Nicaragua in search of fame. At that time he had been dreaming of Balboa's first sighting the distant gleaming billows of the Pacific, and of the host of other explorers — Columbus, da Gama, Livingstone, and the rest "who have gazed first upon some glorious scene and felt the exultant thrill: It is mine. . . ." [59]

In his introductions Peary, who rarely spoke of the North Pole now, could not let the moment pass without a reference to his own discovery. Today was the sixth, he said — the sixth of April, the sixth anniversary of his reaching the North Pole. Six, he reflected, was his lucky number: he had been born on the sixth of May; the expedition on which he had reached the then-farthest north had left land on the sixth of March; the *Roosevelt* had sailed from

New York on her successful journey on the sixth of July; the wireless message about the Stars and Stripes being nailed to the Pole had gone out from Indian Harbor on the sixth of September.

Peary stopped there. He was not known as a religious man; and apparently not until he was reminded of it later did he observe that in Genesis it was recorded that on the sixth day the Creator made man, to "have dominion . . . over all the earth." [60]

Chapter 13

With the North Pole "out of his system" Peary needed something to fill the void — to give him an outlet for his energy. That new interest was aviation, which had aroused his explorer's curiosity several years earlier, soon after Orville Wright's underpublicized first flight in 1903. Not until 1908 did official interest become sufficient to risk awarding the Wright brothers a contract for constructing a biplane — for the United States Army Signal Corps — and Peary could regard the next year, 1909, as particularly momentous for both himself and aviation.

"The same year . . . ," he observed, "marks the closing of one great book of history, and the opening of another. One, the conquest of the North Pole, a four-hundred-year-old book with the last page written by the United States; the other, the great new book of the conquest of the air. . . ." [1]

In 1909, too, the Frenchman Louis Bleriot flew across the English Channel, and Peary's interest was further intensified. "I had a conference with the Wright brothers in Dayton," Peary said, "and realized my place was to help write part of the book of America's progress in the airplane industry. . . ." [2]

Little more than two years later Wilbur Wright died, and Peary wrote a tribute indicative of his intense feeling for aviation:

Wright was more than an inventor, more than a scientist. He was a conqueror and an explorer . . . for he has given to man a new kingdom and a new dominion, greater and grander than that of the earth itself — the kingdom of the air, sacred to God, the lightning, the winds, and the birds, but forbidden to man since the beginning.[3]

Until this time a popular axiom of military strategy had been, "He who commands the sea commands all," handed down from Themistocles, creator of Athenian naval policy, about 600 B.C. Now Peary foresaw a modification: "He who commands the air commands all." The maxim later was credited by many persons to General "Billy" Mitchell, the renowned early advocate of air power, but Peary had used it in speeches and on letterhead stationery at least a year before Mitchell.[4]

After war broke out in Europe in 1914 Peary increased the urgency of his warnings and set out on a Reverelike campaign around the country, pleading with his countrymen to prepare, especially in the air. Through the Aero Club of America, to which he was elected an honorary member in 1913, he called attention to the deficiency. In mid-1916 aerial defenses of the United States were said to rank behind England, Germany, France, Russia, Italy, Austria, Turkey, Bulgaria, Japan, Spain, Switzerland, and the Netherlands.[5] Now, with a passion reminiscent of his devotion to Arctic exploration, he called for rectification. On occasion he invoked resounding scriptural entreaties: "Awake, awake, put on strength," from Isaiah; "Gird ye on every man his sword," from Samuel; "Stand fast, and prepare thee; for the sword shall devour round about thee," from Jeremiah.[6] His pleas were not limited to increased air power, however, for he also urged an expansion of the Navy. In 1916 he remarked that the United States was the "only great two-ocean nation in the world," and that it should have a "two-ocean Navy" for adequate protection.[7] Not even the newly opened Panama Canal could provide passage quickly enough, he declared, to move a fleet from one ocean to another in case of attack.

Peary also proposed size and armament of ships. He suggested a squadron of fast battle cruisers, with fewer guns than battleships but with greater maneuverability and effectiveness. He was fond of comparing the nation to a swordsman: airplanes were the eyes, submarines the guard and parry, battle cruisers the deadly thrust. In advocating battle cruisers as opposed to battleships Peary's fervency was only slightly less than in his espousal of aviation: "I feel very strongly on the matter of battle cruisers," he wrote New York *Times* editor Carr Van Anda.[8] A Senate committee had just voted a reduction — to five — of proposed battle cruisers, and Peary was voicing his opposition to this action, which, he added, resulted from "a hasty interpretation of the North Sea Battle and the stampeding of the committee by the ultraconservative element of the Navy. This element believes nothing but a battleship is any good, and thus far has prevented the Navy's having any battle cruisers."

On another occasion he wrote:

Just as the Russo-Japanese War rang down the curtain on the battleship with primary, secondary, and tertiary batteries, and brought in the all-big gun ships, so this war is ringing down the curtain on the battleship of twenty-two and twenty-four knots, and bringing in the swift battle cruiser of thirty knots and over.

You doubtless recall the feeling of apprehension along the entire Atlantic Coast after [Spanish Admiral] Cervera's squadron started out [during the Spanish-American War] and before it was located.

Compare this with the feeling of security that would come from a fleet of the superb fighters in New York Harbor or Hampton Roads, able to reach any point between Havana and Halifax in twenty-four hours and to meet an enemy three hundred miles east of Bermuda in the same time.[9]

Peary of course invariably gave himself entirely to whatever major project attracted his attention, and this same devotion characterized his involvement in preparedness. In September of 1915 he suggested that he be given active duty "at sea or on shore" and offered to report immediately. "The experience gained in my twenty-three years of polar work is applicable to a winter campaign, particularly the trench warfare, and can be utilized to conserve the vitality and increase the efficiency of troops in the field in winter, in a marked degree." [10]

While Peary was thus urging the construction of a two-ocean navy and exhorting an immediate buildup of two defenses, air and sea, trouble developed on a third front: the old fight with Dr. Cook. For a time Peary was forced to retrench in his battle for preparedness and to shore up defenses against Cook, who had cultivated a few friendly ears in Congress with the deliberate or independent connivance of Peary's old foe, General Greely.

In the House of Representatives Congressman Henry T. Helgesen of North Dakota introduced a bill to repeal the act promoting and retiring Peary with the "Thanks of Congress." Greely supplied details for the arguments used,[11] such as the proven nonexistence of two Peary "discoveries" — The "Peary channel" of northeast Greenland and Crocker Land. Helgesen opened his bill with the words, "Whereas the various alleged Arctic discoveries claimed to have been made at certain times and on sundry expeditions by Civil Engineer Peary have been proven fictitious . . ." [12]

To help him in Congress Peary employed a lobbyist, Lucien Alexander, who had worked in Peary's behalf during the earlier legislative proceedings.[13] Again Peary said little publicly, even in the face of renewed attacks upon him, but privately he wrote memoranda, some apparently only for his own satisfaction; notes to Alexander, giving him pertinent information for use in lobbying against the bill; and an occasional personal letter on the subject. Some of Peary's penciled notes, most of them undated and untitled but in his handwriting, indicate the extent of the anger that again tormented him:

. . . You [Helgesen] have made under the protection of Congress immunity statements which show you to be either a liar or ignorant of the matter, or both. You are now challenged to formally charge to the secretary of the Navy that I did not reach the North Pole, and I will assure your having a court-martial ordered before which you will have an opportunity to make good your charges in responsible form under oath, and where there will be an opportunity to elicit the motives back of your campaign, the sources of your information, and the source of the funds which inspire your activities.[14]

[Greely's] record in the Arctic and his past judgments in regard to geographical matters are not such as to make one inclined to accept him as an authority.[15]

Congressman H[elgesen] is first a deliberate unmitigated and —— liar. He is second the mouthpiece and cat's-paw of a notorious lobby engaged in exploiting Congress for press-agent work in the interest of a vaudeville venture.[16]

Helgesen enjoyed scant success in Congress, and the "vaudeville venture" of Peary's reference failed. A lobbyist on the Cook side, E. C. Post, sued the doctor for $2787.02 nonpayment of money allegedly promised him to create a Washington atmosphere favorable to Cook — but as one newspaper editor commented, "Cook's lawyers say the atmosphere was not very good." [17] In 1917, as a result of counteraction by Peary's lobbyist and his friends, and more directly as a result of the growing fears of United States war involvement, Congress abandoned the renewed controversy. The intense emotion on both sides lingered, however, and the breach between Greely and Peary grew even wider. Contributing greatly to this new rift was a bitter exchange of letters, launched by Greely and publicly exposed in the columns of the Boston *Herald.* Greely, commenting on a *Herald* editorial, wrote the editor that giving Peary credit for establishing the insularity of Greenland was erroneous, and that Greely did not recall "Peary himself has ever claimed to have determined the insularity. . . ." [18] Someone clipped and mailed the letter to Peary, who fired back:

> . . . Insularity is defined as "the state of being an island" (*Century Dictionary*). My sledge journeys overland to Independence Bay and in 1900 round the northern end of Greenland (Cape Morris K. Jesup) and down the east coast determined the insularity of Greenland, as the *Herald* editorial stated.
>
> These expeditions located the northern limit of Greenland, and so reduced the extent of the unknown Greenland East Coast as to make any other conclusion than that Greenland is an island impossible. . . .
>
> The record of Arctic exploration does not show, and I am sure that General Greely himself will not claim, that he ever traversed a mile of Greenland coastline or ever led a serious sledge party in Greenland or elsewhere. [19]

After mailing his reply, long and vehement in its entirety, to the *Herald* Peary remarked, "I am too occupied with matters of present importance to engage in a controversy with G — G — [General Greely] on a subject in which the public is not interested." [20] Greely wrote another letter "to the editor" on the subject, but Peary apparently dropped it after that.

The "matters of present importance" Peary desired to devote himself to referred, of course, to his preparedness campaign. To enhance its effectiveness — and no doubt to further establish his name in American history — he briefly considered, in the summer of 1916, running for the United States Senate, after the death of a Maine senator, although Peary himself had always declared his lack of interest in politics. He discussed the possibility with his attorney and confidant in Portland, Charles Nichols, and the two decided on a course that was indicated later in a letter to Peary from Nichols:

I wrote an article advocating you as a candidate for senator from the state and took it to the [Portland] *Express* office this morning, but they would not publish it as news. They offered to publish the statement as news if it would come from you that would announce yourself as a candidate for senator, but I preferred [for it] to come that others are requesting you to seek the office rather than for you to announce yourself as a candidate.[21]

Two days later news leaked into the office of the *Express* editor that "some businessmen" [22] of Portland were suggesting Peary as a Republican candidate, and the editor queried Peary on his feelings. Peary answered:

I have your telegram asking if I will accept the nomination for U.S. Senator for the unexpired portion of Senator Burleigh's term, if tendered me.

Were your inquiry in regard to a full senatorial term of six years, I should decline without a moment's hesitation. I have no political ambitions.

But if the State of Maine should tender me the nomination for senator to fill the short unexpired term of my friend . . . I should accept with a deep sense of honor and responsibility, and a feeling that during the coming two years of active preparedness, the influence of the position combined with the strength of my desire to do my share, will enable me to be of service to Maine and to the nation. . . .[23]

Peary mapped out his campaign. He would come out "squarely" for national and state Republican platform, promise to work for every Maine project proposed in Washington, and support aeronautics generally.[24] A few days later, however, he faced reality: Nichols had warned him, ". . . You could not get the nomination for senator . . . without a fight . . . and if you announce yourself for a candidate over your own signature you will

have to come in for a fight. Is it worth it?" [25] Peary mused over
the question and decided it was not worth it — as he had done
many years earlier at Bowdoin College when he decided to settle
for second place in his graduating class rather than give up all
outside-of-class interests to try to win first place from a student he
knew to be outstanding — and a bookworm. Now he released a
statement to Maine newspapers: "It would be unwise for me without training to enter at a moment's notice an unaccustomed field,
in a contest against experts in that field, in thorough training and
with perfected organizations. With the developments of the last
two or three days also, my candidacy would mean running against
personal friends. I therefore request that my friends desist from
circulating any petitions for my nomination as senator at the coming special primaries." [26]

He turned his full attention again to preparedness, a subject on
which he spoke with more confidence. He also spoke considerably ahead of his time. In the First World War he foresaw the
utilization of military and naval tactics that were not developed
with adequate sophistication until the Second World War two
decades later. " 'He who commands the sea commands all' still
holds good," he said. "But it has a rival, the command of the air,
without which it is beginning to be valueless." [27] In a 1916 speech
he warned, "An attack upon us must come by sea. Our coastline
as a base gives us an inestimable advantage in aerial warfare, and
will enable us to send out such a veritable cloud of airplanes as
would completely overwhelm and destroy any number of airplanes that could be transported on the deck of a hostile fleet, thus
leaving us in the possession of our eyes and the enemy blinded.
. . . I would to God that I might have the power to transmit to
this audience the intensity of my feeling on the subject." [28]

Peary urged the creation of a Department of Aeronautics with
rank equal to the Navy and War departments: "Our air service is
now handled partly by the Army and partly by the Navy. This

manner — it cannot be called system — is inherently wrong. It means divided and dispersed responsibility. It means diversion of officers from the imperative work of their respective departments at this crucial time. It means that aeronautics is the last and least of the numerous duties devolving upon these officers. . . . While this immediate air preparedness is for a present military emergency, the money and effort expended on our air service will all count toward a great peace air service . . . the carrying of mails; the transportation of passengers and express material; the lifesaving patrol of our coasts. . . ." [29]

As the United States grew ever closer to involvement in the European war, an Aerial Coast Patrol was organized with Peary as chairman. The agency never was to become as large and as effective as Peary desired, but through its work three hundred trained aviators later became available for military service after the United States had entered the war.

With that entry, Peary became even more vehement in his campaign for a speedy military buildup. He criticized the absence of submarines — for defense practice — at the Pensacola base where naval aviators received training, and for the same reason he attacked the absence of airplanes at submarine bases. He denounced a decision to give up all United States claims to Greenland as part payment for the Danish West Indies (the Virgin Islands), observing that "stranger things have happened than that Greenland, in our hands, might furnish an important North Atlantic naval and aeronautical base" and that Greenland, in hostile hands, "could be a serious menace." [30] He lashed out at the people who had refused to listen to him and to other early advocates of preparedness:

Suppose we had begun two years ago, as we should [have] to get ready. . . . Suppose we had followed the almost frantic appeals for a great air fleet, and as a result had possessed when war was declared five thousand airplanes to throw into the scale, what would be the result? But, no, [we have had] procrastination, hesitation, indecision, failure to grasp the meaning, and as a result . . . if the Central Powers win it will be because the United States was too slow.[31]

Peary saved some of his plentiful invective for Secretary of War Newton Baker. On December 10th, 1917, Peary read a story in the Washington *Star* reporting a statement by Baker that the United States must speed its military preparations because of a serious German threat on the Western Front. Peary clipped and saved the article, and he penned a note to accompany it into posterity:

If this man B— from the time he took office had devoted the energies of the War Department to preparing for this country's participation in the struggle (which every intelligent and informed person has known was coming) instead of feeding us on pacifist slop, our soldiers would not now be drilling with broomsticks because the War Department has no rifles for them, nor dying by hundreds of pneumonia because the War Department has not sufficient wool for them, and it would not be necessary for him now to be shrieking to the country to speed up its war preparation.[32]

During the war itself Peary warned of impending U-boat attacks on the East Coast — and even of air attacks on American cities, an event so obviously unlikely in those years of wonderful isolation that people accused Peary of alienating friends of aviation with his exaggeration and sensationalism. Not even many European cities had suffered costly air attacks.

"How this airship nonsense does bring out the nuts!" exclaimed one senator after hearing Peary.[33]

Nevertheless, Peary reiterated his belief that, in the future, "He who commands the air commands all," and in a wartime speech before the Navy League in San Francisco he declared that command of the sea was worthless — impossible, in fact — without command of the air.[34]

If Peary still had doubters then, they vanished quickly with the passing years, and in the early period of the Second World War his prophecy was to be given an enduring stamp of verity, in an ironic way.

On February 19th, 1942, with Japanese air and naval forces on an inexorable advance in the Pacific, planes from Admiral Chuichi Nagumo's carrier fleet raided the Australian port of Darwin and sank a dozen ships caught in the harbor. Among the losses was the United States destroyer *Peary*, named for the civil engineer who had retired a rear admiral.

Chapter 14

ROBERT PEARY at the age of sixty was still an imposing figure. Washingtonians who saw him walking from his home at 1831 Wyoming Avenue toward the Army and Navy Club, where he got his mail daily, observed a lithe, lean, erect man who walked at a lively pace — a man apparently certain of where he was going and unwilling to use unnecessary time getting there.

His face was ruddy and lined, more red than bronze — a result still of that exposure to the bitterness of Arctic wind and sun. His gray handlebar mustache was long and thick, and it usually covered his upper teeth, even when he talked. His blue eyes still appeared veiled by that Arctic squint, but this was a bit deceptive, for Peary was described as "alert, dignified, responsive; his whole personality suggested nobility and a reserve power capable of rising to any height." [1]

Persons who did not know him well were impressed by his silence — a reticence — but when he spoke, his strong positive manner gave full indication of his aggressiveness: his sentences were quick and decided, with each ending clipped. Rarely, now, did he volunteer talk about the North Pole, but when he was asked about his Arctic work he replied in that precise manner of his: "Each time I was knocked onto the ropes," he said once, in response to such a question, "I knew more about the game than I did before I had suffered from defeat. That was experience." [2]

This strength, which had helped Peary endure countless bitter-cold disappointments during his career, was near a waning point. At the end of 1917 he noticed that exertion left him more tired than usual, and he complained of feeling unwell.[3] Doctors diagnosed his illness as pernicious anemia, which was not curable. Undaunted, Peary told his wife, "Jo, we have won many fights. We are going to win this one."[4] Then, with remarkable detachment, he began keeping daily records of his physical condition, as if these data were no more momentous than meteorological or tidal observations:

Monday, January 6th
    Blood examination
    R[ed] 3,010,000
    W[hite] 4,200
    Hem[oglobin] 65 per cent
Tuesday, January 7th
    Talk with [Dr. B.L.] Hardin 4:30 P.M. and physical exam.
    Blood pressure 145
    Heart, stomach, liver, spleen, pronounced
absolutely sound and normal. . . .
Wednesday, January 8th
    Tendency to nausea much of day. . . . Rapid pulse. Am turning in at 9:00 P.M.
    Awake till 11:00 P.M.
Thursday, January 9th
    Awoke early. Threatened nausea. Perspiration at breakfast.
Saturday, January 12th
    . . . Inspection of air station 11:00 to 12:00.
    Group photo 3:00 P.M.
    Distinctly tired feeling.
    Hypodermic injection 10:00 A.M.
    Supper. Mutton chops and baked beans.
    Bed at 8:30. Usual milk and tea 9:00 P.M.

Uncomfortable feeling disappears, but much annoyed by stinging sensation in left nostril preventing sleep till midnight. 11:00 P.M. two spells of rapid racing of heart.

Sunday, January 13th

Near vomiting just before breakfast.

Flush and perspiration after breakfast.

In April, following a blood transfusion, newspaper stories first told of Peary's illness. The New York *Times* reported, "Rear Admiral . . . Peary . . . is . . . greatly increased in strength and rapidly on the way to a full recovery. The malady which required the operation was pernicious anemia, which the admiral's physicians said would steadily reduce his physical strength and lead to death." [5] The *Times* meant to say, of course, that the transfusion, then called an operation, had corrected this condition, but their vagueness proved to be prophetic.

One of the first persons to call at the Peary residence was General Greely, who left his card, with this handwritten note: "Inquiries and best wishes for the admiral's recovery." [6]

At first Peary did indeed show signs of recovery. To get the rest his doctors prescribed for him he canceled all spring appearances, and for several weeks during May he even refrained from attending to his voluminous correspondence, which had become heavier than usual with letters from other anemia victims who hastened to send their own suggestions for treatment. To one such well-wisher Peary wrote details of his illness, and his letter exuded the same optimism that had kept him face-ahead against hardships in his Arctic exploration:

Have rec'd score or more letters from various parts of country from others suffering from anemia who have seen press notices regarding me. None more interesting than yours. Am inclined to feel particularly fortunate: . . . My physician caught me and sent me to bed with my red corpuscles at the two-million count and my coloring matter at 45 per cent. I responded at once to treatment in that I did not swing any lower, in fact made a slight gain. The ratio of gain was so slow, however, that transfusion was advised, not as a dernier resort but with a view to running me up on an elevator rather than compelling me to walk up. I have thus far had three transfusions of 250; 500; and 1100 c.c. at intervals of three weeks. My coloring matter is now 85 per cent and the blood count is 3,300,000. It is possible that I may try another transfusion in order to put me in the 4,000,- 000 class.

While I was on my back practically all the time for eight weeks it was for the purpose of reducing as much as possible any blood destructions from exercise and not because I was unable to get about. On each occasion of going to the hospital for transfusion I have dressed and walked down to my car, walked into the hospital, and returned in the same way at the end of twenty-four hours after the transfusion.

Searching physical examinations by independent doctors have shown that every organ is sound, healthy, and in smooth running order; my appetite is first class, and I sleep like a man who has worked hard all day. My blood pressure, the doctors tell me, is that of a man of forty, and of course all these things have been of the utmost value and assistance to me and the physicians. I have had none of the symptoms of which you speak except, in a slight degree, the abdominal numbness and incipient nausea. I am now up and going about the house freely and go out for an hour or so of each day. Within the past week three doctors independently have stated that I was over the top, out of the woods, every chance for a complete recovery. I have not at any time felt any apprehension in regard to my condition because I could not believe that a perfectly sound, smooth running machine could be put out of commission permanently because the steam pressure had run a bit low.[7]

In June Peary was gratified to learn that his count had gone up to 3,500,000, and he remarked confidently that he looked forward "to qualifying in the 4,000,000 class before long." With buoyant humor he added, "This refers to red blood corpuscles, not to dollars." [8]

By mid-July of 1918 the count was only 160,000 short of his goal; and on August 6th his medical report showed 4,200,000. The doctor appended a note: "Results are better than I hoped for — but you need to be cautious not to lose ground." [9]

Peary, in his diary jottings, was less optimistic and less jesting than he was in letters to his friends. His carefully penciled notes, probably recorded for the doctor's information but nevertheless typical of Peary's obsession with keeping a record of his daily activities, showed these terse notations in September: "Spells of small coughing apparently from stomach. Perspirations. Sudden brief uneasy feelings. Pain across forehead on rising suddenly. Palpitations. Diaphragm spasms preventing sleep until lie on side." [10]

In January of the following year, Peary made his last public appearance, with his old foe General Greely, at a National Geographic Society program honoring Vilhjalmur Stefansson for his Arctic work. After that Peary again turned down invitations, on doctors' orders. Sleeping became fitful; his general condition worsened. Pessimism was evident, as was Peary's remarkable objectivity, in a memorandum prepared for his doctor:

It occurs to me that the last report makes the following two assumptions permissible.

First, that my blood mill has fallen down completely, and that my brief encouraging upturn of last summer was simply the last flash of that physical reserve force which until now I have always had at my command.

Or — second, that our efforts are being neutralized by some hostile influence or condition. . . .[11]

Occasionally Peary read printed accounts reporting cures for pernicious anemia; hopefully he wrote those doctors who purportedly had discovered the cure, but in every case he was disappointed. His own doctors varied their treatment, and once they tried injections of protein over a long period, but nothing helped; not until 1926 was it first to become known that half a pound of liver daily would control the condition. Peary grew weaker as the disease continued its devastation, but he never really resigned himself to death, and on the tenth anniversary of his polar attainment — April 6th, 1919 — he again underrated his plight, publicly, when he told a Washington *Star* reporter, "I can hardly believe as I sit here in my home, surrounded by my family, that the hardships of the polar regions exist. It was hard, I remember, when we were on our way to the Pole, to imagine that there existed any place in the world so fair and quiet a place as home. I suppose that the boys in the trenches had much the same feeling." [12]

In the waning months Bartlett tried several times to make his old leader smile — once at a clipping from the Wichita Falls, Texas, *Times* that had been sent to Bartlett by a friend. It was an advertisement for the "Texas Eagle Oil Company," and it invited, in bold type: "Get Into A Sound Company." Bartlett scribbled a marginal note, "Here's a chance for you to get rich quick," and sent the item on to Peary, who read the text:

"Dr. Cook, the explorer, and a group of well known substantial men are behind this organization. . . . Deposit your money with us with the same confidence you have in your bank. . . . With the eyes of an eagle we have searched and with claws of an eagle we have gripped the oil fields of mid-Texas." [13] The stock sold for ten dollars a share; four years later Cook was to land in jail for similar oil promotions.

Peary's last summer in his "Promised Land," Eagle Island, came in 1919, but he was not able to tramp through the woods the way he used to, and the summer seemed fraudulent. In October he and his family closed their home there for the winter, to return to

Washington, and Robert Peary, Jr., made a parting remark reminiscent of his father of earlier years: "We stay in Washington every winter, but we really live on Eagle Island." [14]

In the Washington winter Peary grew still weaker, despite the transfusions. On February 13th he was given his thirty-fifth and final transfusion, at the Naval Hospital, and on the following day he returned home. Peary asked his doctors about his condition, and they told him he had one week to live. [15]

During that week, until the last few hours, he was alert and responsive, well able to talk. He called his Washington lawyer by telephone to make certain that his will, drawn in 1913, was in such shape that it would give Jo no difficulty. [16] He also summoned his son to the bedside to dictate a last memorandum; but before doing this he dispatched Jo and his daughter Marie, then married and expecting a second child, on a manufactured errand, to avoid any touch of the melodramatic.

To his son he said that he desired Eagle Island to remain in the family, that he wanted his son to keep his Arctic papers and trophies, that he wanted to give Marie one thousand dollars to buy an electric car she had been admiring — with this vehicle Marie could give her son excursions into the open air without having to push a baby carriage on slippery streets. Peary then sought to anticipate every matter of business his wife might encounter. He talked for two or three hours, and when his wife and daughter returned Peary was dozing. His son, hunched over a table, was resting his head on his arms. [17]

Near, now, was the time Jo had foreseen fifteen years earlier — on February 7th, 1905 — when she had written her husband, "I hope you will live to know that you have reached the Pole; then you will be content to die, whether anyone else knows it or not."

Those lines had been written when the finality of death had seemed remote. Now, with the vital minutes ebbing, such detachment was impossible; Jo was to write later, "Although we knew the end was near, yet we were unprepared when it came. But not he. . . ." [18]

She was also to write a revised estimate of her husband's polar discovery.

No one will ever know how the attack on my husband's veracity affected him, who had never had his word doubted in *any* thing at *any* time in his life. He could not believe it. And the personal grilling which he was obliged to undergo at the hands of Congress, while his scientific observations were examined and worked out, although it resulted in his complete vindication, hurt him more than all the hardships he endured in his sixteen years of research in the Arctic regions and did more toward the breaking down of his iron constitution than anything experienced in his explorations.[19]

Eleven years earlier Peary himself had commented on this same subject: "I wonder if you have ever happened to think," he said, "what a nightmare of misrepresentation, animosity, insult, and now of wrangling and haggling this has been since my return with the Pole." [20]

Such a tragedy was not lost on enlightened, sensitive persons. Commented an editor for *The Nation*, at the height of the controversy:

. . . Peary . . . has been defrauded of something which can never be restored to him.,. . . False as it has proved, [Cook's] claim has dimmed the luster of the true discoverer's achievement. He will receive the full acknowledgment that his work merits, in the form of recognition from scientific and other bodies and of a sure place in history; but the joy of the acclaim that should have greeted him at the triumphant close of his twenty-three years' quest can never be his.[21]

About noon of February 19th Peary became delirious and passed into a coma. At 1:20 A.M. Friday, February 20th, 1920, he died. Letters of condolence and tribute poured in from over the world, from General Greely, British explorer Ernest Shackleton, President and Mrs. Woodrow Wilson, Alexander Graham Bell, Fridtjof Nansen — from presidents, kings, geographers, and explorers.

The following Monday Peary was buried in Arlington National Cemetery. En route there, his casket was covered with the flag that Jo had made for him years before, the flag he had carried on all of his Arctic trips and from which he had cut a diagonal strip to leave at the North Pole. Those had been the days of suffering, of work, and of discovery for Peary — the days that, on occasion, he later voiced a yearning for, long after they were gone:

I can hear the eager yelping of the dogs, the shouting of the drivers, and the forward rush of every man and sledge, as after days of weary travel across the ragged sea ice, every man and dog spurts for the shore of that untrodden land lying a few yards ahead in the brilliant Arctic sunlight.[22]

Now, at Arlington, Navy seaplanes and Army aircraft flew over the cemetery. Navy riflemen saluted the Admiral. A Navy bugler sounded taps, and Peary began yet another journey into the unknown.

Notes

Notes

UNLESS OTHERWISE NOTED, all documentary material is from the Peary Papers, which were in the immediate possession of Robert Peary's daughter, Marie Peary Stafford of Brunswick, Maine, when the author was given access to them in 1962 and 1964.

CHAPTER 1

1. Penciled rough draft, dated August 16, 1880, of a letter Peary later copied and mailed to his mother, from Washington, D. C.
2. Genealogy can become wearisome, especially when it is someone else's. In a biography, however, it is expected. On the next page is Peary's genealogical chart, compiled from family records.
3. Statement by Marie Peary Stafford. Mrs. Stafford provided some information of a personal nature not recorded on paper but passed on orally in the Peary family. This information has been used when it meshes with the known facts, and the source has been cited.
4. After Peary became world famous a dispute over the place of his birth arose between residents of Gallitzin and Cresson. Family letters and official records have shown Peary's birthplace to have been Cresson — or, specifically, Washington township, out of which Cresson was created in 1893. After the dispute arose Peary himself always maintained that he was born in Cresson and that his parents had moved to Gallitzin later. Marie Peary Stafford has quoted her father as saying, "Mother said Cresson was my birthplace, and she should know."
5. Letter from Drs. Fitch and Sykes, Pittsburgh, to Charles M. Peary, dated January 21, 1859.
6. Clipping from an unidentified, undated newspaper, but obviously one from Cambria County, Pennsylvania, where Gallitzin is located. Date of Charles Peary's death is given therein as January 28, 1859. The clipping is in the Peary Papers.
7. A recollection of Marie Peary Stafford, to whom Peary mentioned this. The account of her father's boyhood as given here is based largely on

PEARY'S GENEALOGICAL CHART

STEPHEN PEARE
r. Porter, Me.

m. about 1798

JAMES R. PEARY
b. April 2, 1801
d. May 31, 1862
r. Parsonsfield, Me.

MARTHA BEACHAM
r. Parsonsfield and Porter

RICHARD BEACHAM ———— "LORD BEACHAM"

m. Oct. 5, 1825

CHARLES NUTTER PEARY
b. Jan. 1828
d. Jan. 1859

CHARLES NUTTER
b. Dec. 27, 1785, Portsmouth
d. May 1, 1845
r. Porter, Me.

HENRY NUTTER
r. Portsmouth

HENRY NUTTER

m.

ALMIRA NUTTER
b. Feb. 15, 1808
d. Aug. 3, 1887

MRS. OLIVE (TAYLOR) DURGIN
b. Jan. 9, 1778
d. Aug. 24, 1846

EBENEZER TAYLOR

ROBERT EDWIN PEARY
b. May 6, 1856
m. Aug. 11, 1888
d. Feb. 20, 1920

m.

BENJAMIN WILEY
b. Dec. 1775, Andover
d. June 28, 1872
r. Fryeburg, Me.

BENJAMIN WILEY
r. Andover and Fryeburg

WALTER BRYANT
b. Feb. 12, 1740
d. Oct. 2, 1784

WALTER BRYANT
b. Feb. 10, 1710, Great Island, Portsmouth Royal Land Surveyor
d. 1807

JAMES BRYANT
b. about 1660 in England settled at Great Island d. 1720

m.

HONOUR ———
b. Jan. 31, 1678
d. 1767

m. Nov. 17, 1762

ELIZABETH FOLSUM
b. Sept. 10, 1712

m.

MARY WILEY
b. 1827, Fryeburg, Me.
d. Nov. 4, 1900

m. May 4, 1805

WALTER BRYANT
b. July 16, 1765
d. 1856-7

MARY DOLE
b. July 21, 1788
d. Nov. 9, 1777

m.

(2) MARY DOLE BRYANT
b. Nov. 11, 1786, Newmarket
d. Jan. 15, 1849

HANNAH GOODWIN
of Newmarket

her recollections of Peary's own reminiscences, on letters from relatives, and on other material in the Peary Papers.

8. Statement by Marie Peary Stafford.
9. Statement by Marie Peary Stafford.
10. *Sunday School Advocate,* March 22, 1862. Mary Wiley Peary's signature appears on this copy.
11. This note, in pencil, is addressed, "Bertie."
12. Robert Peary to his mother, April 30, 1865.
13. Peary to his mother, February 28, 1868.
14. Peary to his mother, March 7, 1868.
15. Peary to his mother, March 21, 1868.
16. *Ibid.*
17. Peary diary, January 12 and 13, 1873.
18. Peary diary, January 3, 1871.
19. Peary diary, January 5, 1871.
20. Peary diary, April 14, 1871.
21. Olivia Ashley to Peary, July 16, 1871.
22. In Peary's diary for January, 1873.
23. Peary diary, January 13, 1873.
24. This essay, dated February 3, 1872, was titled, "My Studies."
25. From an undated essay, in Peary's handwriting, titled, "Self Reliance."
26. All from Peary's 1873 diary.
27. Peary diary, February 12, 1873.
28. From Peary's 1873 diary.

CHAPTER 2

1. Statement by Janette Wiley, Mary Peary's niece, to Marie Peary Stafford, in a letter dated March 23, 1932.
2. Peary diary, August 19, 1873.
3. Peary diary, March 25, 1875.
4. Peary to Mary Kilby, June 4, 1876.
5. Peary diary, October 17, 1873.
6. In a letter to Herbert L. Bridgman, July 2, 1920.
7. Peary diary, January 8, 1874.
8. George W. Tillson, of La Grange, Illinois, to Herbert L. Bridgman, June 28, 1920. Tillson was the last surviving member of Peary's civil engineering class at Bowdoin.
9. Peary to Mary Kilby, January 28, 1876.
10. Peary to Mary Kilby, May 16, 1875.
11. Peary diary, July 18, 1875.
12. Peary diary, October 31, 1875.
13. Peary to Mary Kilby, June 4, 1876.
14. *Ibid.*
15. Peary to Mary Kilby, September 17, 1876.

16. Peary diary, August 8, 1875.
17. Marie Peary Stafford, *Discoverer of the North Pole,* p. 20.
18. In a letter to Herbert L. Bridgman, June 28, 1920.
19. *Ibid.*
20. Peary to Mary Kilby, June 4, 1876.
21. Peary diary, July 18, 1875.
22. Peary diary, January 21, 1877.
23. Peary to Mary E. Wiley, a cousin, June 17, 1877.
24. Portland High School records show that a "Mary Kilby" was enrolled at the same time as Robert Peary, but in Peary's diaries of high school days he never referred to her by full name.
25. Peary to Mary Kilby, May 6, 1877.

CHAPTER 3

1. In a letter dated August 27, 1877.
2. Peary to Mary Kilby, June 12, 1878.
3. Peary to Mary E. Wiley, August 19, 1877.
4. *Ibid.*
5. In a letter to Mary Kilby, October 24, 1877.
6. Peary to Mary Kilby, October 17, 1877.
7. In a letter dated August 29, 1878.
8. Peary to Mary Kilby, October 10, 1877.
9. In a letter dated February 2, 1879.
10. In a rough draft of a letter, probably to Professor Vose, dated July 25, 1879.
11. Peary to his mother, September 21, 1879.
12. Peary to his mother, February 3, 1881.
13. Peary to his mother, November 2, 1879.
14. In the entry for December 31, 1879.
15. In a letter dated August 16, 1880.
16. On September 2, 1880.
17. On September 6, 1880.
18. From the rough draft of an unaddressed letter dated simply April to July, 1880.
19. From a draft, in Peary's handwriting, dated 1881; no other identification.
20. Peary diary, August 23, 1881.
21. Peary kept a rough draft of this note in his papers. One profile referred to was made from Jockey Cap, near Fryeburg, Maine. The same profile was used to make a mountain finder, which still stands atop Jockey Cap as a memorial to Peary.
22. Letter dated December 14, 1881.
23. Peary to his mother, November 18, 1880.
24. Peary to his mother, October 10, 1880.

CHAPTER 4

1. In a letter dated December 26, 1881.
2. December 17, 1881.
3. December 26, 1881.
4. Undated observations penned by Peary during the journey and saved by him.
5. From the diary for June, 1882.
6. In a letter dated June 14, 1882.
7. Quoted in Marie Peary Stafford, *Discoverer of the North Pole*, p. 45.
8. Peary to his mother, December 15, 1882.
9. In a letter dated October 1, 1882.
10. Penciled rough draft dated September 11, 1881.
11. The letter was completed and dated December 28, 1884.
12. Peary diary, February 4, 1885.
13. Peary diary, February 6, 1885.
14. A. G. Menocal, *Report of the U.S. Nicaraguan Surveying Party*, p. 14.

CHAPTER 5

1. From a typewritten text of Peary's speech, given at the Hotel Astor by the New York Lehigh Club in 1913.
2. This memorandum was found in the front of Peary's 1885 diary, as were the following ones.
3. In a letter dated April 14, 1886.
4. Peary to his mother, June 30, 1887.
5. From Peary's diary.
6. Peary diary, May 31, 1886.
7. *Ibid.*
8. From Peary's diary. In his book, *Northward over the "Great Ice"* (v. 1, p. 5), Peary said he was disembarked at Disco Bay on June 6, not June 7, as in his diary.
9. From Peary's diary.
10. Robert E. Peary, *Northward over the "Great Ice,"* v. 1, pp. xxxiii, xxxiv.
11. Peary, *Northward over the "Great Ice,"* v. 1, p. 11.
12. Peary, *Northward over the "Great Ice,"* v. 1, pp. lxviii–lxix.
13. *Ibid.*
14. Peary, *Northward over the "Great Ice,"* v. 1, pp. 16–17.
15. From Peary's diary.
16. Peary diary, November 10, 1886.
17. Peary to his mother, February 27, 1887.
18. *Ibid.*

CHAPTER 6

1. His salary from the Canal Company was to be four hundred dollars a month. The rest was Navy pay.

2. In a letter dated November 3, 1887.
3. Dated March 10, 1887.
4. Dated September 18, 1887.
5. In a letter dated December 6, 1887.
6. Peary to his mother, December 28, 1887.
7. Peary to F. A. Pellas, January 3, 1888.
8. In a letter dated January 20, 1888.
9. This description of his Managua visit is paraphrased from his letter to his mother, dated January 20, 1888. He specifically mentioned the Greenland sky, indicating the Arctic yearning was not dead, just dormant.
10. From Peary's monthly report [for January, 1888] submitted to General Manager H. C. Taylor of the Canal Company. This report was dated February 2.
11. Peary to General Manager Taylor, February 3, 1888.
12. The man remained drunk in Greytown for several days, precluding Peary's settling the man's account. "He has been out in the streets with only a torn shirt and a pair of drawers on," Peary wrote, with New England disdain, in an undated, unaddressed rough draft of a letter, "and the English consul . . . took him from bed with a Negro woman in one of the miserable shanties in the place and locked him up, with a man to watch him."
13. Peary to his mother, February 29, 1888.
14. In a letter dated May 6, 1888.
15. He made this statement at a meeting of the Explorers Club, reported in the New York *Times*, March 16, 1915, and on other occasions.
16. Josephine Peary to Mary Wiley Peary, October 8, 1888.

CHAPTER 7

1. Marie Peary Stafford, *Discoverer of the North Pole*, p. 78.
2. Dated February 1, 1891.
3. Josephine Peary to Mary Wiley Peary, March 21, 1890.
4. In a letter dated June 2, 1890.
5. From a rough draft of the letter, dated only June, 1890, from "League Island, Pennsylvania."
6. Peary to his mother, March 12, 1890.
7. Peary to his mother, October 27, 1890.
8. In a letter dated May 3, 1891.
9. Peary to Professor Leslie A. Lee, December 21, 1890.
10. Peary to William Wood of Portland, Maine, September 22, 1890.
11. A maxim often stated by her father and remembered by Marie Peary Stafford.
12. The letter was written in late 1890 or early 1891. Later Daly wrote a

letter to the secretary of the Navy supporting Peary's application for a leave of absence, and he used some wording from this letter.

13. In a letter dated May 6, 1891.
14. In a letter dated June 11, 1891.
15. Peary diary, June 15, 1891.
16. Josephine Peary diary, June 17, 1891.
17. Josephine Peary diary, July 14, 1891.
18. Undated memorandum, in Josephine Peary's handwriting, in pencil.
19. Josephine Peary diary, July 14, 1891.
20. Josephine Peary diary, July 16, 1891.
21. Josephine Peary diary, July 24, 1891.
22. Josephine Peary diary, July 15, 1891.
23. Josephine Peary diary, July 21, 1891.
24. Josephine Peary diary, July 22, 1891.
25. Marie Peary Stafford, *Discoverer of the North Pole*, p. 88.
26. Peary diary, August 26, 1891.
27. Peary diary, September 17, 1891.
28. Peary diary, November 24, 1891.
29. John Verhoeff diary, February 20, 1892. Peary always required, in the contract with expedition members, that all diaries be turned over to him at the end of an expedition. These diaries are in his papers.
30. Josephine Peary diary, January 17, 1892.
31. *Ibid.*
32. John Verhoeff diary, March 17, 1892.
33. April 26, 1892.
34. John Verhoeff diary, March 20, 1892.
35. Peary diary, March 3, 1892.
36. Josephine Peary diary, January 29, 1892.
37. Robert E. Peary, *Northward over the "Great Ice,"* v. 1, pp. 203–210.
38. Robert E. Peary, "The Great White Journey," in Josephine Peary, *My Arctic Journal*, p. 227.
39. As quoted in an account prepared by Gibson; this event was dated August 12, 1892.
40. Gibson and Cook found the rocks and the footprints, said Gibson in a diary entry dated August 21, 1892.
41. August 28, 1892.

CHAPTER 8

1. Nansen to Peary, September 29, 1892.
2. In a letter dated June 25, 1893, the day before Peary sailed.
3. Lee recounted this at an unveiling of the John C. Johansen portrait of Peary at the Kane Masonic Lodge in New York, November 29, 1921.
4. Dated January 31, 1893.

5. Quoted from Lieutenant Maury by Peary in a handwritten manuscript, "Brief Outline of a Project for Determining the Northern Limit of Greenland, Overland."

6. Robert E. Peary, *Northward over the "Great Ice,"* v. 2, pp. 93–94.

7. Peary, *Northward over the "Great Ice,"* v. 2, p. 7.

8. In an undated rough draft of a letter to a Mrs. E. S. Starr, through whose help Peary had acquired the pigeons and had planned the experiment in communication.

9. Peary, *Northward over the "Great Ice,"* v. 2, pp. 69–70.

10. Josephine Peary diary entries, September 21 and September 25, 1893.

11. Josephine Peary diary entries, September 21 and September 29, 1893.

12. William Herbert Hobbs, *Peary,* p. 129.

13. Peary, *Northward over the "Great Ice,"* v. 2, pp. 97–100.

14. Peary, *Northward over the "Great Ice,"* v. 2, p. 111.

15. *Ibid.*

16. Peary diary, following an entry headed, "Leave Netiulumi 1 A.M., May 19 [1894]."

17. Peary, *Northward over the "Great Ice,"* v. 2, p. 146.

18. Peary, *Northward over the "Great Ice,"* v. 2, p. 149.

19. Peary, *Northward over the "Great Ice,"* v. 2, p. 151.

20. From Hugh Lee diary, quoted in William Herbert Hobbs, *Peary,* pp. 171–172.

21. In an undated letter; a postscript to that letter was dated June 15, 1894.

22. Quoted in a letter from O. D. Lee of Meriden, Connecticut, to Cyril Adams. A copy of the letter is in the Peary Papers.

23. Lee diary, August 3, 1894. A typescript of the diary is in the Peary Papers. This passage has often been quoted elsewhere, including in Hobbs, *Peary,* p. 142.

24. Peary diary, August 28, 1894. After the *Falcon* had disembarked the return party at Philadelphia the ship sailed again and disappeared at sea.

25. Peary to his wife, September 9, 1894, but not mailed, of course, until later.

26. Peary diary, September 6, 1894.

27. Peary to his wife, September 12, 1894.

28. A phrase used in his diary entry October 8 to October 19, 1894.

29. Robert E. Peary, "Work in North Greenland in 1894 and 1895," in American Geographical Society *Bulletin,* v. 28, 1896, p. 22.

30. So stated in Peary, "Work in North Greenland . . . ," referred to above, p. 21.

31. Peary, *Northward over the "Great Ice,"* v. 2, pp. 291–294.

32. Peary described this feeling in *Northward over the "Great Ice,"* v. 2, p. 301.

33. In a letter to William Herbert Hobbs, November 28, 1934. A copy of this letter is included in the Peary Papers.

34. Peary, *Northward over the "Great Ice,"* v. 2, pp. 446–447.

35. Peary, *Northward over the "Great Ice,"* v. 2, p. 462.
36. Peary, *Northward over the "Great Ice,"* v. 2, pp. 467–468.
37. *Ibid.*
38. Peary, "Work in North Greenland in 1894 and 1895," American Geological Society *Bulletin,* v. 28, 1896, p. 30.
39. From Lee diary. This account was also given by Lee to William Herbert Hobbs in a letter dated November 9, 1935, and used by Hobbs in *Peary,* p. 163. Copies of Lee's diary and his letter to Hobbs are in the Peary Papers.
40. Lee told this story at a meeting of the Kane Lodge in New York, November 29, 1921.
41. Peary, *Northward over the "Great Ice,"* v. 2, p. 522.
42. Peary diary, July 1, 1895.
43. Quoted by Hobbs in *Peary,* p. 166.
44. This letter was dated March 10, 1895, and delivered to Peary after the arrival of the *Kite.*
45. Peary, *Northward over the "Great Ice,"* v. 2, p. 533.
46. Peary, *Northward over the "Great Ice,"* v. 2, p. 535.
47. A sum stated in a letter from Museum Director Bumpers to Josephine Peary, February 16, 1909.
48. In a letter to William Herbert Hobbs, November 9, 1935. A copy is in the Peary Papers.

CHAPTER 9

1. Fitzhugh Green, *Peary: The Man Who Refused to Fail,* pp. 166–167.
2. In a letter to his wife, August 27, 1899; the meeting referred to occurred in October, 1898.
3. Peary diary, January 6, 1899. The entry is in T. S. Dedrick's handwriting; Peary obviously dictated the entry to him.
4. Peary diary, January 18, 1899, in Dedrick's handwriting. Eventually Peary lost eight toes, in two subsequent operations.
5. Hobbs mentioned this quotation without documentation in his biography of Peary (p. 213). Since then it has appeared in numerous other books and articles. Neither Peary nor Dedrick, the only two men at Fort Conger capable of keeping literate diaries, mentioned the quotation, but one would not expect Peary to. Inside the cover of Peary's diary beginning April 4, 1901, is an inscription, with no elaboration, obviously printed by him: *"Inveniet viam, aut faciet,"* which is in the third person singular of the verb, not first person: "He will find a way or make one."
6. From a typescript, undated and untitled.
7. From an undated, untitled rough draft of a manuscript, in pencil and in Peary's handwriting.
8. Peary discovered, after he had returned to the *Windward,* that he had lost a day in calculation sometime during his journey. According to the *Windward* crew, he returned there February 27, not February 28.

9. Dated August 27, 1899, at Etah.
10. Peary diary, May 9, 1900.
11. Peary diary, May 16, 1900.
12. *Ibid.*
13. As quoted earlier, in Chapter 5.
14. Dated August 28, 1900.
15. Dated January 23, 1901, aboard the *Windward.*
16. In a letter dated August 14, 1899, from Atlantic City, New Jersey.
17. Peary diary, July 12, 1900.
18. Peary diary, December 20, 1900.
19. The contracts did not designate No. 1 and No. 2 assistants. Furthermore, although Henson's position was never so exalted as some authors later were to claim, he had much more experience than Dedrick in Arctic work.
20. Peary mentioned, in a diary entry of November 20, 1900, that Dedrick had complained to him about the ridiculing.
21. Dedrick's original diaries later were turned over to Peary and are now in the Peary Papers.
22. From a penciled draft, in Peary's handwriting, in his November, 1900, diary.
23. Related in both Peary's and Dedrick's diaries. Dedrick's letter of resignation was dated April 13, 1901.
24. These instructions were dated April 4, 1901, the day before Peary's departure.
25. Dated April 4, 1901.
26. In a letter dated simply March, 1900 — but not delivered for more than a year.
27. Letter dated July 9, 1900.
28. Letter dated July 6, 1901. Peary's mother died November 2, 1900.
29. Dated August 21, 1901.
30. In a letter from Peary dated August 24, 1901.
31. Peary diary, September 8, 1901.
32. Peary diary, October 5, 1901.
33. Peary diary, October 29, 1901.
34. Robert E. Peary, *Nearest the Pole,* p. 341.
35. Peary diary, April 21, 1902.
36. Peary diary, April 25, 1902.
37. Peary diary, May 16–17, 1902.
38. Peary diary, May 24, 1902.
39. Peary diary, June 6, 1902.
40. Letter dated December 22, 1902.

CHAPTER 10

1. Fitzhugh Green, *Peary: The Man Who Refused to Fail,* p. 233.
2. On September 28, 1903.

3. Dated November 14, 1902.
4. Dated September 5, 1903.
5. Letter dated March 1, 1905, from Thorntown, Indiana.
6. Letter dated June 19, 1905, from Glennville, Georgia.
7. Letter dated July 15, 1905, from West Hoboken, New Jersey.
8. Josephine Peary to her husband, June 17, 1904.
9. From undated, untitled typed notes used for his 1904 lectures.
10. Peary to Robert T. Collier, the magazine publisher, January 14, 1904.
11. Peary diary, August 2, 1905.
12. Robert E. Peary, *Nearest the Pole*, p. 4.
13. Peary diary, July 31, 1905.
14. Peary, *Nearest the Pole*, p. 14.
15. Peary diary, July 30, 1905.
16. Peary diary, August 28, 1905.
17. Peary, *Nearest the Pole*, p. 46.
18. Peary, *Nearest the Pole*, p. 68.
19. Noted in Wolf's diary, September 22, 1905.
20. These menus were recorded by Dr. Wolf in his diary, November 15, 1905; the recollection of Peary's reaction to musk ox steak appeared in a later general entry.
21. As recorded in Wolf's diary, December 25, 1905.
22. Peary, *Nearest the Pole*, p. 93.
23. Peary, *Nearest the Pole*, p. 102.
24. Peary, *Nearest the Pole*, p. 131.
25. Peary, *Nearest the Pole*, pp. 134–135.
26. Peary, *Nearest the Pole*, pp. 144–146.
27. Peary, *Nearest the Pole*, pp. 146–147.
28. Peary, *Nearest the Pole*, pp. 168–169.
29. Peary, *Nearest the Pole*, p. 207.
30. William Herbert Hobbs, *Peary*, p. 297.
31. Donald B. MacMillan, *Four Years in the White North*, pp. 87–88.
32. Peary, *Nearest the Pole*, p. 224.
33. Peary, *Nearest the Pole*, p. 240.
34. Robert A. Bartlett, *The Log of "Bob" Bartlett*, p. 166.
35. Peary diary, August 13, 1906.
36. Peary diary, August 18, 1906.
37. Peary diary, August 19, 1906.
38. In a letter dated May 18, 1906, but not delivered until months later.
39. From a typescript of the speech, which was delivered December 15, 1906.

CHAPTER 11

1. Robert E. Peary, *The North Pole*, p. 10.
2. From a typescript fragment, undated, in the Peary Papers.

3. In a letter dated August 8, 1907.
4. As remembered by Vilhjalmur Stefansson in a personal interview, June 25, 1858. Stefansson also mentioned this in his writings.
5. As quoted in a letter from Nichols to Herbert L. Bridgman, July 8, 1920. A copy is in the Peary Papers.
6. J. E. Weems, Race for the Pole, discusses this further (p. 37).
7. As in a letter dated December 17, 1907.
8. Dated November 17, 1907.
9. These orders, signed by Acting Secretary of the Navy Truman H. Newberry, were dated July 2, 1908.
10. In a letter dated March 25, 1907.
11. Letter dated May 12, 1908.
12. Peary, The North Pole, p. 27.
13. Peary, The North Pole, p. 29.
14. Fitzhugh Green, Peary: The Man Who Refused to Fail, p. 286.
15. The name of this village has been spelled various ways, by different writers, as have most Eskimos names. The most frequently used spelling appears here.
16. Peary, The North Pole, p. 76. Peary kept a copy of this letter, which was dated March 17, 1908, "On the Polar Sea northward from Cape Hubbard." The letter instructed Franke to wait until June 5, 1908, and if Cook had not returned by that date to make his way southward and take passage on a whaler. The letter concluded with a statement that Cook was bound for the North Pole.
17. Dated August 13, 1908.
18. A receipt for this, signed by Franke August 17, 1908, was found in Peary's papers.
19. As stated in a letter to Herbert L. Bridgman August 17, 1908. The letter, signed by Peary, was handwritten by Ross Marvin. Obviously it was dictated to Marvin, who was expedition secretary.
20. As quoted in an article in the Bangor, Maine, Daily News, May 15, 1937, based on an interview with Mrs. Wardwell. Wardwell's statement is confusing. Actually Cook said later that he left Etah with ten Eskimos. Four of them, he said, went onto the sea ice with him — and two of these turned back after the first few marches.
21. This order has been quoted in print in varying versions. It is reproduced here from an order, either the original or a copy that Peary made for his files, that Peary kept in his papers.
22. In a letter dated July 15, 1908.
23. In a letter dated August 17, 1908.
24. Peary, The North Pole, p. 77.
25. Peary diary, December 22, 1908.
26. Peary, The North Pole, p. 215.
27. Ibid.
28. This account of Peary's journey across the frozen Arctic Ocean has been pieced together from Peary's "North Pole diary," in the Peary Papers,

from his book *The North Pole,* and from diaries, and the following books, written by other expedition members: Robert A. Bartlett, *The Log of "Bob" Bartlett;* George Borup, *A Tenderfoot with Peary;* Matthew A. Henson, *A Negro Explorer at the North Pole;* and Donald B. MacMillan, *How Peary Reached the Pole.* This account first appeared in a chapter of *Race for the Pole,* by J. E. Weems, published in 1960 and thereafter used in part in an article in *American Heritage* (April, 1962) entitled, "Peary or Cook: Who Discovered the North Pole?" It appears here with some revision and with the addition of material from the Peary Papers not previously available.

29. Borup, *A Tenderfoot with Peary,* p. 162.
30. Borup, *A Tenderfoot with Peary,* p. 163.
31. Borup, *A Tenderfoot with Peary,* p. 164.
32. Peary, *The North Pole,* p. 224.
33. Peary, *The North Pole,* p. 225.
34. Peary diary, March 8, 1909.
35. Peary, *The North Pole,* p. 229.
36. Peary, *The North Pole,* p. 230.
37. Peary diary, March 10, 1909.
38. Peary, *The North Pole,* p. 231.
39. This note, either a copy or the retrieved original, is in the Peary Papers, dated March 11, 1909, from "fourth camp."
40. He gave this estimate, "not less than twelve miles," in *The North Pole,* p. 232. In his diary for March 11, however, he noted, "Sixteen miles made good?" This was a reflection of Peary's inherent optimism. Occasionally his diary estimates proved to be overly cheerful, and he was forced to scale them down later.
41. Peary, *The North Pole,* p. 233.
42. Peary, *The North Pole,* p. 234.
43. Emphasizing the inconsistency of Eskimos names, Peary once spelled this name "Sigloo" in his diary and "Siglu" in an Eskimos census at the end of *Nearest the Pole.* In *The North Pole* it was spelled "Seegloo."
44. Peary diary, March 14, 1909.
45. The original copy, dated March 25, 1909, and signed by Marvin, is in the Peary Papers.
46. Peary diary, March 27, 1909.
47. Peary, *The North Pole,* p. 261. Peary did not mention the incident of the ice break in his diary, but he did not write an entry for March 29, 1909, when he would have entered it. He later recounted the story from memory; it appears in entirety in *The North Pole,* pp. 259–262.
48. Peary, *The North Pole,* p. 263.
49. Peary diary, March 31, 1909.
50. *Ibid.*
51. Peary, *The North Pole,* p. 266.
52. Peary diary, April 1, 1909.
53. From Peary's copy, dated April 1, 1909, and signed by Bartlett, who had

probably written the memorandum a day or so in advance to save time:
He left blank spaces for latitude observation, weather description, and
estimated number of days required to reach the Pole. This information
was entered, by Bartlett, later — when it had become available — but
with another pencil. This seeming inconsistency was to be noticed and
questioned by a congressional committee during hearings on a bill to
promote Peary to admiral.

54. Peary, *The North Pole*, p. 268.
55. From a notation adjoining Peary's diary entry of April 1, 1909. Peary
later polished the wording and used it in a book (*The North Pole*, p.
269), a frequent practice of his.
56. Peary, *The North Pole*, p. 269.
57. Peary, *The North Pole*, p. 270.
58. All of these entries are quoted as they appeared in Peary's original
"North Pole diary," with the exception of style changes as noted in the
Acknowledgments section.
59. Matthew Henson, *A Negro Explorer at the North Pole*, p. 132.
60. *Ibid.*
61. Henson, *A Negro Explorer at the North Pole*, p. 135.
62. Peary, *The North Pole*, p. 287.
63. Peary diary, April 6, 1909.
64. Peary, *The North Pole*, p. 291.
65. Another example of the inconsistency, in spelling Eskimo names. In *The
North Pole* Peary spells it two ways: Ooqueah and Ookeah.
66. As quoted in *The North Pole*, pp. 296–297.
67. Peary, *The North Pole*, p. 301.
68. Peary, *The North Pole*, p. 302.
69. Henson, *A Negro Explorer at the North Pole*, p. 140.
70. Peary diary, April 9, 1909.
71. Peary, *The North Pole*, p. 316. In a diary entry of April 22–23, 1909,
Peary used a similar statement without credit to Ootah: "The devil must
be asleep or his attention taken up by troubles with his wife, or we
should never have got back so comfortable."
72. Peary diary, April 22–23, 1909. This entry has been widely quoted, but
as originally entered by Peary and quoted here it differs somewhat from
the other versions.
73. These notes were entered at random on blank pages and were not entered under any specific date.
74. Peary, *The North Pole*, p. 318.
75. From an undated, untitled manuscript of miscellaneous notes, in pencil
and in Peary's handwriting.
76. Peary spelled it Itookashoo in this entry.
77. Peary diary, August 8, 1909. Under the same date Dr. Goodsell, in his
diary, also mentioned this news of Cook but gave no indication that he
was aware, either, of Cook's North Pole claim.

78. Cook himself spelled these names Etukishuk and Ahwelah.
79. The original manuscript, in Borup's handwriting, is in the Peary Papers.
80. Also in Borup's handwritten manuscript, referred to above.
81. According to a signed and witnessed statement made by Cabin Boy Pritchard, who was at Annoatok when Cook arrived. The original statement is in the Peary Papers.
82. From Borup's manuscript reporting the interrogation.
83. As stated in an undated, untitled manuscript of reminiscences prepared by Robert Bartlett and kept in the Peary Papers.
84. From the original of the telegram, dated September 6, 1909.
85. As stated in Bartlett's manuscript of reminiscences, mentioned above.
86. This telegram, also dated September 6, 1909, was addressed to the Associated Press in New York.
87. Dated July 16, 1909. Josephine Peary wrote out this letter six times, as she did most letters to Peary while he was in the North, for dispatch on six different whaling ships. One of them, she reasoned, would reach Etah or another point in Greenland where Peary's mail could be left for forwarding.
88. From "A Godspeed to Peary," read by Richard Le Gallienne at a farewell dinner for Peary given by Herbert L. Bridgman June 20, 1898.

CHAPTER 12

1. Used in a letter to a friend, Frank H. Norton of New York City, October 12, 1909.
2. As recalled by Freuchen's friend Vilhjalmur Stefansson in a personal interview June 25, 1958.
3. Pittsburgh *Press*, September 26, 1909.
4. This letter was dated October 13, 1909, from "The New Hotel English, Indianapolis," and was found in the Peary Papers with many others similar in tone — attesting to Peary's openness, at least at home, in regard to keeping records on the controversy.
5. In a letter to Thomas Hubbard, June 8, 1910.
6. A description used by publisher Benjamin Hampton to Peary's attorney Charles Nichols in a letter dated November 8, 1909. Hampton had purchased Peary's North Pole story for use in his magazine, and in the interest of promoting it he urged Nichols to persuade Peary to appear more in public.
7. Hubbard advised Peary from the first that he ignore Cook; this specific advice was contained in a letter to Peary dated February 16, 1911.
8. Peary to Edward N. Crane, December 31, 1909.
9. Peary to J. Scott Keltie, July 22, 1910.
10. Peary to Robert A. Bartlett, March 22, 1911.
11. In a letter dated December 6, 1910.

12. This information appeared in a letter dated November 22, 1909.
13. Letter dated October 26, 1909.
14. The decision was announced on December 21, 1909, and appeared in newspaper stories around the world.
15. From a copy of the minutes of the committee meeting, which was held on December 24, 1909. Club officials now refuse to give out information on this subject; these quotations came from a copy kept in the Peary Papers. After the 1909 action various newspapers reported the action, and these stories corroborated the minutes as retained in the Peary Papers.
16. The Peary-Cook dispute over attainment of the North Pole is the subject of a book, *Race for the Pole*, by J. E. Weems, and is not detailed again here.
17. As stated in a letter from Society President Leonard Darwin to Peary, December 5, 1910.
18. A receipt for $280 "in full payment of services rendered as expert computers" was signed March 13, 1911, and delivered to Peary.
19. From their "Computations of the Observations" sent to Peary.
20. As quoted in a news story of December 24, 1909, in the London *Times*.
21. From "Rasmussen's Report of the Account of Peary's Eskimos," a manuscript transmitted from Copenhagen by United States Minister Maurice F. Egan to the Department of State. A copy is in the Peary Papers.
22. In a letter to Peary dated October 3, 1910.
23. Peary said this in a letter to Thomas Hubbard dated January 16, 1911. In it he enclosed clippings from Philadelphia papers of January 14 and 15 reporting Macon's appearance at the commissioning of the battleship *Arkansas*. Macon was "father of the sponsor" of the battleship, Peary noted, and traveled to Philadelphia in the company of a large Navy contingent. Peary claimed Macon's close association with the Navy had resulted in Macon's violent opposition to Peary.
24. In a letter dated February 5, 1911.
25. This letter was dated January 10, 1911. A copy was sent to Peary later, presumably by Foss.
26. This was the culmination of efforts by Peary to secure formal recognition of his accomplishment. For a detailed account of the arguments against him and the arguments in his favor see *Race for the Pole*.
27. Letter dated April 1, 1911.
28. From the presentation speech by Society President Leonard Darwin, May 4, 1910. The gold medal had been designed by the wife of Antarctic explorer Robert Scott.
29. In the United States Peary also received medals or other awards from the following organizations in recognition of his polar attainment: National Geographic Society, Chicago Geographic Society, Canadian Camp of New York City, Geographical Society of Philadelphia, Peary Arctic Club, Explorers Club of New York City.
30. Letter dated October 28, 1909.

31. Fitzhugh Green, *Peary: The Man Who Refused to Fail*, pp. 368–369.
32. L. M. Harte, in the Portland *Sunday Press and Times*, September 28, 1913.
33. *Ibid.*
34. The publishing agreement was dated December 11, 1909.
35. These inconsistencies are detailed in *Race for the Pole*. The fact that Thomas, who later became a well-known dramatist, was ghost-writer for *The North Pole* was not publicized, although the work was carried out with the knowledge and approval of the publisher. Several letters from Thomas found in the Peary Papers prove conclusively that Thomas helped Peary with the book. On May 3, 1910, Thomas wrote Peary, who was in England part of that month, "I am not at all satisfied with the extent of the material you gave me concerning what you did at the Pole. . . . That thirty hours at the Pole is what we have been working up to. . . . I wish you would send me an account of every single thing you did there. What the others did. What you said. . . . And there is one more thing I wish respectfully to urge on you and that is the importance of scrutinizing all the proof with the utmost care, remembering that every enemy you have in the world [is] sure to go over your book with a fine-tooth comb for the purpose of picking flaws in it. And only you, yourself, can prevent . . . technical errors or misstatements. . . ." Elsewhere in the papers was found a receipt, signed by Thomas June 21, 1910, for "eleven weeks work on North Pole book at fifty dollars per week, including revision and proofreading of entire volume. $550."
36. The agreement with *Hampton's* was dated November 4, 1909.
37. In a letter to Peary dated January 8, 1914. Knopf also sent a copy of Conrad's new novel *Chance*.
38. In a letter to President George H. Brimball of Brigham Young University, August 9, 1915.
39. From the text of a speech given at Norton, Virginia, July 3, 1915.
40. In a letter to Peary dated February 15, 1912.
41. This copy of Peary's answer is kept in his papers, but with no date.
42. The original draft of this telegram is in the Peary Papers.
43. Dated March 11, 1912.
44. *Ibid.*
45. When the National Geographic Society presented its gold medal to Amundsen, Peary served as toastmaster and made the actual presentation.
46. A recollection of Marie Peary Stafford.
47. This request from *The Bookman* was dated December 4, 1913; Peary's reply, the following day.
48. A recollection of Marie Peary Stafford.
49. In a letter to the American Book Company of New York, February 20, 1912.
50. In a rough draft of a letter dated December 19, 1912, reporting a change of address, to The Burlington.

51. In a letter dated February 27, 1912.
52. From a rough draft of an undated letter, probably written in 1914.
53. This project was urged on Peary by Ralph Ingraham of Orange Park, Florida, in a series of four letters dated February 17, May 14, and June 11, 1911; and June 16, 1912. Peary answered only the first one.
54. As shown in a letter from F. A. Stokes to Peary dated July 26, 1911, and in a telegram from Peary to Stokes dated July 28, 1911. The idea of the contribution originated with Peary.
55. Peary's contract with Henson was an oral one, but Peary asserted that Henson was well aware of the terms. All other expedition contracts were written, and all contained clauses restricting lecturing and writing by the member concerned.
56. In a letter from the Reverend George A. Holbrook to Herbert Bridgman, dated July 2, 1920. Bridgman solicited the comment for a projected biography of Peary, later deposited the letter in the Peary Papers.
57. From a copy of the invitation which was sent out.
58. *Ibid.*
59. From the rough draft of the letter, in Peary's writing, dated only 1881, referred to in Chapter 3.
60. Genesis, chapter 1, verse 26.

CHAPTER 13

1. In a letter dated June 15, 1912, to Henry Woodhouse for use in an Aero Club memorial service for Wilbur Wright.
2. In a speech before the Cleveland City Club March 24, 1917. Peary, of course, spelled it "aeroplane," as did everyone else then.
3. *Ibid.*
4. As noted by various writers including — most recently — the author of a tribute to Peary in the Washington *Star* of April 6, 1942 — the thirty-third anniversary of the North Pole attainment. The maxim appeared on stationery of the Aero Club, of which Peary was an official, in 1916.
5. As noted in a release by the National Editorial Service dated July 10, 1916, and based on information provided by the Aero Club of America.
6. In a speech at the Economic Club dinner in New York City, December 13, 1915.
7. These and the accompanying remarks are from a speech at the Sphinx Club of New York City, March 14, 1916.
8. Letter dated July 10, 1916.
9. From an undated, untitled rough draft, in Peary's handwriting, in the Peary Papers.
10. Stated in a letter to Secretary of the Navy Josephus Daniels, September 6, 1915. A similar letter went to the Bureau of Navigation, which then served in the same capacity as the Bureau of Naval Personnel today.
11. A comparison of the Greely scrapbooks, kept in the National Geographic

Society Library, with Helgesen's speeches, as recorded in the *Congressional Record*, will show this link clearly. Moreover, a confidential Navy Department letter (Ridley McLean, office of the Judge Advocate General, to Lucien Alexander, August 7, 1916) reported that Helgesen, who conducted research against Peary in the Hydrographic Office, "had someone behind him interested in the other side of the controversy." This same letter said the Navy's attitude toward the renewed controversy was "hands off."

12. House Joint Resolution 287 dated August 2, 1916.
13. Peary agreed to pay Alexander five hundred dollars a month and expenses not to exceed fifty dollars a month, according to a memorandum from Alexander September 27, 1916.
14. This rough draft was dated September 10, 1916. There is no indication of how, or whether, it was used.
15. This rough draft was dated September 20, 1916.
16. Undated rough draft.
17. In the Lancaster, Ohio, *Gazette*, October 7, 1916.
18. In the edition of August 9, 1916. Greely's letter was dated August 5.
19. In the Boston *Herald* edition of August 18, 1916.
20. Undated, untitled penciled note in Peary's handwriting. Perhaps it was more of a memorandum to himself, such as was occasionally found in his diaries.
21. Letter dated June 22, 1916.
22. Words used in a telegram from George W. Norton, Portland *Express* editor, to Peary, June 24, 1916, asking Peary if he was willing to run.
23. In a night letter to Editor Norton of the Portland *Express*, June 25, 1916.
24. As stated in an undated memorandum, "Plan of Campaign," found in the Peary Papers.
25. In a letter dated June 22, 1916.
26. Dated July 2, 1916.
27. From an undated manuscript.
28. Quoted from a speech by Peary at the annual meeting of the American Academy of Political and Social Science in Philadelphia, April 29, 1916.
29. From an article in *Army and Navy News*, quoted by Congressman Murray Hulbert of New York in the House of Representatives May 1, 1917. Hulbert joined forces with Texas Senator Morris Sheppard in an attempt to establish a Department of Aeronautics with a secretary having cabinet rank.
30. From a copy of a "letter to the editor" sent in 1916 to various newspapers.
31. From a rough draft, in pencil and in Peary's handwriting, identified as "[Washington?] *Star* article."
32. Both the clipping and the handwritten comment are in the Peary Papers.
33. Mentioned in the Boston *Herald*, April 11, 1918.
34. Reported in the San Francisco *Chronicle*, April 12, 1917.

1. Written by Elsa Barker (who worked with Peary on the *Hampton's* magazine article), in the Baltimore *Sun*, February 22, 1920. This description is based on information in her *Sun* article and in an article by J. E. Jones in the *Times Review*, January 11, 1917.
2. *Times Review*, January 11, 1917.
3. First news reports of Peary's illness appeared in April, 1918; but his diaries show that he had become aware of his condition at least three months earlier.
4. Fitzhugh Green, *Peary: The Man Who Refused to Fail*, p. 401. This is also a recollection of Marie Peary Stafford.
5. Edition of April 10, 1918.
6. Dated May 3, 1918.
7. In a letter to the Reverend Thornton F. Turner of New York City, May 27, 1918.
8. In a letter to Herbert Bridgman, June 11, 1918.
9. An observation of Peary's doctor in Portland, Maine, Dr. Elmer H. King, who attended him during his visits to Eagle Island.
10. Undated notes in with other material dated in September, 1918.
11. A memorandum found among material dated January, 1919. The original probably went to Dr. B. L. Hardin or Dr. H. F. Strine, his physicians in Washington.
12. Printed in the Washington *Star*, April 6, 1919.
13. Wichita Falls, Texas, *Times*, May 19, 1919.
14. Portland *Herald*, October 5, 1919.
15. A recollection of Marie Peary Stafford.
16. According to a statement by Josephine Peary in a letter to Charles Nichols, March 8, 1920.
17. These are recollections of Marie Peary Stafford.
18. In a letter to Charles Nichols, March 8, 1920.
19. An undated, untitled note, in ink, in Josephine Peary's handwriting.
20. This note, in pencil on lined tablet sheets, was for some reason apparently dictated by Peary to his wife; the handwriting is hers.
21. In the issue of December 23, 1909.
22. In the *American Museum Journal*, May, 1912.

Bibliography

Bibliography

As STATED, this biography has been based largely on material in Peary's personal papers, and on personal interviews in connection with research into that material. Individual items from the papers have been cited in "Notes on the Chapters," and the information is not repeated below. In addition to this, however, certain books, and other publications, have been used, and are listed below. A good many more books and articles, many critical of Peary, have been read, but are not listed. A complete bibliography of these items can be found in the author's earlier book, *Race for the Pole*.

BOOKS

Bartlett, Robert A. *The Log of "Bob" Bartlett*. New York: Putnam's, 1928.

Borup, George. *A Tenderfoot with Peary*. New York: Stokes, 1911.

Green, Fitzhugh. *Peary: The Man Who Refused to Fail*. New York: Putnam's, 1926.

Henson, Matthew A. *A Negro Explorer at the North Pole*. New York: Stokes, 1912.

Hobbs, William Herbert. *Peary*. New York: Macmillan, 1936.

MacMillan, Donald B. *How Peary Reached the Pole*. Boston: Houghton Mifflin, 1934.

MacMillan, Donald B. *Four Years in the White North*. Boston: Hale, Cushman, and Flint, 1933.

Menocal, A. G. *Report of the U.S. Nicaraguan Surveying Party*. Washington: Government Printing Office, 1886.

Peary, Josephine Diebitsch. *My Arctic Journal*. New York: Contemporary Publishing Company, 1893.

Peary, Robert E. *Nearest the Pole*. New York: Doubleday, 1907.

Peary, Robert E. *The North Pole*. New York: Stokes, 1910.

Peary, Robert E. *Northward over the "Great Ice."* 2 v. New York: Stokes, 1898.

Peary, Robert E. *Secrets of Polar Travel*. New York: Century, 1917.

Stafford, Marie Peary. *Discoverer of the North Pole*. New York: Morrow, 1959.

Weems, John Edward. *Race for the Pole.* New York: Holt, 1960.

OTHER PUBLICATIONS

American Museum Journal, May, 1912.
New York *Times* files.
Peary, Robert E. "Ice Navigation." *Century,* September, 1917.
Peary, Robert E. "My Plans for Reaching the Pole." *Harper's Weekly,* July 9, 1904.
Peary, Robert E. "Sledge-traveling." *Century,* November, 1917.
Peary, Robert E. "Work in North Greenland in 1894 and 1895." American Geographical Society *Bulletin,* v. 28, 1896.

Index

Index